Walter Farquhar Hook, Walter Hook

The Church and Its Ordinances

Vol. 2

Walter Farquhar Hook, Walter Hook

The Church and Its Ordinances
Vol. 2

ISBN/EAN: 9783337003234

Printed in Europe, USA, Canada, Australia, Japan

Cover: Foto ©Lupo / pixelio.de

More available books at **www.hansebooks.com**

THE CHURCH

&c.

VOLUME II.

BY

WALTER FARQUHAR HOOK, D.D. F.R.S.

LATE DEAN OF CHICHESTER

EDITED BY

THE REV. WALTER HOOK

RECTOR OF PORLOCK

IN TWO VOLUMES : VOLUME II.

LONDON
RICHARD BENTLEY & SON, NEW BURLINGTON STREET
𝔓ublishers in 𝔒rdinary to 𝔓er 𝔐ajesty the 𝔔ueen
1876

CONTENTS

OF

THE SECOND VOLUME.

SERMON		PAGE
XVIII.	THE VISITATION OF THE SICK	1
XIX.	THE ORDINATION OFFICES	23
XX.	MUTUAL FORBEARANCE RECOMMENDED IN THINGS INDIFFERENT	47
XXI.	'TAKE HEED WHAT YE HEAR'	74
XXII.	'PERIL OF IDOLATRY'	89
XXIII.	THE NOVELTIES OF ROMANISM	122
XXIV.	INVOCATION OF SAINTS	151
XXV.	'THE MOTHER OF MY LORD'	189
XXVI.	AURICULAR CONFESSION	218

SERMON XVIII.*

ON THE VISITATION OF THE SICK.

'*Is any sick among you? Let him call for the Elders of the Church, and let them pray over him.*'—St. James v. 14.

THE office of the Church, which comes this day under our notice, is that appointed for the Visitation of the Sick. It is an office which brings the Church into our chambers, to mingle with our domestic concerns, and to weep with them that weep. And though not a public office, yet it is one in which we, all of us, either have been or shall be interested. Some among us there doubtless are, who have already been benefited by sickness and sorrow; who look back to the time when, in obedience to the divine direction in our text, they sent for the Presbyters of the Church to pray over them; there are some, perhaps, who can date their conversion from that affliction which was to them a blessing in disguise. Who is there that expects to escape the ills to which all flesh is heir? Who but must feel that the time may come, and come soon, when he shall lie on the bed of languishing; when his limbs, however strong, will be feeble; his body racked

* [Preached at the consecration of Morpeth Church, 1842.]

with pain, and his proud spirit humbled by the prospect before him, of an eternity of misery or of bliss?

Now the formulary which is provided in our Prayer Book for the Visitation of the Sick, is one which has been used from a remote antiquity: all the directions and prayers are to be found in the most ancient manuals, while some of them may be traced to the primitive ages. And, assuredly, this adds to their affecting solemnity. It is an affecting thing to the imaginative mind, when stretched upon the bed of sickness, to feel that we are receiving consolation through the self-same formulary by which so many departed spirits, now in the triumphant Church, have been comforted and consoled; and colder natures cannot reprove the sentiment in our case, since the service, though ancient, was, at the Reformation of our Church, revised, and whatever was not authorized by 'Holy Scripture and ancient authors' abscinded. How powerful this service has been in kindling a holy fervour of feeling, in enabling those who have been tortured with bodily suffering to forget their agonies for a while, and to catch even a foretaste of the joys of heaven, those among us can tell, who having been reduced by disease to the gate of death, have availed themselves of the office;— yes, they can tell, that in speaking as I do, I speak the words of soberness and truth. Although, therefore, this office is performed in private, it is one in which we all are interested.

It is sometimes asked whether a Clergyman is tied to this service. And the question is to be answered by enquiring, under what character the Clergyman is sent for. A Clergyman may visit us as a private friend; and a private friend may join his prayers with ours, and pray with us, and pray for us. But if you send to him as a Presbyter, if you call upon him to visit you as a ministerial act, then, of course, he is bound to use this service, and this service only,—the service by which he, as a Clergyman, is to officiate. The practice of the Clergy frequently is, to use this service, when the illness is protracted, once a week or oftener; paying, in the meantime, friendly visits, in which, not acting officially, they are at liberty to act as they see fit. But so far as anyone expects any species of sacramental benefit from the prayers of the Church, he will seek for them under this form, and require its use from his Pastor.

The office commences with a Salutation and the shorter Litany, which are followed by the Lord's Prayer and two collects, the one for support under the affliction, and the other for the sanctification thereof. Then follows an Exhortation, the most perfect model of a sermon that we possess: but, since the same sermon often repeated would be wearisome, latitude is given, and the minister may use 'any like form.'

The articles of the Apostles' Creed are rehearsed to the sick man, that he may know whether he doth believe as a Christian man should, or not;—the Apostles' Creed containing, not everything that we ought to know and believe to our soul's health, but the very least that we can believe, and be called a Christian. It is that Creed, without believing the articles of which a heathen cannot be baptized. Then the minister is directed to examine the sick man, 'whether he repent him truly of his sins, exhorting him to forgive, from the bottom of his heart, all persons that have offended him; and if he hath offended any other, to ask them forgiveness; and where he hath done injury or wrong to any man, that he make amends to the uttermost of his power. And if he hath not before disposed of his goods, let him be admonished to make his will, and to declare his debts,—what he oweth, and what is owing to him; for the better discharging of his conscience, and the quietness of his executors. But men should often be put in remembrance, to take order for the settling of their temporal estates while they are in health.' 'These words before rehearsed,' continues the Rubric, 'may be said before the minister begin his prayer, as he shall see cause.' 'The minister should not omit earnestly to move such sick persons as are of ability, to be liberal to the poor. Here,' the Church proceeds, 'shall the sick person be moved to make a special confession of his sins, if he feel his conscience troubled with any weighty matter. After which confession, the Priest shall absolve him (if he humbly and heartily desire it) after this sort': 'Our Lord Jesus Christ, who hath left power to His Church to absolve all sinners, who truly repent and believe in Him, of His great mercy forgive thee thine offences; and by His authority committed to me, I absolve thee from all thy sins, in the name of the Father, and of the Son, and of the Holy Ghost. Amen.'

Then follow a prayer, the seventy-first Psalm, and the Benedictions.

It is observable here, that the Church makes a

twofold provision for the sick. If the Priest or Elder of the Church is sent for to a person who has been under grace, and who has led a godly life, the service, without reference to Confession or Absolution, is to be employed,—a calm, a soothing, a quieting service. But if there is reason to suppose that the sick man's conscience is troubled with any weighty matter, he is to be moved to confess; and in so moving him, the minister is left to his own discretion, to use what words and to refer to the topics he may consider best adapted to the case; and after Confession, the sick person may have, if he desires it, Absolution.

The fact that, both here and in the exhortation to the Holy Communion the duty of Confession is recognized, the fact that Absolution is directed to be given in the most direct form,—these facts are seized upon by the Protestant opponents of the Church of England, and made grounds of cavil. But from the facts, observe, we cannot escape. There they are, Confession and Absolution, just as they were before the Reformation, in our office for the Visitation of the Sick; there they are, Absolution in the very terms used by the Roman Catholic Priesthood, as well as by our own: there they were left when our Prayer Book was revised by the Reformers of Edward the Sixth; there they were still left by the Reformers of Elizabeth's reign; still were they left by those who revised the Prayer Book in the reigns of James the First, and Charles the Second. There is no ground, therefore, for what is sometimes said, that they were left there at the time of the Reformation to conciliate the Romanists; for they have been continued there at all subsequent reviews or reformations. However they may be designated, there they are, forming part of that Sacred Book, to all and everything 'contained and prescribed in and by which,' the Bishops and beneficed Clergy of the Church of England declare 'their unfeigned assent and consent.' No man, except the most ungodly of all men, can indulge in those idle declamations, with which some of our so-called religious publications abound, against Confession and Absolution, who has given his unfeigned assent and consent to all and everything contained in and prescribed by the Book of Common Prayer.

We cannot alter the facts. The Church, in the Homily on Common Prayer and Sacraments, remarks, that 'Absolution is no such Sacrament as Baptism and the Communion are.' This we must maintain; but as to any condemnation of Confession and Absolution, from this, as consistent Churchmen, we must abstain: to the principle, the Clergy give their unfeigned assent and consent. Nay, upon this principle the Church has legislated; for in the 119th canon it is provided, that, 'if any man confess his secret and hidden sins to the minister,' that minister shall not be bound to present the delinquent to the ecclesiastical court; but 'is strictly charged and admonished, that he do not at any time reveal and make known to any person whatsoever, any crime or offence so committed to his trust and secrecy, except they be such crimes as by the laws of this realm his own life may be called in question for concealing the same, under pain of irregularity.'

It would be very wicked on our part were we to

conceal from you these facts, assuming, as is popularly done, your ignorance of the Prayer Book. It is, indeed, a misfortune, that some of those who dogmatize upon the Church, are most ignorant of what the Church really teaches; but we, who are churchmen indeed and in truth, neither sympathizing with Rome nor symbolizing with Geneva, must never shrink from expounding and abiding by the principles of the Prayer Book, however unpopular they may be to either party.

The question with us is simply, what does the Church of England teach: not what, in our private judgment, she ought to teach.

The Church of England, at the Reformation, did not abolish the practice of Confession. How, indeed, could she, when Scripture is so plain upon the subject? 'If we confess our sins,' according to St. John, 'God is faithful and just to forgive us our sins, and to cleanse us from all unrighteousness.'* 'He that covereth his sins shall not prosper; but whoso confesseth and forsaketh them, shall have mercy.'† In the Acts of the Apostles we read, 'Many that believed came and confessed, and shewed their deeds.'‡ 'Confess your faults one to another; and pray one for another, that ye may be healed.'§

But what, at the Reformation, the Church of England did, was this,—while insisting upon the duty of Confession, she contended also, that Confession to God only was sufficient; that there is no necessity to confess to the Priest. Confession to the Priest she

---

* 1 St. John i. 9. † Prov. xxviii. 13.
‡ Acts xix. 18. § St. James v. 16.

recommends, in the Exhortation to the Holy Communion, 'if any of you cannot quiet his conscience, but requireth further counsel and advice'; and she moves the sick man to make a special confession of his sins, 'if he feel his conscience troubled with any weighty matter.' But she refuses to consider it necessary to salvation. Expedient it is for some; necessary to none: it may be a help to edification; it is not a point bearing upon salvation: it is a comfort to many, and in their sickness and sorrow they may be moved to it; but it will not affect the salvation of any.

This is what was asserted at the Reformation of our Church, and is its doctrine still. And this is the point of difference, with respect to this doctrine, between the Church of England and the Church of Rome: the Church of Rome, in the assembly of Trent, has adjudged it 'necessary by the divine law, to confess all and single mortal sins which anyone does remember, or can recollect by due and diligent self-examination.' *

The difference between the Church of England and the modern Church of Rome is this, that while in the 16th century both Churches admitted the necessity of a reformation, the Church of Rome, in the assembly of Trent, conducted her reformation on the principles of the medieval Church, which she represents, and the Church of England reformed herself on the principles of the primitive Church. Thus, with respect to the practice of Confession, the Church of Rome, representing the medieval Church, has declared it to be necessary to salvation,—making it a Sacrament,

* Sess. xiv. c. 5.

such as Baptism and the Lord's Supper: the Church of England, as I have shown, regards it only as in some cases expedient. Nothing, indeed, can be more clear than the fact, that the principle of the primitive Church, with respect to Confession, was accordant with our own. St. Chrysostom, in the fourth century, exhorting men to repentance, says, 'I bid thee not bring thyself upon the stage, or to accuse thyself to others; but I advise thee to observe the Prophet's direction, Reveal thy way unto the Lord,—confess thy sins before God,—confess them before the Judge, praying, if not with thy tongue, yet at least with thy memory; and so look to obtain mercy. It is better to be tormented with the memory of thy sins now, than with the torment that shall be hereafter. If you remember them now, and continually offer them to God, and pray for them, you shall quickly blot them out; but if you forget them now, you will remember them against your will when they shall be brought forth before the whole world, and be publicly exposed upon the stage before all—friends, enemies, and angels.'

You will observe here, how St. Chrysostom, while insisting upon the duty of Confession, without which self-examination cannot be properly performed, contends also that Confession to God is sufficient. In another place he says more plainly still, 'It is not necessary that thou shouldest confess in the presence of witnesses, after thy sins be made known in thine own thoughts; let this judgment be without any witness; let God only see thee confessing.' Again he says, 'I beseech you, make your Confession continually to God. For I do not bring thee into the theatre of thy fellow-servants, neither do I constrain thee by any necessity to discover thy sins unto men: unfold thy conscience before God, and show Him thy wounds, and ask thy cure of Him. Show them to Him who will not reproach thee, but only heal thee. For although thou confess not, He knows all. Confess, therefore, that thou mayest be a gainer. Confess, that thou mayest put off thy sins in this world, and go pure into the next, and avoid that intolerable publication that will otherwise be made hereafter.' *

These quotations will serve to show that the primitive Church, like the Church of England at the present time, while holding Confession to be a duty absolutely necessary, considered Confession before God alone sufficient, when by such Confession the conscience could be satisfied.

It is with deference to this principle that we must understand an ancient writer, who says that 'throughout Scripture we are taught to confess our sin, continually and humbly, not only to God, but to holy men, and those that fear God;'† not of necessity, but as an act expedient to be performed. Thus another writer, under the name of Clemens Romanus, bids every one, into whose heart either envy or infidelity has slily

---

* See Bingham, book xviii. chap. iii., for the quotations here made.

† Bingham quotes this passage, as if it might be St. Augustine's: but it is now ascertained to be from a Homily of Cæsarius of Arles, a writer of a century later. Cæsar. Serm. lvi.

crept, 'not to be ashamed, if he has any care upon his soul, to confess his sins to the Bishop or Minister presiding over him, that by the word of God and his saving counsel he may be healed.' *

When the discipline of the Church was strict, it was expected that anyone who had committed any glaring offence, before joining in the general Confession, should make a special declaration of his fault, that the congregation might decide whether he were in a fit state to receive the Holy Communion; of which at that time, everyone who named the name of Christ partook, unless he were positively forbidden. As the world began to mingle with the Church, some very dreadful sins were thus exposed, and scandal brought upon the Church. It was then determined, that if a person had any doubt upon his mind as to the propriety of his receiving the Holy Sacrament, instead of confessing his sin to the whole congregation, he should make his Confession privately to the Priest; and it was left to the Priest to decide as to the fitness of his state to receive or not. In process of time it became very usual thus to consult the Priest; and in the end the Church of Rome made that compulsory, which at first was optional. And the Church of England, at the Reformation, restored her children to their primitive liberty; and while her Priests are, or ought to be, ready to give ghostly counsel and advice to those who confess to them, it is left optional both to them and to the laity, whether they will confess their sins to man

---

* Rufini Vers. Epist. ad Jacob. c. xi. Cotelcr. Patr. Apost. i. 618.

or not. The system of the middle ages, adhered to by the Church of Rome, had been found to lead to gross hypocrisy: when all were compelled to confess, many, pretending to do so, concealed some sins, and various abuses were the result: the system of the primitive Church, which afforded a model to us, while compelling no one to this discipline, provides, nevertheless, for those whose over-fraught hearts would break, if there were no one at hand to whom they might open their grief.

In the quotations I have given from St. Chrysostom, he alludes evidently to what appears to have been a prevalent opinion, that when, at the day of judgment, Satan will stand, the accuser of the brethren, to expose our sins, he will not be permitted to lay to our charge those that we have confessed in this world; our confession of them now rendering the exposure of them at the great day unnecessary. Whether the direction, that we are to move the sick person to a special confession of his sins, have reference to this opinion, I know not; to those who hold it, the comfort will be great to open their grief here, to avoid that shame which must be theirs, when standing at the judgment seat,—there every thought, as well as word and work, will be revealed.

And such a person, whether clerk or layman, may humbly and heartily desire to receive Absolution, which, on his Confession and contrition, no Clergyman has a right to refuse. He will rejoice to hear from the mouth of God's ambassador, that God has pardoned him for all the sins he has acknowledged and confessed,—that

He will blot them out of His remembrance, and remember them no more. He knows full well that there are unconfessed and unremembered sins, sins of his youth and sins of his riper years, sins of his soul and sins of his body, negligences and ignorances, evil things done to please others, and evil things done to please himself, all sufficient to condemn him, unless he had 'an Advocate with the Father, Jesus Christ the righteous, who is the propitiation for our sins;' he therefore joins, with a thankful heart, in that prayer for pardon which follows the Absolution, and which has been used in the Western Churches in this place for thirteen hundred years.

Against this Absolution, to which we give our unfeigned assent and consent, the very form still used in the Roman Catholic Church, no reasonable objection can be urged by those who, on the principle of the Prayer Book, have regard to Sacramental Religion. They who deny that Regeneration is conveyed to the soul by the Holy Ghost through the waters of Baptism, sanctified to the mystical washing away of sin; those who deny that, through the Eucharist, the body and blood of Christ are verily and indeed taken and received by the faithful, can consistently repudiate this Absolution: but are they consistent in affirming their unfeigned assent and consent to all and everything contained in and prescribed by the Book of Common Prayer? If you do give assent and consent to the Book of Common Prayer, you believe that by the affusion of water, remission of sins is given: you also believe that remission of sins is conveyed through the elements of bread and wine duly consecrated; and to suppose that a similar effect may be wrought by the word of a person commissioned by God, as His ambassador, to speak to you in His name, is only a following out of the same principle, and will be readily received, when the minister informs you, that, when he was ordained, the Bishop, in Christ's name, conferred this authority upon him, in these words;—' Receive the Holy Ghost, for the office of a Priest in the Church of God, now committed unto thee by the imposition of our hands. Whose sins thou dost forgive, they are forgiven; and whose sins thou dost retain, they are retained:' the words of our blessed Saviour, as found in the twentieth chapter of St. John's Gospel.

But why does there lurk in some minds, even when admitting that the Church has the power to remit or retain sins through the administration of the Sacraments, a jealousy of this Absolution, conveyed, not through water or the consecrated elements, but by word of mouth? It is because people imagine, though it is a vain imagination, that the efficacy of the ordinance is supposed to depend upon the will or caprice of an individual. But this is not more the case than in the instance of Baptism and the Eucharist, and is not the case at all. In every case it is God who remits the sin. But as God can delegate to man a power to work wonders above the course of nature, so can He delegate that power which belongs absolutely to Him, the power of remitting, to whom He will: but when He delegates this power to man, He does so conditionally, and man only acts ministerially. When St. Paul had power to work miracles, he could not work a miracle how or when he pleased. It was not for his own sake, but for that of others, that the power was given to him, and he could only act as God was pleased to direct. So, though the Bishops of the Church of England impart to the Clergy authority to remit or to retain sins, and although in so doing they act by commission from God, yet God does not limit His own powers. He has ordained that man should be brought into union with Him, through Christ the only Mediator; that man should be brought into union with Christ the Head, by union with His mystical body the Church; that union with the mystical body should be effected by Baptism, preserved by the Eucharist, and in subordination to this, by the other ordinances of the Gospel. Hence He has commissioned persons to administer these ordinances; but He is not tied to the means, and may save those who from these ordinances are excluded. While at the same time, though our Lord, as the general rule, has promised that He will bind in heaven what is bound on earth, it does not follow that, because the outward and visible sign is administered, the promised grace will be conferred upon unworthy receivers; we know, on the contrary, that 'the wicked, and such as be void of a lively faith, although they do carnally and visibly press with their teeth, as St. Augustine saith, the Sacrament of the body and blood of Christ, yet in nowise are they partakers of Christ; but rather, to their condemnation, do eat and drink the Sacrament of so great a thing.'* This principle is applicable to

* Article xxix.

every ordinance. If it be received unworthily, God, who knoweth the heart, will not ratify in heaven, what His Minister, administering His ordinance, hath done on earth. He gives us the rule, without debarring Himself from making an exception to it. Precisely so, it is only on the contrite that the words of Absolution take effect.

We know that God will pardon the contrite heart. 'A broken and a contrite heart, O God, Thou wilt not despise.'* If you believe this, why take offence because God's Minister, by the authority which God gives him, declares this to have taken place? If you deceive Him, and are not contrite, you receive no benefit from the Absolution; if you are contrite, you have the liberty given you of asking the declaration of your forgiveness from God's Minister. He cannot give you the blessed Eucharist every time he visits you, but in the intervals he can give you this blessing, which is part of the blessing of the Eucharist, by word of mouth.

Will anyone say, if this be so, if it is our contrition which is accepted by God for the sake of our Lord Jesus Christ, that Absolution is a work of supererogation? Let us see. Suppose you had been a traitor to your country, and that you were dwelling in a foreign land; suppose also, that you had repented of your sin, and that proof of your repentance had been conveyed to your sovereign; suppose, moreover, that from the general expression used by your injured sovereign, you felt sure that he would receive you again into favour; would you not, nevertheless, feel it satisfactory, before

* Ps. li. 17.

returning to your country, to have some formal writ made out and duly signed by the ambassador of your sovereign residing in the strange country in which you had taken up your abode? However certain you might feel of the favour of your sovereign, still you would think it expedient to have your pardon signed and sealed with the customary forms: you would not feel grateful to the ambassador, your gratitude would flow entirely to the sovereign his master; the act of the ambassador would be merely ministerial, but of his ministerial services you would avail yourself. If the ambassador were to refuse to act, he would be punished, and his evil deed would not damage you; but you would feel, if he were prepared to act, that your reception by your sovereign would not be what you would desire it to be, were you to despise the regulations he has made; and you would seek from his ambassador a certificate, or such document as might be legally necessary.

Thus, at all events, thinks the Church of England. Before the Reformation, as in the present Church of Rome, auricular Confession was required ere Absolution was given; and Absolution was necessary to qualify a Christian to receive the Holy Communion. At the Reformation, as I have pointed out, though Confession was retained, it was not considered necessary to make any special Confession to a priest, although such Confession was allowed. Confession to God only being required, care was taken to insert a form of Absolution in the Office for the Holy Communion:—a general Confession, and then the Absolution, the declaration in

God's name by God's ambassador, of forgiveness to the contrite. But not only this. On the same principle, a general Confession, not intended to supersede your private Confession either to God only, or to man also, was introduced into the daily service of the Church; and daily, every parish priest is directed to pronounce the Absolution. The pardon is thus, as it were, handed over to you by God's ambassador day by day, if day by day you draw nigh with a humble, lowly, penitent, and obedient heart.

In the Visitation of the Sick, where the pastor is brought into contact with the soul of the individual, the offices both of Confession and of Absolution are more special; but still it is left to the discretion of the sick person whether he will or will not avail himself of the help here offered. You are not compelled to accept this service. Let everyone be fully persuaded in his own mind. But let not those who do not avail themselves of what is offered as a privilege, malign those who do; for to this Confession and Absolution the Bishops and Clergy of the Church of England still give their unfeigned assent and consent.

I pass now to the consideration of an objection made from another quarter: the Romanist censures us for neglecting in this ordinance to anoint the sick with oil. If the anointing of the sick with oil were an ordinance of our Church, we should observe it, and at the commencement of the Reformation it was retained. But the Church has power to loose as well as to bind, and to this ordinance we are bound no longer. We vindicate for the Church of England the right to regulate the ordinances by which the Catholics of England are to be bound. But if it be said that St. James, while exhorting us when sick to call for the Presbyters of the Church, that they may pray over us, adds, that they should anoint us with oil; we have, in defence of our Reformation, to say, that as we reformed our Church, not on medieval but on primitive principles, we are justified in concluding that this injunction of St. James had no reference to a permanent ordinance, for in the primitive Church no such ordinance existed. The original object of the anointing was to 'save,' or to procure miraculous recovery to the infirm; and therefore the Church of England, in reforming her offices, was at liberty to loose us from this observance, which she apparently has done, to avoid that error of the middle ages which the Church of Rome has retained, by which a temporary ceremony has been converted into a Sacrament.

And here, my brethren, having brought to a conclusion my observations upon these two objections to that office, from two opposite extremes, it may not, perhaps, be irrelevant, if I remind you, that the only safe course on our part, in these days, is to abide humbly by the teaching of the Church of England. We have men taking the foreign Reformers for their guide, and they seek to undermine your Church on the one side, and we have also men who take the schoolmen rather than the Fathers, or rather the scholastic divinity diluted through Romish publications, for their guide; and these, though opposed to the foreign Reformers and Puritans, unite with them in the damage they do to our Church; the one class explain away our Baptismal Office to reject regeneration; the other explain away our Office for the Holy Communion, to bring in the Sacrifice of the Mass; while latitudinarians, half infidels, still remain in our Church availing themselves of these disputes to explain away almost every doctrine of Christianity. You see the sin of all these persons; it is pride, presumption, setting themselves up as judges. Be it ours, my brethren, to act more humbly and more wisely. Let us seek to ascertain what the Church of England really teaches, and let us humbly suppose that the Church of England may be wiser than ourselves, how wise soever we may imagine ourselves to be. Our lot has been cast in the Church of England; she is our guide, given to us by our God; we know that she does not lead us into any immoral act, any infringement of God's revealed law; let us yield to her guidance. Even if we do not see at once her wisdom on the one hand in rejecting Extreme Unction, or on the other in retaining the Confession and Absolution, let us have the modesty to suppose that her decision may be more correct than our own; and if we do not now, we shall perhaps hereafter see that she was right, even where, in our presumption, we once may have thought her to be wrong. Be not followers of men; heed not what is said by Bishop, Priest, or Deacon, if they follow not the Prayer Book; study your Prayer Book; be the Church your guide, and so will you come to a right understanding of Scripture. Do not set yourselves up as judges of the Church, where she differs from other Churches, for it can only encourage pride to the peril of your soul.

Guided by this principle, we cannot, at all events, go far out of the right course; it is a safe course for our souls to pursue, though a humble one. If the time shall come when the proper authorities shall see fit to organize some fresh reform in our Zion, then we may listen to what is said by our opponents on either side; but as this is not now the case, let us seek to act conscientiously as members of the English Church; and if we act up to her precepts, if we follow the example of her saints, if we duly avail ourselves of the privileges she offers, and of the means of grace which God provides in her for the renovation and sanctification of our souls, we shall be prepared when the hour of sickness comes, or as the day of death approaches, for that office which has this day come under our consideration. The Church will then send peace to our house, and by her Minister speak comfort to our souls: not only will she remind us that there should be no greater comfort to Christian persons than to be made like unto Christ, by suffering patiently adversities, troubles, and sicknesses; for He Himself went not up to joy, but first He suffered pain; He entered not into glory before He was crucified; not only will she remind us that our way to eternal joy is to suffer here with Christ, and our door to enter into eternal life is gladly to die with Christ, that we may rise again from death, and dwell with Him in everlasting life; but she will also enable us to eat His flesh, and to drink His blood, so that our bodies may be made clean by His body, and our souls washed through His most precious blood, and that we may evermore dwell in Him, and He in us.

Yes, for the Church of England, when compelled to forego that primitive practice of carrying the Holy Sacrament from the church to the sick man's house, because persons were forced to worship the bread and wine, still acting according to what was also a primitive practice, has permitted the Minister, who has the cure of souls in each parish, reverently to minister the Holy Communion in any convenient place in the sick man's house.

I address those now in health, who may, ere long, fall sick, and will, ere very long, die ; and I would invite them to study the Office to which I have called their attention this day, that they may be able to realize, in their time of need, the consolation it provides.

SERMON XIX.*

ON THE ORDINATION OFFICES.

Then said Jesus unto them again, Peace be unto you: as my Father hath sent me, even so send I you. And when he had said this, he breathed on them, and said: Receive ye the Holy Ghost. Whose soever sins ye remit, they are remitted unto them; and whose soever sins ye retain, they are retained.—St. John xx. 21-23.

THE three offices, the first, for the ordering of Deacons; the second for the ordering of Priests; and the third, for the consecration of Bishops, form what is commonly called the ordinal of the Church of England. To this form of making, ordaining, and consecrating of Bishops, Priests, and Deacons, and to all and every thing contained therein, the Clergy are required to give their unfeigned assent and consent. The rite of Ordination is not a Sacrament in the same sense as Baptism and the Lord's Supper are Sacraments; but it is thus spoken of by the Church of England in the first part of the Homily on Common Prayer and the Sacraments: 'Though the ordering of ministers hath this visible sign or promise, yet it lacks the promise of remission of sins, as all other Sacraments besides the two above-named do. Therefore, neither it, nor

* [Preached at the consecration of Morpeth Church, 1842.]

any Sacrament else, be such Sacrament as Baptism and the Communion are.' It was not, as I observed on a former occasion, by lowering the other ordinances, called by Hooker, 'Sacramentals,' that the reformers sought to distinguish between them and the two Sacraments of Baptism and the Eucharist, but by speaking of these two as necessary to salvation. They who are not jealous of the exclusive pre-eminence of these great mysteries or Sacraments, Baptism and the Supper of the Lord, are those who can afford to elevate the other ordinances to their proper and relative position. Low views of the two great Sacraments, occasion low views of every other rite of Christianity, and even of the fundamental articles of faith.

As in the three offices of Baptism, so in the three offices of the Ordinal, the same general features may be traced, with the alteration in detail rendered necessary by the change in the respective position of the parties participating in the rite. In each office there are certain enquiries addressed to the congregation and to the candidates, to certify the qualifications they possess for the office they seek, so far as they are ascertainable by any but the all-searching eye of God. These enquiries, forming the introductory part of each Service, are accompanied with prayer: this is followed by the administration of the rite, the outward and visible sign being the imposition of hands, with words varied according to the order to be conferred: each Service concludes with prayer and benediction. One important point each office has in common with the others: for each office, for that of Deacon, Priest, and Bishop, a Divine institution is claimed.

Thus, in the form for Ordering Deacons it is said, 'Almighty God, who by thy Divine Providence hast appointed divers Orders of Ministers in thy Church, and didst inspire thine Apostles to choose unto the order of Deacons the first martyr St. Stephen,' &c. In the Ordering of Priests, the prayer runs thus: 'Almighty God, giver of all good things, Who by thy Holy Spirit hast appointed divers Orders of Ministers in thy Church, mercifully behold these thy servants, now called to the office of Priesthood.' And in the Consecration of a Bishop: 'Almighty God, giver of all good things, Who by thy Holy Spirit hast appointed divers Orders of Ministers in thy Church, mercifully behold this thy servant, now called to the work and ministry of a Bishop.' From which prayer, as a learned author remarks,* thus used in every form of ordination, it is manifest that the Church believes them to be several and distinct orders; for it would be absurd, not to say blasphemous, to give it as a reason why we may repeat God's blessing on the ordination of each, 'because He has appointed divers orders in His Church,' if each were not one of those distinct and divers orders.

Recommending the perusal of these offices in private, that you may clearly understand what the Church teaches upon a subject concerning which much ignorance prevails, I shall proceed to make a few miscellaneous remarks on some of the peculiarities of each office, to which, in the perusal, I would direct your attention. In the office for Ordering Deacons: 'Before

* Brett, quoted by the Hon. and Rev. Arthur Perceval, in his letter to the Bishop of Winchester.

the Gospel, the Bishop sitting in his chair shall cause the oath of the Queen's supremacy, and against the power and authority of all foreign potentates, to be ministered unto every one of them that shall be ordered.'

Now, it is very important to take notice of the terms of this oath, which is entitled, 'The oath of the Queen's sovereignty,' as regards what it does not contain, as well as what it does contain. 'I, A B, do swear, that I do from my heart abhor, detest, and abjure as impious and heretical, that damnable doctrine and position, that princes excommunicated or deprived by the Pope or any authority of the See of Rome, may be deposed or murdered by their subjects, or any other whatsoever. And I do declare, that no foreign prince, person, prelate, state, or potentate, hath, or ought to have, any jurisdiction, power, superiority, pre-eminence, or authority, ecclesiastical or spiritual, within this realm.' *

Such is the oath which was necessary in the days of the Reformation, and which is unfortunately necessary also in these days, to protect the liberties of our Church against the aggressions of the Romish pontiff and the intrigues of his partisans. But I call attention to this oath, because by the enemies of the Church it has been so misrepresented as to lead persons to suppose, that the Church of England has transferred the power of the Pope to the Sovereign, a thing which we expressly repudiate. The papal jurisdiction is suppressed: but, be it observed, it was suppressed some time

* This oath is not now administered during the service, but privately, in the presence of the Bishop. Clerical Subscription Act, 1865.

after the supremacy of the English Sovereign over all causes and persons, ecclesiastical as well as civil, was asserted: this was asserted as an inalienable right of the English Crown by the ministers of Henry the Eighth, the Gardiners and the Bonners, who took part in the persecutions of queen Mary's reign, or rather, were the chief instigators of them. In asserting the supremacy of the British Sovereign, we claim for her only that power which before the French Revolution the kings of France exercised over the Gallican Church, and to which the Spanish Church still submits. A wrong impression is conveyed to men's minds by a term never used in our Church itself, that the Queen is the head of the Church: properly explained, there may be no objection to the term, if by head is meant the political head; still as a matter of fact, though the title of head of the Church of England was assumed by Henry VIII., yet such was the offence given by this title, that Queen Elizabeth renounced it. Hence, too, it became necessary to explain, in Article XXXVII. that 'the king's majesty hath the chief power in this realm of England, and other his dominions, unto whom the chief government of all estates of this realm, whether they be ecclesiastical or civil, in all cases doth appertain, and is not, nor ought to be, subject to any foreign jurisdiction. Where we attribute to the king's majesty the chief government, by which titles we understand the minds of some slanderous folks to be offended; we give not to our princes the ministering either of God's Word or of the Sacraments, the which thing the Injunctions also lately set forth by Elizabeth our queen do most plainly testify; but that only prerogative which we see to have been given always to all godly princes in Holy Scriptures by God Himself; that is, that they should rule all states and degrees committed to their charge by God, whether ecclesiastical or temporal, and restrain with the civil sword the stubborn and evil doers. The Bishop of Rome hath no jurisdiction in the realm of England.'*

The object was to assert the majesty of the law against the usurpation of the Pope, and to place the Church of England under the same control of the civil power, to which all other communities are bound to submit.

The next point to which I would call your attention is, the two questions asked of Deacons, the first of which is not repeated in the Ordering of Priests, or Consecration of Bishops. 'Do you trust that you are inwardly moved by the Holy Ghost, to take upon you this Office and Administration, to serve God for the promoting of His glory, and the edifying of His people? Do you think that you are truly called according to the will of our Lord Jesus Christ, and the order of this Realm, to the Ministry of the Church?'

The principle involved in these two questions thus placed in juxtaposition is one of general application. Upon almost all our deliberate actions it may be brought to bear. Good thoughts and holy desires are the inspiration of God the Holy Ghost; but all thoughts that we may think to be good, and all de-

---

* See Queen Elizabeth's Injunctions.

sires that we may imagine to be holy, are not really so: the devil may suggest a thought and desire apparently good, and this may be to us a temptation. We must therefore 'try the spirits.' We must compare our inward inclinations with those providential circumstances under which we are placed; and when we find that, without violation of any law, without deviation of rectitude, we are enabled to do what we desire to do, then we attribute the desire to the inspiration of God. The providence of God, and the grace of God will correspond, since both are the effects of the one Divine will.

A man has a strong inclination to become a preacher of the Gospel—how is he to discern whether this inclination comes from God? If this desire is of God, and not a temptation of the enemy, intended to make him set up his will against the will of God, the way will be opened to him by Providence to acquire sufficient learning, and to realise those acquirements which the Bishop may require before he will ordain a candidate. If no facilities are provided, if such studies cannot be pursued, then the internal moving is not of God, and the desire must be overcome, that to the will of God, plainly opposed to our own will, we may submit and say, 'Father, not my will, but Thine be done.' But woe, still greater woe, to that poor wretched being, who, because facilities of preparation are provided, because friends and parents wish him to undertake the sacerdotal office, because some worldly benefice may be secured—ventures to present himself to the Bishop without any inward call, without an earnest desire to spend and be spent in his Master's service. If, where outward circumstances are unfavourable, the inward desire is to be restrained, much, much more must we refuse to avail ourselves of favourable circumstances from without, if there be no inward call. It is a dreadful sin to have recourse to this ordinance unworthily! Oh! awful thought, that many may have received this rite to their everlasting condemnation! Oh! what tears of repentance must be shed, what years of unmitigated labour passed, by those whose hearts, converted after their ordination, awaken to a sense of their sin! Awful thought for the clergy, whether Bishops, Priests or Deacons; a thought so awful that it induced St. Chrysostom to fly to the desert to escape consecration, since he thought it so difficult for a Bishop to be saved! But with respect to the laity, our twenty-sixth Article, written for their comfort, affirms that, ' Although in the visible Church the evil be ever mingled with the good, and sometimes the evil have the chief authority in the ministration of the Word and Sacraments, yet forasmuch as they do not the same in their own name, but in Christ's, and do minister by His commission and authority, we may use their ministry both in hearing of the Word of God and in receiving of the Sacraments. Neither is the effect of Christ's ordinance taken away by their wickedness, nor the grace of God's gifts diminished from such as by faith and rightly do receive the Sacraments ministered unto them; which be effectual, because of Christ's institution and promise, although they be ministered by evil men. Nevertheless, it appertaineth to the discipline of the Church, that inquiry be made of evil ministers, and that they be accused by those that have knowledge of their offences, and finally being found guilty, by just judgment be deposed.'

Alas! that this principle is so often reversed, that men refuse to bring an evil minister to justice, and yet decline his ministrations, thereby committing a double offence; neglecting their manifest duty to the body of Christ, which requires the amputation of a corrupt member, and at the same time, while neglecting a duty, committing an act of schism. It is our duty to God and His Church to bring our evil minister to judgment; but so long as he holds his credentials, the wickedness of an ambassador does not vitiate his ministerial acts. He acts in the name of the sovereign, and the sovereign, while he punishes the ambassador himself, will ratify all his acts legally performed.

The question relating to the inward call is not repeated in the Ordering of Priests, because the question relates to the whole ministry, and consequently need only be made on the first entrance into the same.

In the form of administering this ordinance, there is a difference in each of the three offices: in the Ordaining of Deacons, the Bishop alone lays on his hands; in the Ordering of Priests, the Priests who are present unite with the Bishop in the imposition of hands; in the Consecration of a Bishop, all the Bishops act with the Archbishop. In the Greek Church the custom for the Priests to lay on hands at the ordination of a Priest, does not prevail; and it is not essential to the ordinance. But in a well regulated Church, a Bishop does nothing without consulting his Priests, and they ought especially to be consulted on the admission of any Deacon into their own order, an order very little inferior to that of the Bishop, and possessing very nearly the same privileges; the Priests who are present at an ordination, being properly those of the cathedral church, represent the second order of the clergy. In the consecration of a Bishop, care is taken to secure the attendance of at least three Ministers in episcopal orders, besides the Archbishop or his representative. The Epistle is to be read by one Bishop, the Gospel by another, and the elect is to be presented by two. The sanction of a synod of Bishops was always considered necessary to a consecration, to prevent the possibility of persons being introduced clandestinely into that sacred order; and to constitute a synod, there must be present three Bishops at the least.

Deacons are ordained on the sole responsibility of the Bishop, who lays 'his hands severally upon the head of every one of them, humbly kneeling before him;' and he says, 'Take thou authority to execute the office of a Deacon in the Church of God, committed unto thee; in the name of the Father, and of the Son, and of the Holy Ghost.' The Bishop delivers to every one of them the New Testament, saying, 'Take thou authority to read the Gospel in the Church of God, and to preach the same if thou be thereto licensed by the Bishop himself.'

In the Ordering of Priests, the Bishop, with the Priests present, laying their hands severally on the head of everyone that receiveth the Order of Priesthood, the receivers humbly kneeling on their knees, the Bishop says, 'Receive the Holy Ghost for the office and work of a Priest in the Church of God, now committed unto thee through the imposition of our hands. Whose sins thou dost forgive, they are forgiven; and whose sins thou dost retain, they are retained. And be thou a faithful dispenser of the Word of God, and of His holy Sacraments; in the name of the Father, and of the Son, and of the Holy Ghost. Amen.' Then the Bishop delivers to every one of them, kneeling, the Bible into his hand, saying, 'Take thou authority to preach the Word of God, and to minister the Holy Sacraments in the congregation where thou shalt be lawfully appointed thereunto.' In the Consecration of Bishops the form is nearly the same, only the power to forgive and retain sin having been already conferred, it is not imparted again, the Bishop possesses that authority through his former ordination; therefore the Archbishop and the Bishops present, lay their hands upon the head of the elected Bishop, kneeling before them upon his knees, the Archbishop saying, 'Receive the Holy Ghost for the office and work of a Bishop in the Church of God, now committed unto thee by the imposition of our hands. In the name of the Father, and of the Son, and of the Holy Ghost. Amen. And remember that thou stir up the grace of God which is given thee by this imposition of our hands; for God hath not given us the spirit of fear, but of power, and love, and soberness.'

It is important to bring these facts before you, for as ordinations and consecrations are not often in these days publicly performed, nor when publicly performed, always in the cathedral, the generality of people are not aware of the great powers which the Bishops assert, and the authority which they give to the Priests. Perhaps a portion of the ill-will, with which consistent Churchmen are regarded, would be mitigated were these facts more fully known. It is certain that we are at present sending men to Rome by our putting a latitudinarian construction upon a Catholic Ritual. The Prayer Book teaches one thing; the popular religion is opposed to the plain teaching of the Prayer Book; and the system of explaining away the plain meaning of the Prayer Book, must have a demoralizing tendency, while persons taught by the Prayer Book to believe what they may not venture to express, are of course alienated from the Church of England. Let us seek to be consistent, neither explaining away one Sacrament to satisfy Puritans, nor refining upon the other to gratify Romanizers; still less let us put a non-natural sense upon our ordinances to wile latitudinarians to our fold, whose presence is only an impediment to the growth of godliness.

You will observe that every Bishop, in that office, to all and everything contained in and prescribed by which, they, as well as the other clergy, give their unfeigned assent and consent, exercise the power of conferring the Holy Ghost by the imposition of their hands. He uses the words of our Lord Himself when He incorporated His Apostles, and gave them the Holy Ghost to sanctify their ministry, to which He hath promised His own presence even unto the end of the world. In vain do men seek to evade the teaching of the Church. Before the Reformation these same words were used: and they were understood in their natural sense; and no honest man may put a non-natural sense upon them, the Church not having giving the slightest intimation of her intention of interpreting the words, since the Reformation. But that the grace is given by the Bishop is unequivocally asserted in the Consecration of Bishops, in which these words occur, as you have just heard, 'Remember that thou stir up the grace of God which is given thee,'—how?—' by this imposition of our hands.' The imposition of hands is the outward and visible sign, through which this grace, the reception of the Holy Ghost for the work of the ministry, is given.

Oh! what presumption is here, what awful presumption, as it must seem to those who reject sacramental religion, and deny the Apostolical Succession. To others there is no difficulty in understanding how grace may pass through this channel, however unworthy; for they believe that through the elements of bread and wine, duly consecrated in the Eucharist, grace may pass to the souls of the faithful; and if grace, then the Holy Ghost in His character of the Comforter, since of all grace He is the Author. The grace, of regeneration in Baptism, the grace of the Lord's body and blood for the strengthening and refreshing of our souls, these blessings are conveyed to our souls through the outward and visible signs in these two great Sacraments of the Gospel: and we who receive the teaching of the Church in this respect, can understand how grace for the ministry, which can only be efficacious through the Holy Ghost assisting those who minister in God's name, may be conveyed through the imposition of hands; the Bishop being only the instrument made use of by God, even as water in the font, or as bread and wine in the Eucharist.

So too can we understand the power of remitting and retaining sins, as conferred by the Bishop upon the Priests he ordains: waiving for the present all consideration of special absolution; what is Baptism? 'I believe one Baptism for the remission of sins;' that is one article of the Christian faith professed by all in the Nicene Creed; in administering this Sacrament then, the authority to forgive sins is exercised. What is the Sacrament of the Lord's Supper? 'This is My blood,' saith our Saviour, 'which is shed for you and for many for the remission of sins.' When the Eucharist is administered, this power is again used; and St. James directs the sick to send for the Presbyters of the Church; 'the prayer of faith shall save the sick, and if he have committed sins they shall be forgiven him.'* This whole office is indeed described by St. Paul, 'God was in Christ, reconciling the world unto Himself, not imputing their trespasses unto them, and hath committed unto us the word of reconciliation.'† In refusing, on just grounds to administer these ordinances, they retain sins; but since nothing is to be left to private judgment, for such refusal an appeal is permitted to the Bishop; as for example, in the case of refusing the

---

* St. James v. 14.   † 2 Cor. v. 19.

Holy Eucharist to anyone. And this branch of the sacred Office is subject to casual limitations, limitations perhaps overstepped by those of the Clergy who refuse to a people desirous of advancing in godliness a weekly Communion, which every member of the English Church has a right to demand of his priest.

You perceive how that they have no difficulty with respect to this portion of the Prayer Book, who held in sincerity what the Prayer Book teaches in her other offices. But those who reject the teaching of the Church, those who, to conform to the other Offices of the Church, receive them in a non-natural sense, must resort to the same artifice here, must have recourse to a non-natural sense of the ordinance, and so benumb their moral sense, learn to equivocate, and do despite unto the Spirit of truth.

It is only by believing in the fact of the Apostolical Succession, that we can acquit the Bishops and Clergy of the Church of England of arrogance the most sinful. What sinful arrogance in Bishops to take upon themselves the power of giving the Holy Ghost, to make themselves channels of grace, to give to sinful men authority to remit or retain sins, unless they be authorized to do so by Him, who only is the fountain of grace, and who only can forgive sins. When did God our Saviour give to any individual, exercising the office of a Bishop, the authority to do this? Has He spoken to him by miracle? No; but as the Church has always believed, and as you read in the words of our text, Christ our God has given this authority to a certain body by Him incorporated, and like all such bodies possessing a perpetual succession. If a Bishop acts as he does in the Ordination Services, on the ground of his belonging to that holy order which our Saviour Christ, the great Shepherd and Bishop of souls, instituted under the circumstances described in our text, his conduct is intelligible, even to those who will not admit the existence of the fact. But to deny the fact, and yet to use these words, is indeed to blaspheme; to say that the Church of England does not hold the doctrine of the Apostolical Succession, is to accuse the Church of England of blasphemy in her Ordinal; but to all and everything contained in and prescribed by the Form of Making, Ordaining, and Consecrating Bishops, Priests, and Deacons, the Clergy of the Church of England solemnly declare their unfeigned assent and consent.

Sin is an offence against God: God only, therefore, can absolve, but the power is communicable. The Priests absolving through these agencies, we regard the Priest only as one of the agents; and we mean that it is God who absolves, the Priest's power being merely a delegated, ministerial, conditional power. But all depends upon the fact, that he has received this delegation. The Church of England instructs every Bishop to speak as one to whom such power has been delegated, and who can, through the Holy Ghost, hand on the power, and delegate others; which is the whole principle of the Apostolical Succession.

If men will not accept this truth, they must remain in that dilemma to which I have referred: but we are sometimes desired to produce evidence that the Church of England has formally, and in express terms, asserted this doctrine in some of her formularies since the Reformation.

But the real question is, not whether she asserts, but whether she denies it. If she admitted it before the Reformation, and has not denied it since, it is a doctrine of our Church. The Church of England does not date from the Reformation; if indeed it did, it would be no Church at all. The Catholic Church was at the Reformation not destroyed in this country, but reformed; medieval corruptions and innovations were repudiated, but the Church remained as she was; even as Naaman, when cleansed of his leprosy, was still Naaman,—the same as he was before, though purified. Until the period of the Reformation never did a community of Christians exist, which doubted of the necessity of episcopal ordination, which implies, as all admit, the Apostolical Succession. 'Of the distinction among the governors of the Church,' observes Dr. Isaac Barrow, ' there was never, in ancient times, made any question; nor did it seem disputable to the Church, except to one malcontent Aerius, who did indeed get a name in story, but never made much noise or obtained any vogue in the world. Very few followers he found in his heterodoxy; but all, Arians, Macedonians, Novatians, Donatists, &c. maintained the distinction of orders among themselves, and acknowledged the duty of the inferior Clergy to their Bishops. And no wonder, seeing it standeth upon so very firm and clear grounds; upon the reason of the case, upon the testimony of Holy Scripture, upon general tradition, and unquestionable monuments of antiquity, upon the common judgment and practice of the greatest saints, persons most renowned for wisdom and piety in the Church.'

I repeat it, that unless we would unchurch ourselves, the question really to be asked is, not where has the Church of England in her public documents asserted this great truth, but where does she repudiate it? From the first foundation of our Church, whether the founders were the British Bishops, or Augustine of Canterbury and his Missionaries, this, the undoubted doctrine of Christendom, was the doctrine also of the Church of England; and nowhere does the Church of England stultify herself by rejecting this Catholic verity. The sectarian requires the express declaration of his sect for what he receives as doctrine: but we are not sectarians. What was held by our Church before the Reformation, is held by the Church now, unless by subsequent definitions an alteration is asserted,—just as the Canons are still in force in our ecclesiastical courts, although ordained long before the Reformation, except when they are overruled by subsequent enactments,— and one reason why those who desire to avoid all sectarian notions, are so desirous to retain the ancient ceremonies, even when not expressly enjoined in the present Prayer Book, is to keep up in men's minds the knowledge of the fact, that our Church was not founded at the Reformation; and to connect the Church since the Reformation, with the Church before the Reformation; a reformation implying, that things remain as before, except upon the points reformed. This is the principle involved in the present controversy about ceremonies; all admitting that ceremonies are in themselves things indifferent, they still dispute because the one party desires to regard the Reformers as the founders of our Church, and the other,—believing that the Church hath no human foundation, that to ascribe to it a human foundation, is to pronounce it to be, not a Church, but a sect,—desire continually to remind men that it is a portion of that very congregation of faithful men which was incorporated under the Apostles,—Christ Himself being the chief corner-stone,—which existed long in its purity, which was corrupted in the middle ages, which was reformed three hundred years ago, and now exists among ourselves, whether well or ill administered, the very Church of Christ.

Such persons would argue thus: the doctrine of Apostolical Succession is a doctrine of the Catholic Church, the Church of England is a branch of the Catholic Church, this, then is her doctrine.

But if it be necessary to silence those who regard the Church of England as a sect, we are prepared to meet them on their own ground. The Preface to the Ordinal forms part of that Book, to all and everything contained and prescribed wherein the Clergy give their unfeigned assent and consent. It commences thus, 'It is evident to all men reading the Holy Scriptures and the ancient authors, that from the Apostles' time there have been these orders of ministers in Christ's Church; Bishops, Priests, and Deacons. Which offices were evermore had in such reverend estimation, that no man might presume to exercise any of them, except he were first called, tried, examined, and known to have such qualities as are requisite for the same, and also by public prayer, with imposition of hands, were approved and admitted thereunto by lawful authority. And therefore, to the intent that these orders be continued, and reverently used and esteemed in the Church of England, no man shall be accounted or taken to be a lawful Bishop, Priest, or Deacon, in the Church of England, or suffered to execute any of the said functions, except he be called, tried, examined, and admitted thereunto, according to the form hereafter following, or hath had formerly Episcopal Consecration or Ordination.'

Now you must see at once how this formulary silences those, who, being mere sectarians, conform to the Church of England with sectarian feelings, and on this principle feel that they may reject the doctrine of Apostolical Succession. It is evident to all men reading the Holy Scriptures and the ancient authors, that from the Apostles' time there have been these orders of Ministers in Christ's Church, Bishops, Priests, and Deacons. But what did those ancient authors mean by the word Bishops? They meant, as all will admit, ecclesiastical rulers to whom exclusively pertains the power to ordain. This point cannot be denied. The assertion of the Church, then, is this: that from the Apostles' time this order existed, the order of Bishops, as distinguished from the other orders; she also states that evermore, even from the Apostles' time, the Bishops, as well as the other Clergy, were admitted to their office by public prayer and imposition of hands. It is admitted that Ordination is an office which has always belonged exclusively to the episcopal order, where episcopacy exists, and our Church affirms that this order has existed from the Apostles' time. Therefore as our present Bishops were all ordained by Bishops, so by Bishops were their predecessors consecrated, up to what period? The Church answers, up to the Apostles' time; the Apostles, being themselves ordained by Christ, ordained the first generation of Bishops, and Bishops, from that time to this, have ordained men to succeed them in the episcopal office, and this is what is called the Apostolical Succession; a fact in history, and a fact necessary for us to insist upon, because it is only by this fact, that the Clergy can prove that they have authority from Christ Himself, the King of kings, and Lord of lords, to act as His ambassadors. He said to the Apostles, 'As My Father hath sent Me, even so send I you:' the Apostles said to the Bishops whom they appointed to be their successors, 'As Christ sent us, so do we send you:' and down to the present hour, this is the office of Bishops; as they were sent by those who had power to send, so these, in their turn, send others, and they use the words which Christ the Bishop of souls, Himself used, when first giving the commission, handing to others both the grace and the authority which He has Himself imparted to His Church. So it is that the Church on earth, in her baptisms and her ordinations, is compared to that luminary which is placed in the firmament to rule the night; daily diminishing and daily increasing; our brethren departing from us to the Church triumphant, and their vacant places filled; so that by a continual accession of children and of fathers, the visible Church is continued to the end of the world.

Of this Church we are members; some of us set apart for the ministry, but many more to be ministered unto; but whether ministers, or those that are to be ministered unto, all forming but one Church. We, my brethren, are ordained for you; for your regeneration, renovation, edification. It has been by means of one of our order that the infant you saw so lately at the font, has received spiritual regeneration; that infant was brought here a child of wrath, it has been taken hence a child of grace; it has been born again of water and the Holy Ghost; it is a new creature. It is now a member of Christ, a child of God, and an inheritor of the kingdom of heaven. And this marvellous change has been wrought through the ministry of one of our order. It was by means of one of Christ's ministers that you received the spirit of strength in your Confirmation. It is by means of us that, in the Holy Eucharist, your spiritual life is renewed, and nourished, and sustained; and you are built up in your holy faith. It is for you, my brethren, that we have been ordained; your duty is to receive, with all readiness of mind, our ministrations; our duty is to take heed to our ministry that we fulfil it. And to do our duty, both we and you need God's special grace, which must be sought for by diligent prayer. Consider how much we need your prayers. Consider the heavy responsibility that is laid upon us. These are the words addressed by the Bishop to every candidate for the priesthood: 'We exhort you in the name of our Lord Jesus Christ, that you have in remembrance, into how high a dignity, and to how weighty an office and charge ye are called, that is to say, to be messengers, watchmen, and stewards of the Lord; to teach and to premonish, to feed and provide for the Lord's family; to seek for Christ's sheep that are dispersed abroad, and for His children who are in the midst of this naughty world, that they may be saved through Christ for ever. Have always therefore printed on your remembrance, how great a treasure is committed to your charge. For they are the sheep of Christ, which He bought with His death, and for whom He shed His blood. The Church and congregation whom you must serve, is His spouse, and His body; and if it shall happen the same Church or any menber thereof, to take any hurt or hindrance by reason of your negligence, ye know the greatness of the fault, and also the horrible punishment that will ensue. Wherefore consider with yourselves the end of your ministry towards the children of God, towards the spouse and body of Christ; and see that you never cease your labour, your care and diligence, until you have done all that lieth in you, according to your bounden duty, to bring all such as are or shall be committed to your charge, unto that agreement in the faith and knowledge of God, and to that ripeness and perfectness of age in Christ, that there be no place left among you, either for error in religion, or for viciousness of life.'

Brethren, is not our responsibility great, far greater than yours? And who is sufficient for these things? No one by himself. No not a St. Paul nor a St. John by himself, without the grace of God. But blessed be God, 'His grace is sufficient for us'; surely then, brethren, you will not refuse us your prayers; we need them. If St. Paul needed the prayers of the brethren, surely we need them more; and it is on this account that the Church, in her tender love for our souls, before the candidates for the priesthood receive the imposition of hands, requires the people to offer up prayers in their behalf. If you look at your Prayer Books, you will see that after several questions have been put by the Bishop, and answered by candidates, and after a short benedictory prayer by the Bishop, there follows this rubric, 'After this the congregation shall be desired secretly in their prayers to make their humble supplications to God for all these things, for the which prayers there shall be silence kept for a space.' These prayers should not only be offered up by the people at the time of Ordination, but they should never cease. Pray then, for us, my brethren, that we may not have entered into the ministry to our condemnation; and that you yourselves may not suffer loss by our unfaithfulness.

SERMON XX.*

MUTUAL FORBEARANCE RECOMMENDED IN THINGS
INDIFFERENT.

'*One man esteemeth one day above another, another esteemeth every day alike. Let every man be fully persuaded in his own mind. He that regardeth the day, regardeth it unto the Lord, and he that regardeth not the day, to the Lord he doth not regard it. He that eateth, eateth unto the Lord, for he giveth God thanks; and he that eateth not, to the Lord he eateth not and giveth God thanks.*'
—Romans xiv. 5, 6.

WE are assembled this day to assist in the consecration of a building which has been dedicated to the service of Almighty God by one of the most devoted of His servants, grateful for the privileges of his election in Christ Jesus; and the chief pastor of the diocese hath come in God's name to accept the offering, and to leave the divine blessing behind,—a blessing which will, I trust, especially rest upon him who, by founding this church, has given proof of his love towards the Saviour who died to save him, and of his zeal for the glory of his God. May he be blessed in his going out, and his coming in, and whatsoever he putteth his hand unto.

And remembering that Mary, when it was not in

---

* [Preached at the consecration of the Church of St. John the Baptist, Hawarden, July 22, 1843.]

her power to do much to evince her devotion towards her divine Master, yet anointed His feet with ointment and wiped them with her hair, other members of the founder's family, each according to his or her ability, have made offerings for the adornment of this sanctuary. There has indeed been no utilitarian Judas here, who, dwelling in a lordly palace, has begrudged the expenditure encountered for the honour of God; but on the contrary, everything has been done to render the place meet for the performance of our ritual in an orderly and decent manner.

And it is because in these days the question has been started,—what is orderly and decent?—that for this occasion I have selected the words of my text as the subject of my discourse. We have here a golden rule for our guidance in things indifferent. Among the early Christians, converts from the Jews and Gentiles, some there were of the former class, who thought it to be incumbent upon them to observe the Jewish customs. This, of course, they did not do as if they were a means of justification, for then they would have been rebuked at once for impugning that great doctrine which lies at the root of Christianity; justification by faith; but they acted thus for edification, or for self-discipline, or from a reverential feeling of attachment to forms and ceremonies formerly ordained by their God and long observed by their ancestors. But this observance of the ancient customs was condemned by many as an encroachment upon the 'liberty whereby Christ had made them free.'* The one party blamed

* Gal. v. 1.

the other for superstition, and this again was blamed for laxity of conduct and irreverence. Both parties were admonished in the spirit of love by the Apostle: 'Him that is weak in the faith receive ye, but not to doubtful disputations, for one believeth that he may eat all things: another who is weak, eateth herbs. Let not him that eateth despise him that eateth not; and let not him that eateth not judge him that eateth; for God hath received him. Who art thou that judgest another man's servant? to his own master he standeth or falleth. Yea he shall be holden up; for God is able to make him stand. One man esteemeth one day above another: another esteemeth every day alike. Let every man be fully persuaded in his own mind. He that regardeth the day regardeth it unto the Lord, and he that regardeth not the day, to the Lord he doth not regard it. He that eateth, eateth unto the Lord, for he giveth God thanks, and he that eateth not, to the Lord he eateth not, and giveth God thanks.' *

The things alluded to in this passage, not having been ordained in the Christian Church, were to Christians, things indifferent; it was a thing indifferent whether men did, or did not, observe the Jewish regulations as to food; whether they did, or did not, keep the Sabbath and other days held sacred by the Jews; these were open questions, with respect to which men, animated by the same motive—love to God—arrived at conclusions most different. And with either party the Apostle pleads for mutual toleration and forbearance.

* Rom. xiv. 1-6.

In our own Church we can produce an analogous case. There are in our calendar what are styled red letter days, and black letter days: the first are festivals, noted by being printed in red, for which a service is appointed, and the observance of which (since the observance is enjoined by competent authority), is no longer to us, who are members of the Church, a thing indifferent: the black letter days, on the contrary, are festivals for which no service has been appointed in our Church since the Reformation, but which, being retained in the calendar, some of our brethren still observe in private, and even feel an obligation so to do. Now, in this case the very words of the Apostle are applicable: 'One man esteemeth one day above another, another esteemeth every day alike. Let every man be fully persuaded in his own mind.' It is an open question, let each man act according to his persuasion of what is expedient to be done.

With respect to all forms and ceremonies and external observances, we may lay down two rules which will be understood by all who are capable of reflection; namely, first, that forms and ceremonies, and external observances are in themselves things indifferent; and secondly, that when they are appointed by competent authority in the Church, they cease to be any longer indifferent, but upon the members of the Church they become obligatory. 'If any minister shall omit to use the form of prayer, or any of the orders and ceremonies prescribed in the communion book, let him be suspended; and if after a month he do not reform and submit himself let him be excommunicated; and then if he will not submit himself, within the space of another month, let him be deposed from the ministry.'*

The argument of the Apostle, therefore, is not applicable to the observance of the Lord's day, or of the other fasts and festivals, the observance of which is ordained by the Church; it is only applicable to those fasts and festivals, or other observances which, not being expressly enjoined, individuals, out of piety, impose upon themselves. And it would be well indeed if on all such subjects, each side would regard the other side as consisting of weaker brethren; only let it be the regard not of contempt but of charity, which will terminate not in recrimination but in mutual forbearance.

We perceive, then, with respect to the forms, ceremonies, and outward observances of the Church, wherein we are bound, and wherein we are at liberty. Where the directions of the Church are plain and unequivocal, the honest man and true Christian will not question, but obey; where there is a doubt as to the intention of the Church, each man must exercise his own judgment; 'let him be fully persuaded in his own mind,' and the liberty which he claims for himself, let him extend to others.

There must be some scope, within certain limits, for the exercise of the private judgment, since it is impossible for any directions to be so definite and minute as to render a difference of opinion impossible. Two persons may be sincerely desirous and dutifully prepared

---

* Constitutions and Canons Ecclesiastical of the Church of England. Canon xxxviii.

to obey the directions of the Church, and yet from the circumstance just alluded to they may be found to vary in their mode of carrying their intentions into effect. For example, two clergymen may intend to observe the rubric which directs the priest humbly to present the alms and other devotions of the people collected at the Eucharist upon the holy table, and yet the question may arise as to the mode in which this act of humility is to be performed, one thinking it necessary, and the other not, to present the alms on his bended knee. So again two clergymen may wish to obey the Church as to the position of the priest at the time of consecrating the sacred elements, but the one may interpret the rubric as directing him to stand in the front of the altar, and the other may suppose that the intention of the Church is that he shall stand at the north side. These are minor points, things in themselves indifferent, but they are adduced to illustrate my meaning when I say that something must be left to the private judgment; and for that judgment therefore a guide is necessary.

In seeking for guidance some persons will reason thus: I must strictly adhere to what the Church ordains, but where the letter of the Prayer Book is not quite clear, or where certain observances have fallen into disuse, I am guided in my interpretation of what the Church intends, by the custom which I found to prevail at the time of my ordination, a custom which received the sanction of my diocesan. When a man so argues, all we can say is, 'let every man be fully persuaded in his own mind:' only, such a person, on his own principle, must be prepared to obey his diocesan, when that diocesan absolutely withdraws the sanction which it was presumed that he tacitly gave, and thinks proper to insist on a closer observance of the letter of the law.

But there are others who, conceding the point that, in the mode of observing the regulations of the Church, something must be left to the private judgment, and that an exact uniformity in all details cannot be expected and is not to be desired, refuse, nevertheless, to take for an authority the practice of the preceding generation,—who lived in an age of laxity and indevotion. They contend that to ascertain the mind of the Church of England, we must enquire into the customs that prevailed when our offices were reformed and reduced to their present shape. They would direct their enquiry not to the customs of the last age, but to the age which preceded the reformation; for, the reason why some of our rubrical directions are less clear than they might be is, that they who translated and re-arranged our offices, presumed that the clergy of our Church would continue to act, after the reformation, as they had done before, except where special directions were given; just as the canons received in our Church, before the reformation of it, are still binding, except where they contravene canons and statutes subsequently ordained. As an instance of what I mean I may refer to the alternate mode of chanting and of saying the Psalms, for which no directions are given in our Prayer Book, for none were needed; the reformers of our ritual knew that the clergy would, as a matter of course, act in this respect as they had been accustomed to do before the reformation commenced.*

Here again, with respect to this mode of proceeding, we may say, 'Let every man be fully persuaded in his own mind.' It is not, indeed, to be denied that these different ways of interpreting the ritual when the rubrics are doubtful, must, among other things, prove the existence of two different schools in our Church, nor is it to be denied that these different schools must continue, until what is now indefinite is made definite by the only authority which can effect this, namely, a convocation; † yet there seems no reason why on this

* In the Act for extinguishing the authority of the Bishop of Rome the following passage occurs:—
'Provided always, and be it enacted, That neither this Act, nor any thing or things in the same repeated, mentioned, or composed, be in any wise prejudicial, hurtful, or degrading to the ceremonies, uses, and other laudable and politic ordinances, for a tranquillity, discipline, concord, devotion, piety, and decent order heretofore (*i.e.* before the Reformation) in the Church of England used, instituted, taken, and accepted, nor to any person or persons accordingly using the same or any of them.'

† The government of the Church has always been monarchical, but it has never been a despotism. The Church is not governed by Bishops alone but by Bishops acting with the advice of the Presbyters and the consent of the laity. The inspired Apostles themselves consulted the Elders, Acts xv. 6. That there should be discontent, therefore, among the clergy when they find their Bishops endeavouring to govern the Church, not by the advice of the Presbyters, but by the authority of Parliament, is a thing not to be wondered at. Hence the desire evinced in so many quarters to have a convocation summoned for the despatch of business. But many will demur to a petition for this purpose addressed to the houses of Parliament. Convocation is not dependent upon Parliament, but has an authority of its own, and all that is required is the consent of the Sovereign, to whom the petitions should be addressed. The friends of the Reformation should remember the indignation with which Queen

account these two schools should regard each other with bitter and hostile feelings; there seems to be no reason why they should not act towards each other according to the golden rule of charity laid down in our text.

But it is a notorious fact that the most angry and bitter feelings are excited against those who act on the principle to which I have alluded last; and these angry feelings, upon examination, are excited, because the result of acting upon this principle has been found to be, that it makes the appearance of our sanctuaries and the ceremonies of our service approximate much more nearly to what we see in Catholic churches on the Continent, than to what we witness in places of worship pertaining to Protestant Dissenters at home. And the fear is entertained, that by such a proceeding, therefore, men may be led to Romanism. It is, indeed, obvious to reply that the contrary course has a tendency to lead men to Protestant Dissent, since a well-regulated mind would prefer no ceremonies to ceremonies rendered unmeaning by a careless observance of them. And it is still an open question in our Church which is most to be deprecated, Protestant Dissent or Romish Dissent.

Nevertheless, as the primitive Christians watched

Elizabeth resented the interference of Parliament in matters of religion. These things were to be settled by herself and the convocation of the Clergy. And no true Churchman will consent, though he may be compelled to yield, to the authority of a Parliament, in the affairs of religion, composed as our Parliaments now are of men professing any religion, or no religion, and many members of which are the avowed enemies of the Church.

with jealousy whatever had a tendency to lead men back to Judaism, so will the true-hearted member of the Church of England regard with more than jealousy anything which has, in his opinion, a tendency to bring back our Church into that slavery to the Pope, and those abominations of Romanism, from which, by the wisdom of our Reformers and the struggles of three centuries, she has been so happily rescued.* I speak

* It is, indeed, much to be lamented that there are persons in connexion with the Church of England who value too lightly the great movement in our Church, known as the Reformation, which took place three centuries ago. It is true that the Reformation is merely an event in our history, and as the Bishop of St. David's, with consistent charity, remarks, every man is free to form and express his own opinion on the advantages and disadvantages which have resulted from that great movement. But surely everyone who is acquainted with the real, not the imaginary, state of the Church of England before the Reformation, must see cause to bless God that this Church has been reformed. And even if we admit the charges which are brought of a want of reverence in the mere establishmentarian, of secularity in our higher ecclesiastics, and of ignorance of the Gospel as well as a want of charity in the so-called Evangelists, still it ought to be borne in mind that these faults exist in the unreformed branches of the Church, and that in every branch of the Church these faults will continue to exist, as accidents, until human nature becomes very different from what it now is. If in some few things the Romanist may have the advantage over us, yet in most things the balance is in our favour.

Let what is going on in Ireland at the present time open the eyes of men to the real character of Popery. The defenders of Romanism have called upon us to admit that in the Romish Church there is, what we have not, unity and discipline, and this point has been too easily conceded. But where is the unity and discipline now? The Romish clergy are preaching up bloodshed and rebellion, and almost every crime; and either no attempt has been made by ecclesiastical authority to restrain them, and then the whole Romish Church is involved in the guilt of these wicked priests, or else

strongly on this point as I ever have done and ever will do, for be the doctrines of the Church of Rome mitigated or evaded to any extent by those of her divines, who are breathing the purer atmosphere of England, and are brought into proximity to the English Church, which is the purest branch of the Church Catholic now in existence; still, by the sanction which the Church of Rome gives to the practice of bowing down to graven images, and to the invocation of saints, but above all to the blasphemous prayers with which, in her accredited books of devotion, her members insult the mother of our Lord, the Church of Rome is involved in no less a sin than that of idolatry. We admit, indeed, that the Church of Rome is still a portion of the Lord's temple, but it is like the temple of Jerusalem in the time of Manasseh,—' the temple in which evil is done in the sight of the Lord, like unto the abominations of the heathen, and all the host of heaven is worshipped and served.'*

But while thus contending, the question still occurs, on what ground is it presumed that a recurrence to the ancient ceremonies of the Church will bring men to Romanism? The persons who go over from us to Rome,

the boasted discipline of their Church is powerless, and their discipline is at an end.

We might refer even to the much more respectable Romanists of England, and enquire whether the tone and temper exhibited at the meetings of the so-called 'Catholic Institute' are not almost, if not altogether, as contrary to the spirit of true religion as any of the most objectionable of the meetings which are held in Exeter Hall. They seem, indeed, to be ready to imitate all that is bad in Protestantism, while they reject the good.

* 2 Chron. xxxii. 2, 3.

in spite of the idolatry of the Romish Church, go, as they tell us, from disgust at our irreverence, our inattention to devotional observances, our neglect of those forms and ceremonies, not over-burdensome, which our clergy are endowed to observe; and they imagine that the Romish Church is, in these respects, superior to our own: it is not then on account of our return to the ancient usages of the Church of England, but on account of our neglect of them, and on account of the polemical spirit in which religion is too often made to consist rather than in acts of devotion that those weaker brethren, whose lapse all who have a just abhorrence of idolatry must deplore, have departed from the light of the Church of England and betaken themselves to the thick darkness of the Church of Rome.

And if this be the case,—if it so be, that our want of attention to these things of minor importance be a stumbling-block in a brother's way, we are bound in charity to remove it: and in so doing we shall be acting on the very principle according to which our Church was reformed. It is said that when Queen Elizabeth ascended the throne she found that at least two-thirds of her subjects, though willing to renounce the supremacy of the pope, were attached to the usages of the ancient Church, and would rather become Papists than renounce them.* And how did that wise

* 'Divisa autem omnis Anglia in tres partes ex tribus una non erat eo tempore hæretica, nec cupiebat aut probabat mutationem religionis, nedum postea, cum sectæ perniciem esset experta.' Sandus *De Schism. Angl.* p. 290. The same statement was made by Creighton, a Scottish Jesuit, in 1586. See Strype. *Annals*, iii. 604.

Queen, to whom under God we are indebted not only for securing to our Church the blessing of the Reformation, but for saving it from the destruction which less wise reformers would have brought upon it,—how did she meet the difficulty? It was by doing that very thing which is now complained of as likely to send men to Romanism! Her mode of conciliating the minds of men hostile to the great spiritual movement of the age, and of encouraging other Churches to reform, was, by maintaining the grandeur of ceremonial worship at the very time that she rejected whatever had a tendency to encourage idolatrous practices. This she did by the authority which the Church had confided to her, and under the advice of those illustrious primates, Parker and Whitgift. She was compelled by circumstances at the commencement of her reign to prefer to high places in the Church many who had imbibed ultra-Protestant prejudices while resident in foreign lands, but she, at the same time, prevented them from perverting the Catholic Church in this country into a mere Protestant sect.

The liturgy of the Church, according to Dr. Heylyn, was, at the commencement of her reign, altered for the express purpose of conciliating those weaker brethren who regarded the Church of Rome with too favourable an eye: 'by leaving out an offensive passage against the Pope, restoring the old form of words accustomably used in the participation of the Holy Sacrament: the total expunging of a rubric which seemed to make a question of the real presence; the situation of the Holy Table in the place of an altar; the reverend posture of kneeling at it, or before it, by all communicants, the retaining of so many of the ancient festivals, and finally by the vestments used by the Priests in their ministrations.'*

* The whole passage as it occurs in Heylyn is so important to the argument of the text, that it is here transcribed for the reader:—

'Nor were these years less fatal to the Church of England, by the defection of the Papists, who till this time had kept themselves in her Communion, and did in general as punctually attend all Divine offices in the same, as the vulgar Protestants. And it is probable enough, that they might have held out longer in their due obedience, if first, the scandal which was given by the other faction, and afterwards the separation which ensued upon it, had not took them off. The Liturgie of the Church had been exceedingly well fitted to their approbation, by leaving out an offensive passage against the Pope; restoring the old form of words accustomably used in the participation of the holy Sacrament; the total expunging of a rubric which seemed to make a question of the real presence; the situation of the holy table in the place of the altar; the reverend posture of kneeling at it, or before it, by all communicants; the retaining of so many of the ancient festivals; and finally, by the vestments used by the priest or minister in the ministration. And so long as all things continued in so good a posture, they saw no cause for separating from the rest of their brethren in the acts of worship. But when all decency and order was turned out of the Church, by the heat and indiscretion of these new Reformers; the holy table brought into the midst of the Church like a common table; the communicants in some places sitting at it with as little reverence as any ordinary table; the ancient fasts and feasts deserted and Church vestments thrown aside, as the remainders of the superstition of the Church of Rome; they then began visibly to decline from their first conformity, and yet they made no general separation, nor defection neither, till the Genevan brethren had first made the schism, and rather chose to meet in barns and woods, yea, and common fields, than to associate with their brethren, as in former times. For, that they did so, is affirmed by very good authors, who much bemoaned the sad condition of the Church, in having her bowels torn in pieces by those very children which she had cherished in her bosom. By one of which, who must needs be of years and judgment at the time of this schism, we are first told what great con-

It was her wise and charitable policy, in this respect, which brought down upon her head the fierce wrath of the fiery Puritans: Neal, their historian, entirely agrees with the statement of the author just quoted, though he alludes to the fact with very different feelings; he says: 'Her majesty was afraid of reforming too far: she was desirous of retaining images in churches, crucifixes and crosses, vocal and instrumental music, with the old Popish (he should have said Catholic) garments: it is not therefore to be wondered at, that in revising the Liturgy of King Edward, no alteration was made in favour of those who now began to be called Puritans, from attempting a purer form of worship and discipline than had yet been established. The queen was more concerned for the Papists:'* that is, according to the admission of this historian, she desired to reconcile them to the Catholic Church, reformed as it had been under her auspices, while she was determined not to yield to those caprices of the ultra-Protestants, which originated rather in an uncharitable hatred of Rome, than in the pure love of truth.†

tentions had been raised in the first ten years of her Majesty's reign, through the peevish frowardness, the outcries of such as came from Geneva against the vestments of the Church, and such like matters. And then he adds, that being crossed in their desires touching those particulars, they separated from the rest of their congregations; and meeting together in houses, woods, and common fields, kept there their most unlawful and disorderly conventicles.'—*Heylyn's History of the Presbyterians*, p. 259.

* Hist. of Puritans, i. 129.

† 'The abuse of a thing doth not take away the lawful use of it. Nay, so far was it from the purpose of the Church of England to forsake and reject the Churches of Italy, France, Spain, Germany,

If, then, such was the principle by acting upon which our Church was placed in its present position, those members of our Church cannot be accused of inconsistency who pursue a similar course; nay, if the report be true that there are in our Communion some who still regard the Romish Church in too favourable a light, we may appeal to the result of this principle in the reign of Queen Elizabeth as a justification of our still acting upon it, since the majority which, at its commencement, inclined to Romanism, had, before its termination, dwindled into a minority; and we have the testimony at the same time of the French Ambassador to the wisdom of this procedure, who, on hearing

or any such like Churches in all things that they held and practised that as the apology of the Church of England confesseth, it doth with reverence retain those ceremonies which do neither endamage the word of God nor offend the minds of sober men ; and only departed from them in those particular points wherein they have fallen both from themselves in their ancient integrity, and from the apostolical Churches which were their first founders.'—*Canons of the Church of England*, Canon xxx.

The opposite system was adopted by many persons in the last century. As the Romanists were not to be won, the attempt was made by the discountenance of Catholic ceremonies, and by the addition of dissenting hymns to our service, to conciliate Protestant dissenters. But this was the deed of individuals acting upon their private judgment, and not any decree of the Church, and consequently the result has been unsatisfactory. Persons whose principles are those of Protestant dissent have conformed to the Church, under the notion that the Church differs very little from the leading dissenting sects. When the principles of the Church are fairly acted upon, these persons are first surprised and then exasperated. They are surprised to find the Church very different from what they thought it to be, exasperated at perceiving that unless they can prevent those principles from being carried out, they must, if consistent, become dissenters.

the service of the Church of England performed, remarked, 'that if the reformed Churches in France had kept the same order, there would have been thousands of Protestants more.' And with this testimony that of the historian of the Puritans is found to accord, when, as a reason for the conformity of those whose tendency, in the early days of this reign, was to Romanism, he assigns the fact which he thus states (and which, as an historical statement, and as showing that the same objections were urged against us then as now, is most valuable), 'the service performed in the Queen's Chapel, and in sundry Cathedrals, was so splendid and showy that foreigners could not distinguish it from the Roman, except that it was performed in the English tongue.'*

And now, having digressed to meet an objection, which by those who, like him who is now addressing you, regard the Reformation as a blessed event in the history of our Church, and who view with abhorrence the malpractices of the Church of Rome, will not be deemed unimportant, I shall revert to the rule of charity laid down in our text. We there find the Apostle urging men to mutual forbearance on the ground of their being united in principle,—their common principle being a desire to please the Lord. 'He that regardeth the day, regardeth it unto the Lord, and he that regardeth not the day, to the Lord he doth not regard it. He that eateth, eateth unto the Lord, for he giveth God thanks; and he that eateth not, to the Lord he eateth not and giveth God thanks.'

* Neal's Hist. of Puritans, i. 144.

And let me ask, may not a similar appeal be made in these days, to those who, on the one side endeavour to reduce our services to the greatest simplicity which a conscientious adherence to the Rubric will allow; and to those on the other side who desire to introduce all that ceremonial grandeur, which the Church permits, if she does not enjoin it; and by which to the disgust only of the Puritans, the early days of the Reformation were, as we have seen, distinguished?

May we not remind those who are true Christians, not angry and bigoted polemics, that, however different their conclusions and their practice in this respect may be, they are both animated by one and the selfsame feeling, even a holy jealousy for the honour of the Lord? In the one great principle both parties are united, that Christ is our all in all; on Him we depend for all we have and for all we are, and for all we hope for; not on our works do any of us trust for salvation, but on Christ and Christ only, Christ crucified, Christ glorified; Christ once crucified for our redemption; Christ now glorified and constantly interceding for us, and sending down unto us the Holy Ghost, the Comforter; in these great principles we are all united; that we are by nature wretched, sinful, damnable, children of perdition, a mass of corruption, so that to render our salvation possible nothing less would suffice than the incarnation and bloodshedding of our God; that, again, to make us meet for the heaven thus purchased for us, nothing less would suffice than the indwelling of God the Holy Ghost, to regenerate and sanctify and work a spiritual miracle upon our nature; the coming

IN THINGS INDIFFERENT.

of this Paraclete being one of the blessed results of the atoning sacrifice of the Cross.

And if we find, as find we do, that there are good men who are opposed to forms and ceremonies and devotional observances, lest the minds of men should be brought to rest upon them as an end, and thus become distracted from Christ,—where is the pious heart that cannot and will not sympathise with those fears? Where is he that will not admit that men may become formalists as much by attending to outward ceremonies, as by placing their religion in the hearing of sermons? The holy principle ought to be respected even by those who, through the same principle, are brought to the very opposite conclusion; they ought to admit that there may be piety even where there exists an abhorrence of its outward expression.

But the same rule of charity is to be applied to those, on the other hand, who, with regard to the ceremonial worship, insist upon its importance; their zeal for the ceremonies of the sanctuary is to be ascribed to the existence of that very principle which we have recognised in their opponents, and which we claim as a ground for forbearance and charity: they value the outward forms because they think that instead of leading men from Christ, they bring them to Him;—they see Christ in everything sacred, and they desire to be surrounded by signs and symbols which may constantly recall their thoughts, too apt to wander, unto Him in whose presence they stand or kneel. They rest not in the outward form, but they use the form as men use glasses to assist their vision: as the best of glasses will be of no avail if the eye be blind, so they know that if the heart be unsanctified the most impressive ceremonies will be useless; but when the heart is right with God, then by the use of a form it may learn to concentrate itself upon some fact of revelation which, without such form, could be but dimly seen. If they love the Church, it is not from partisanship, still less from a degrading worldly notion of its being connected with the state, but because it is the body of Christ, 'the fulness of Him that filleth all in all;' if they love the services of the sanctuary, it is because they are the voice of the spouse addressing Christ, and if they love the ceremonies of the sanctuary it is because they can, by observing them, act, as Mary did when she anointed our Saviour's feet, and, by little actions, evince their devotion to Christ, their only Master; they know that it is only faith in Him which gives efficacy subjectively to the very sacraments themselves, and that it is His presence only that can make them objectively the means of grace.

Nay, those who will regard the case not as polemics, but as true Christians, will perceive that to ceremonial worship, reality of faith will of necessity lead, in the ordinary course of things; as it has led in all branches of the Church, except where some external impediment is permitted to oppose itself. He who really believes that the Lord Jesus Christ is verily and indeed present, in an especial manner, according to His own most gracious promise, wherever His disciples are gathered together in His name; he who regards this promise, not as a mere figure of speech, but as a reality,—he will need no prompting as to his reverential deportment in the house of God; what he would do if the Lord Jesus stood visibly before him, that he still does, because he really believes Him to be, truly, though invisibly, present: he who really believes that the Lord Jesus Christ is perfect God as well as perfect man, the two natures co-existing in the same divine Person, will not think scorn of the obeisance which the Church enjoins when he utters the name of Jesus, the name by which He who is our Lord and our God was known, when for us men and our salvation He was made man: he who really believes that when he enters God's house he comes into the more immediate presence of the King of kings and Lord of lords, to whom in public worship the Church's homage is proffered, in communion with angels and archangels, and all the company of Heaven; that man will feel with St. Paul that in such a connexion the smallest matter becomes of importance, while he will desire that all things may be done with a relative decency and order, such as would prevail in the house of an earthly sovereign, where all things will be of the choicest and best. Never will the font be desecrated, or the holy table be left unadorned by those who really believe what the Church teaches, that the sacraments are not mere badges of Christian men's profession, but effectual signs of grace, signs by which God doth work invisibly in us, and by means of which grace is conveyed to souls, in which no impediment to its reception exists.

And here in passing we may remark that, from what has been said, it is clear that we act indiscreetly when we seek to enforce ceremonial observances, before we have created the appetite to desire them. Until men have become worshippers of God, not mere hearers of sermons, the observance of the ceremonies of the Church may only make them formalists. Whereas, if by diligence and prayer we succeed in making people really to have before their eyes the truths they are willing to profess, the tendency of their minds will not be to complain that our ceremonies are too many, but to desire that they may be more numerous.

It is this feeling, carried perhaps to an extreme, which induces some persons to adopt what may be called private ceremonials, points of ceremony which they impose upon themselves without any directions of the Church. As externals in devotion are nothing, when interior religion is wanting, the Church of England, in her wisdom and piety, enjoins upon us no observances but those which the decencies of public worship require; and as ceremonies, when not enjoined, are among things indifferent, she leaves it to each individual to impose the observance of such upon himself, or to refrain from them entirely, as may conduce best, in his own opinion, to his edification. To the first Prayer Book of Edward the Sixth we are referred, as our authority in ceremonials, and there we find a rubric which is in perfect accordance with the spirit of our text: 'as touching kneeling, crossing, holding up of the hands, knocking upon the breast, and other gestures; they may be used or left, as every man's devotion serveth, without blame.'*

* Rubric at the end of Prayer Book.

But although on this ground toleration may be demanded for such persons as avail themselves of the liberty in which both the Gospel and the Church allow them,—these very persons ought on the other hand to have a regard for the prejudices of others to whom these observances give offence, either because they are a tacit censure of themselves, or because they have been taught to look upon them as superstitious and as symbolizing with Rome. In many who are given to theological discussion, but whose hearts are not softened by the grace of charity, these obsolete observances give rise to the most angry feelings; and in others they create a prejudice against the truths of which they are intended to be the outward and visible signs. And if such be their effect, they who know the value of the outward sign should remember that God sees the heart; that the heart may be humbled though the head do not bow, and if the outward act be restrained from a motive of charity, God will be better pleased with the charitable neglect, than with the haughty observance of a ceremony which, under altered circumstances, may be useful to ourselves and harmless to others. On either side, there ought to be forbearance; let either side have charity towards weaker brethren. But if we permit our private fancies to interfere with the order of the congregation, then indeed we deserve not allowance but censure. Perfect uniformity in divine worship we cannot, for reasons assigned in this discourse, expect; a congregation advanced in spirituality will require and adopt more of ceremonial worship than one which has not been so well instructed : and the rule we should each lay down for ourselves ought surely to be, to follow the custom of that Church in which we may chance to be worshipping, in all those minor details which are not positively enjoined by the rubric: we should not neglect to kneel, because we happen to be in a congregation where it is the evil custom irreverently to sit, when prayers are offered unto the Lord God omnipotent, for this is a ceremony which is not among the things that are indifferent to us, since it has been enjoined by the Church. But let us take a ceremony, not enjoined, but frequently observed,— that, for instance, of turning to the east when the creed is rehearsed; if, being present in a church where this custom is observed, we were to turn to the west, this would be an outward and visible sign of a proud and perverse heart within; but then the same thing is equally true, if when this custom is not observed, we make a point of evincing a superior knowledge by turning in a manner different from the rest of the congregation.

Let it not be said that these things are beneath the notice of a Christian: the worldly philosopher may assert this, but not so the true Christian. He who reads the eleventh chapter of St. Paul's first Epistle to the Corinthians, in which an inspired Apostle devotes a chapter to the consideration of the proper apparel of women when they come into the presence of God and His holy angels, will perceive that the minute details of ceremonial worship are worthy of engaging a Christian's attention; and although it may be truly said that forms and ceremonies are but as the scaffolding to the building, yet let it be remembered that without a scaffolding such a goodly edifice as that in which we are now assembled could scarcely have been reared. It is not till the building is completed that the scaffolding is removed; and let me ask where is the member of the Church Militant who will venture to say that he is completely built up in Christ Jesus? Where is the man who is not like the Church itself, of which he is an atom, in a state of edification?

It is indeed, and let us never for a moment forget it, to build us up in grace and knowledge until the great and terrible day of the Lord, that every ordinance of the Church is intended, and all the writings and preachings of her ministers designed. And woe be to us, if in us this end be not accomplished. However wisely you may dogmatize upon what you deem to be God's pure and unadulterated word, however ceremoniously you may keep the ordinances, however ardent your feelings, however strong your assurance, whatever may be your orthodoxy, these things,—if they have not terminated in good works; if you have said 'Lord, Lord,' but given no heed unto that Lord, who hath declared that the dead shall be judged according to their works, and that before His judgment seat we must all appear; if, as is the manner of too many, you have talked about Christianity but not led Christian lives; if your knowledge has been without love, a cold coruscation playing round the head not warming the heart; if this be the case, then,—as it will be worse for Chorazim and Bethsaida than it will be for Sodom and Gomorrha,—the mercies you have neglected, the knowledge of which you have boasted, your fiery zeal or your cherished but unused privileges,—will only tend to your greater condemnation, will only serve to add a keener sting to the pangs of remorse in hell. Yes, to have enjoyed so much of divine illumination as to have seen the right path in which nevertheless you neglected to walk; to have experienced the constraining motions of the Holy Ghost to godliness but only to have rejected them; to have heard the sweet songs of Sion, but only with the carnal ear; to have felt interested in the decencies of the sanctuary, but never to have penetrated beneath the external form; to have discussed deep points of theology, but never to have realised them to your soul; to have stood at the very gate of heaven, to have caught a glimpse of its everlasting glories, and yet to have been shut out; to have been dashed down into the bottomless pit from the very threshold of Paradise, and there to find the waters of baptism only adding to the fury of the eternal flame, and the spiritual food intended to strengthen and refresh the soul converted into a deadly poison, not because in itself less holy, but from the unworthiness of the recipient; to look up to the realms of bliss, and seeing there the saints in glory, to feel that their crown was almost within your grasp, that you did but just miss the path to those realms of light and life,—surely this,—the thought, I repeat it, of having been dashed down to perdition from the very gate of Heaven,—this will be in itself a Hell.

Oh! my brethren, gifted, privileged, blessed as we are, let us remember that this may be the condition of any one of us. We may fall from grace, we may perish everlastingly, we may become a castaway; and we are in danger of this until God has our entire heart, until we love the Lord our God with all our heart and all our mind and all our strength.

And when we do thus love the Lord our God, then we shall walk in His commandments and ordinances blameless; or if peradventure there be some who shall be prejudiced against those ordinances which are not in strictness deemed obligatory, in them, and in all of us, love to God will conduce to brotherly love, and it shall be no longer said to our disgrace, 'See how these Churchmen hate'; Ephraim shall not envy Judah, and Judah shall not vex Ephraim; we shall not each see in a brother Churchman, according as his private judgment accords with, or is opposed to, our own, either on the one side a semi-papist, or on the other a mere pharisee: but whether we desire, in the place where God's honour dwelleth, simplicity or grandeur; whether we fear that ceremonial worship may lead men from Christ, or whether we regard it as a means of bringing them to Christ, mutual allowance and mutual forbearance will prevail, and we shall rejoice in the thought that we are all connected by love to Jesus the only Saviour, and zeal for God the Blessed Trinity, while our joy is heightened by the thought that the hour is fast approaching when many who are now kept apart by mutual suspicions, or the artifices of Satan,—will be united in love, a love which will never end, there, where all disputings as well as sorrows shall cease.

SERMON XXI.

'TAKE HEED WHAT YE HEAR.'

St. Mark iv. 24.

OF the great importance of the ordinance of preaching, it must, in these days, be unnecessary to speak. That its importance ought not to be exaggerated, so as to elevate it, out of proportion, above other ordinances of religion, must be evident to all. To show you precisely its value, will be, by God's blessing, my purpose this day.

It is to be feared that many entertain an exaggerated notion of the importance of this ordinance, owing to the prevalent custom among some persons of applying to the delivery of sermons those passages in Scripture which speak of preaching. But the slightest consideration must convince you that the character of oral preaching must have been very different before the Scriptures were written, from what it has been since. Faith could come by hearing, and by hearing only, before the Scriptures of the New Testament were delivered ;—at that time an Apostle either went himself, or sent a bishop, priest, or deacon, to tell the people what?—precisely what inspired men afterwards wrote, and we now read, in the Holy Scriptures. The preachers were then infallible men, moved by the Holy Ghost to declare to the people the way of salvation.

And the people were directed to place implicit reliance on what they heard, just as we are now to place implicit reliance on what we read in the Bible, so that if an impostor was to come, with whatever pretences of wisdom or knowledge, he was to be rejected, if he spake contrary to what had been preached. Though we, or 'an angel from heaven,' says the Apostle, 'were to preach any other Gospel to you than that we have preached, let him be accursed;'* an anathema which no modern preacher, I presume, whether Romanist or ultra-Protestant, would venture openly to declare, though, alas! it is insinuated by too many. You see —before the Bible was written, and while the preachers (whether an Apostle, like St. Paul, or apostolical men, like St. Mark and St. Luke) were miraculously inspired —preaching supplied the place of the Scriptures of the New Testament, and instead of referring to the New Testament, which was not written, men could only refer to the preaching of these infallible teachers. So that, strictly speaking, what those teachers, moved by the Holy Ghost, uttered was the Word of God.

But the case was different when by these inspired men the several Books of the New Testament were composed, when miraculous inspiration was withdrawn, and the canon of Scripture had been arranged and authenticated by the Church. Then the only real Word of God was the Bible,—the only true preaching of the Gospel, in the Scriptural sense of the word, was the reading of the Bible to the people. And thus we

* Gal. i. 8.

find that among the very earliest Christians, after the departure of the Apostles, the service of the Church consisted, not in the delivery of sermons, as among us, but in the devout reading of Scripture (which they regarded as the true preaching of the Gospel), with prayer, and with the administration of the Eucharist. They attended Church regularly to hear the Word of God, as preached in his infallible Scriptures, they prayed for all those things that were necessary for their souls, as well as their bodies, and they sought for the Gifts of the Holy Spirit, through the appointed means of grace.

And this deep reverence for Scripture is still retained in the Church of England. During the middle ages the practice of thus making the reading of Scripture a prominent part of divine service fell into disuse. At the Reformation this office was restored to its primitive prominence and importance. While by the two hostile extremes,—by Romanists through their legends, and by ultra-Protestants through their exclusive devotion to sermons,—the reading of Scripture, that is the preaching of the pure unadulterated Gospel, is nearly if not entirely set aside, by the Church of England four chapters of the Bible are appointed to be read every day, while provision for sermons is only made once in the week ; all additional sermons being a freewill offering on the part of the clergy to the people, and a freewill offering which ought not to supersede what is of equal or even greater value, catechetical instruction. So prominently does the Church of England, like the primitive Church, bring forward the Scriptures.

But this preaching of the pure unadulterated Gospel, this Scriptural preaching, without any admixture of human inventions; this reference to Scripture and to Scripture only, will not alone suffice. At a very early period, the delivery of sermons, also explanatory of Scripture, was found to be necessary. For heretics appeared, who drew conclusions the most erroneous from Scripture, and under the seeming sanction of holy writ doctrines the most iniquitous were propagated. Hence it became necessary for the clergy not only to read the Scripture to the people, but in order to guard against the sophistry of heretics, to explain it to them, by pointing out the precise meaning attached by the universal Church to the portion of Scripture they had heard. They said, first hear the plain unadulterated Word of God, and next hear the sense in which it has always been understood, from the beginning; and this was the origin of preaching by the delivery of sermons. Sermons were intended, not to supersede Scripture, but to explain Scripture. And such was the general character of the sermons delivered in the primitive Church. The sermons of the Fathers are almost entirely expositions of the Scripture, and this it is which renders these writings so peculiarly valuable: they show with respect to every passage of Scripture of which the meaning is ambiguous or doubtful, the sense in which it was understood from the first days of Christianity. Hence it is that you hear the Fathers so loudly declaimed against by those who would introduce novelties into religion, or adhere to human system; hence it is that you find them respected by all who obey the Scriptures and ask for the old ways that they may walk therein; for we know that the Christian Religion was once and once for all delivered to the saints, and that whatever is new must be erroneous.*

If at an early period of the Church this kind of preaching (preaching by the delivery of sermons) became necessary, it is as necessary, or even more necessary in our own times, when all kinds of false doctrines are promulgated under the pretence of being Scriptural. A most important ordinance, then, is this of preaching. I am not wishing unduly to decry the ordinance of preaching, but I merely wish to prevent you from applying to modern sermons all that is said of preaching in the Bible, which refers to the preaching of infallible men, and thus from elevating preaching above Scripture —human inventions and traditions, above the inspired Word of God. I would have you to make a clear distinction between Scripture and man's interpretation of Scripture; I would have you to remember that what Scripture says is infallibly true; but man's interpretation of Scripture—(and preaching, in the modern sense of the word, is this and merely this)—is fallible; I would warn you against the common practice of saying this man does, or this man does not, preach the Gospel, for he only preaches the Gospel who reads to you the plain words of Scripture, just in the order in which we find them in holy writ; what is added may be a Scriptural interpretation, or may not be Scriptural interpretation, it may be a true interpretation, or it

---

* Bishop Pearson, Preface to Exposition of the Creed.

may be a false interpretation; but still it is only an interpretation or explanation and nothing more; and to speak of this explanation or interpretation, as of necessity the preaching of the Gospel (because you happen to think that what the preacher says is conformable with Scripture), to the exclusion of any other interpretation, is not only the height of arrogance, but is a mere begging of the question; since the dispute between two preachers, who both of them appeal to Scripture, but deduce from Scripture very opposite conclusions, is, which of the two declares in very truth the mind of the Spirit? To take upon yourself then to decide this is to arrogate to yourself the office of judge, before you have proved your competency, or received your authority to act as such. All such modes of thinking and of acting are, I repeat, of a very injurious tendency; because it leads people to confound two things which are in themselves perfectly distinct—two things which ought to be kept perfectly distinct—the infallible Word of God and man's very fallible comment thereupon; the genuine Gospel of Christ, with some religious system of man's devising, which you may think to be consistent with Scripture, which you may think that you can prove from Scripture, but which, after all, since you are but fallible creatures, may not be consistent with Scripture: but which it is at all events most dangerous to speak of as Scripture, since it may bring upon you the punishment denounced on those who handle the word of God deceitfully.

Now if this be so, you see, my brethren, the need there is to warn men that they take heed what they hear. Suppose, just for the sake of argument, that there were no other obligations to induce a conformity to the Church of England; suppose, for the sake of argument (what we can, by no means, suppose as a real fact), that we were to regard instruction as the main thing to be thought of in attending a place of worship, and that we were at liberty to select our place of religious instruction, it would become a question of the most solemn nature, warned, as we are, to take heed what we hear, to ascertain the precise measures adopted by the preacher, whose teaching we should determine to attend, in order to ascertain in all instances the real meaning of the Bible; for though he says he preaches the Gospel, he may not really do so. Some preachers assert that they explain Scripture according to the system of Calvin; but why should Calvin's system be more right than the system of anyone else? Some assert that they explain Scripture according to the system of Arminius; but why should Arminius be more right than Calvin? Different sects take for their denomination the names of their founders, to announce the system they adopt in the interpretation of Scripture. Now, all these parties, though they preach the most opposite doctrines, assert of these opposite doctrines that they are each of them Scriptural, and declare of themselves that they preach the Gospel. But among these oppositions of doctrine how shall you decide which is in the right? Each claims Scripture to be on his side; each quotes Scripture; and how are you to determine what is of necessity the true meaning of Scripture more than another? Some person perhaps will say that he has prayed to be enlightened by the Holy Spirit, and therefore he is sure that his interpretation is the true one. But such a person ought in charity to admit that he to whose interpretation of Scripture he is opposed, may have prayed likewise to be enlightened by the Holy Spirit; and if he has done so, what gain we by this position? Wesley we know prayed and pronounced himself to have been assured by the Spirit, and consequently to be infallibly certain, that Whitfield was wrong; and Whitfield prayed and felt as infallibly assured and certain that Wesley was wrong. Even Socinus prayed and thought that his God-denying heresy was infallibly right.*

It is, indeed, essential that on this point we should have a clear notion. That the assistance of the Holy Spirit is necessary to them that would understand Scripture aright, who that knows anything of man's evil heart can for one moment doubt? who can doubt, who has the slightest acquaintance with Scripture itself? 'The natural man receiveth not the things of the Spirit of God: for they are foolishness to him: neither can he know them because they are spiritually discerned.'† 'No man knoweth who the Father is, but the Son, and he to whomsoever the Son will reveal Him.'‡ The promise is made that His children shall be taught by God Himself. And in vain, my brethren, will you give your nights and your days to the study of Scripture, unless the Holy Ghost be thus present

---

* See also the awful instance of the deistical writer, Lord Herbert of Cherbury, in Leland's *Deistical Writers*, vol. i. p. 470.
† I. Cor. ii. 14. ‡ St. Luke x. 23.

with you, to write the truths of Holy Writ upon the tablets of your hearts; in vain will you read unless likewise you pray; and most assuredly those who, being communicants, pray earnestly for the enlightening of the Spirit while they read, will have the Holy Ghost for their Helper, for to them, for their crucified Saviour's sake, He has promised his assistance.

But here comes the question, What kind of assistance has He promised? Has He promised to make the illiterate man a skilful critic? Has He promised to confer the gift of tongues on those who are unable to read the Scriptures in their original language? Has He promised to enable those to read who have never learnt to read? These things He does not do, and by not doing these things, He declares that it is not to our intellectual, but to our moral nature, that He promises His assistance. The Holy Spirit will inspire the prayerful Christian with a spiritual perception of the truths which he has intellectually discerned, that is, with such a view of them as shall produce a suitable impression upon the mind, and a corresponding effect upon his heart and life; but He will not inspire a man to know precisely the meaning of this or that particular passage of Scripture. He will inspire a man with a wish to believe and to do whatever Scripture reveals or ordains, with the wish and the ability to eradicate the corrupt passions and prejudices which make him hostile to the truth; but He will not bestow upon him the abilities of a critic, a linguist, and an antiquarian, so as to enable him dogmatically to decide between two systems of doctrine, both claiming to be Scriptural, which is really so. That the intellect is clearer, when the moral temper is good is doubtless true, and thus indirectly He may be said to influence the intellect; but further than this we go not, and they who refer to some favourite commentator or preacher, as if in his interpretation of Scripture he must be correct, act clearly on the principle of the papists when they refer to the pope as an infallible interpreter of holy writ.

How, then, shall plain men act, who have not time or ability for a critical investigation of Scripture, but who are aware that they ought to take heed what they hear? Let them hear the Gospel, as the Church delivers it. Let them hear, with the Prayer Book as well as the Bible in their hand; let them study their Prayer Book thoroughly, not only the Morning and Evening Services, but all the Offices, the Baptismal Office, the Office for the Holy Communion, the three Creeds, and the Ordination Offices. Let a man take his Prayer Book as his guide in the interpretation of Scripture, and with respect to the meaning of Scripture he cannot greatly err.

But I have alluded before to the absurdity of taking for our guide any human systems, and here the objection may be retorted upon me, that I am myself enforcing a human system in the Prayer Book. In answer to this, let me remind you of what our Prayer Book is. The English Prayer Book is not the composition of a few reformers who lived a few centuries ago, but it is the translation and re-arrangement of Greek and Latin Rituals of the remotest antiquity, such as have been in use throughout the Church universal from time immemorial. Our Prayer Book was in all its essential parts in use here in England from the earliest ages, long before the Reformation. But during the middle ages, through papal influence, certain innovations and superstitious observances had crept into it, and all our reformers did was, after comparing the liturgy then existing with the ancient liturgies, with Scripture, and with those interpretations of Scripture which the Fathers have handed down to us, as the interpretations received from the very foundation of Christianity, to cut off from it all innovations, which had been ignorantly adopted by some, or introduced with bad designs by others, and then to translate it into English. And thus the value of the Prayer Book, considered as a guide in the interpretation of Scripture, consists in its having embodied the doctrines which were carefully preserved by the early Church, as the very doctrines received from the Apostles, when the inspired Apostles preached by word of mouth, before the Scriptures of the New Testament were composed, and which were handed down from age to age, with the most jealous accuracy, until by the intrigues and jealousy of the popes of Rome the unity of the Church universal was destroyed. This is our strong point against the Romanists, that we have kept 'the faith once delivered to the saints' without diminution and without addition. And is it not a probability amounting to a moral certainty, that when we find that, like the two parts of a cloven tally, these doctrines thus preserved correspond entirely with Scripture, we have then ascertained the precise determinate sense of Holy Writ? that when, for instance, the tradition of the Church universal, preserved in our Prayer Book, and traced up for its origin to the inspired Apostles, tells us of the Divinity of our Lord, we are amply justified in applying all those passages in Scripture to prove his Divinity, to which Socinians would attach a different meaning? that when this tradition, preserved in our Prayer Book, sanctions the practice of infant baptism, we have a right to quote in favour of our practice those passages of Scripture which relate to the baptism of households and of nations, let Anabaptists say what they will? that we may prove in like manner the lawfulness of our making the Lord's day to supersede the Sabbath? The Prayer Book, like the tradition it embodies, adds nothing to the doctrines received in the Bible, for woe be to us if we add thereto or take therefrom ; the Prayer Book reveals no new doctrine, but it is of indispensable use as explanatory of Scripture, as rendering definite the meaning of Scripture, as unfolding to us the great system which the Bible has made known.*

* The reformed Church of England, in short, claims for her own that rule of faith, which the ancient Church ever professed before the times of division between east and west, and the erection of the papal power. 'Anathema to him,' said St. Ambrose, 'who adds anything to the Divine Scriptures, or diminishes aught from them.' (Council Aquil. § 36.) 'But we condemn those also,' said his brother Bishops, 'who are adversaries to the truth as it was established at the Nicene Council.' (Ibid. § 58.) So speaks the Church of England, taking the Nicene Creed, and the other two Creeds of the primitive Church, as true expositions of 'the faith once for all delivered to the saints.' The ancient Church everywhere received the decisions of the four first general councils as entitled to the greatest deference, composed as they were of delegates from all the Christian world, and each in strict accordance with

The Church then, you will observe, has the Scripture itself read in all her services, which is, strictly speaking, Gospel preaching; she directs that in the interpretation of Scripture, as delivered from the pulpit, deference shall be paid to the Prayer Book; and the wise layman, who studies his Bible with the light of his Prayer Book, will certainly never fall into dangerous error, never be guilty of heresy, as embodying the doctrine and discipline received from apostolic times. And why? Because this is the rule, to which the Scripture itself has promised the blessing of inward satisfaction and peace of mind. 'Stand ye in the ways, and see, and ask for the old paths, which is the good way; and walk therein, and ye shall find rest for your souls:' rest, in the resting place of truth; safety, from the paths of the destroyer!

And thus, my brethren, I have laid before you a rule, of the wisdom of which you will be the more and more persuaded, the more you reflect upon it. It is a rule, by the observance of which you will be kept steady to your profession, and not be among those who are carried about by every wind of doctrine; as must

each other. This peculiar deference was paid to them by the early English Church, before the popes had intruded their canon-law, and asserted their rights to supreme civil and ecclesiastical power. So that on this point the doctrine of Ælfric's time was in perfect unison with the statute determining heresy, drawn up with the advice of the Bishops of the reformation. (Ælfric's Past. Epist. § 23, 29. Stat. 1 Eliz.) And what can be more intelligible in itself, or more consistent with right reason, than this rule, which the Prayer Book everywhere embodies? Who can hope to gain credit even with reasonable men, who sets himself not only against the faith of the present Church, but against the general consent of the Church from the time of the Apostles?

be the case with all who, not taking heed of what they hear, run first to one sect and then to another, thinking that because in some points all are agreed, there can be no material difference between any. Among the trials of our present probationary life this is one, that we acquire the knowledge of the truth slowly and gradually. We are therefore through life to be reading and meditating on our Bible, to gain a nearer insight into the truth; we ought daily to be adding to our spiritual knowledge as well as our spiritual experience.

It is not sufficient to say (as I hope you all can do), 'I believe on the Lord Jesus, I rely for salvation on the alone merits of the crucified Lamb of God, I seek for sanctification only by his Spirit, and through his Ordinances and Sacraments; I hold the foundation, and that is enough.' Upon that foundation you ought to build gold, and silver, and precious stones; you may build thereon wood, hay, stubble. But what says the Apostle? If the former be the case, you will have your reward, if the latter, you will suffer loss.* It is into all the revealed council of God that we are to enquire, as it is all His commandments that we are, in intention, to obey. Nay, it ought to be our wish, in all, the very slightest particulars, to seek to discover the Divine Mind. Yes, if we really love the Lord Jesus, this will be our desire in small things as well as in great—in all things. If we do indeed, and with all our hearts, believe in all that He did, and suffered, to achieve our salvation; if we are accustomed to contemplate him, as in his glory, so in his humiliation, as at

* I. Cor. iii. 12—15.

the right hand of power, so also in the cradle, and amidst his enemies and persecutors and slanderers, and in his passion on the cross; if we are accustomed to hold communion with him in the Eucharist, and being one with him by a living faith to partake of his Spirit ; then ours will be no niggard service ; then we shall not divide our duties into the essential and the non-essential; even in the slightest particular we shall delight to show our devotion, love, and gratitude to the Lord Christ ; we shall dread the charge of irreverence far more than that of superstition; we shall not only worship him, but seek to worship in the very manner in which the first Christians worshipped him, since that manner received the approbation of the inspired Apostles; nay, we shall, being in communion with the saints of God, both those who are departed and those who are still in the flesh, wish to agree in all their recorded practices, so that, as I said before, we ought to be continually enquiring, continually adding to our faith knowledge, and passing on from one degree of spiritual knowledge to another ; and since our duty is this, since it is our inclination encouraged by the Spirit of God, since we are, for this purpose, both to read Scripture and to hear sermons, the rule becomes indeed an important one—take heed what and how ye hear.

SERMON XXII.*

'PERIL OF IDOLATRY.'

'*Little children, keep yourselves from idols.*'—I. St. John v. 21.

The consecration of this Church is a subject for rejoicing, and this for a twofold reason. It is, in the first place, always a cause of Christian joy, when provision is made in the wilderness for dispensing the bread of heaven, and when the wells of salvation are opened afresh, that people may draw thence the waters of life; but there is an additional and an especial ground for rejoicing in the good work this day accomplished by the mercy of God, since in this district Romanism is rife, and the advocates of that system are said to be particularly active.

That Romanism is gaining ground in England is the boast of the Romanists themselves, and it is at the same time the complaint of Protestants; and when two opposing parties are agreed, the one in asserting and the other in admitting the same fact, to maintain the contrary would be hazardous; and it is impossible to deny that there are many and obvious reasons why we should expect that Romanism, at the present time, and for a short season, should increase; and why ' little

* [Preached at the consecration of Clifford Church, in the diocese of York.]

children,' persons of gentle dispositions, and of that childlike simplicity which is the result of a conscious integrity of purpose, who are unversed in the arts, or disgusted by the violence of controversy, should be in danger of being led astray.

The Roman sect has in this country been lately advanced to a new position. It has been placed by the Legislature on the same footing as all other forms of dissent, and consequently the Romanists are now better able than they formerly were to obtain a hearing for themselves.

And not only have they obtained a right to speak, but there are also circumstances in the times which render men willing to hear them. The opinion is prevalent that all men have a right to exercise their private judgment in choosing a religion for themselves; there are many proud spirits who would scorn to 're-ceive their religion from their mother or their nurse;' but, before a choice based upon the exercise of the private judgment can be fairly made, all parties ought surely to be heard; and it would be real illiberality were we to refuse to admit that, *à priori*, the Romanists are as likely to be right as the followers of Calvin or the disciples of Luther. They, therefore, who are seeking the truth, and go to all places of worship, determining hereafter to remain where they 'get most good,' and find the greatest comfort, will visit the Romish in common with other chapels.

But the Romanists have a further advantage. Owing to the removal of the political disabilities, a greater degree of intercourse has taken place between

Romanists and Protestants, and friendly relations between them have been often established. Then, again, in consequence of the increased facilities for visiting the Continent, the English mind has become accustomed to many of the peculiarities of the Romish system. Much in that system has been discovered to be practically good; and, in many instances, the ceremonies which have been uncharitably sneered at as mummeries have been, upon examination, found to be ordinances pregnant with deep meaning. This intercourse with Romanists has led also to the discovery that many of the traditional stories prevalent in England concerning Romanism have no foundation in fact, being the inventions merely of malignant wickedness, zealously received by malignant credulity, and so often repeated as to have assumed the appearance of an undoubted truth. But when once we have made the discovery that we have wronged a person or party, by having believed what is not the truth with respect to him or them, if we have a spark of generosity in our nature we are not only anxious to do justice to that person or party, but also to their self-vindication on other points we are inclined to listen favourably; and hence Romanism has obtained not only a hearing, but a favourable hearing. The case against the Romanist having been overstated, candid minds are suspicious of all the anti-papistical statements made by Protestants, and the Romanist may fairly say, 'If on one point you have been satisfied with my explanations, why not listen to my explanation on other points, which you will probably find equally satisfactory?' Thus it is, that though falsehoods may seem to profit a controversialist for the time, they will in the end do damage to his cause. God will not permit His cause to be maintained by weapons taken from the armoury of Satan.

Then again we may trace the progress of Romanism to the fact, that Protestant sects and parties, which were formerly distinguished for asceticism and self-denial, have gradually become worldly and self-indulgent. The Protestant religious world can no longer be regarded as self-denying; it denounces amusements prevalent in the world, which it calls profane, but only to supply their place by amusements peculiar to itself, which are the more offensive from their being connected with a form of godliness. We have the bitterness, without the austerity of the Puritans, their self-sufficiency without their pure morality, their ostentation, without their piety, their phraseology, without their contempt for creature comforts. Without entering into the question whether asceticism and austerity be or be not desirable in the professors of godliness, there are, and always have been and always will be, some minds in which religion will take this turn; and if these find the shadow only of asceticism, lingering in the once ascetic sects of Protestants, and see the thing itself wholly discouraged by English Churchmen, while they find the substance in the Romish sects, they will naturally incline to Romanism, and receive with gladness those devotional books and exercises which minister to their emotions of thoughtful sadness.

The temper, too, exhibited by the Protestant world at the present time assists the Romanist in palliating that portion of the past history of his Church, which excites against her our strongest prejudices and our just indignation: namely, the persecutions to which the Reformers generally, and the Reformers of the English Church in particular, were exposed in the sixteenth century. On this point, indeed, we do not find the modern Romanist in general attempting to defend himself, further than to maintain, what can scarcely be denied, that by party violence the facts have been sometimes exaggerated. Here he only seeks a drawn battle: he contents himself with saying, 'If we were intolerant in an intolerant age, were you any better? If we persecuted under Mary, did not you persecute under Cromwell? And if you reply, that you censure the Puritans of Cromwell's time, we rejoin, that we censure the Papists in Queen Mary's time. And, as regards the state of things at present, if you point to the toleration now obtained for Romanism in England, we point to the toleration of Protestantism in Roman Catholic countries and even in Rome itself.'

This seems to be a fair argument against Protestantism in the abstract, and against mere Protestants, and, as I have already hinted, it obtains the greater force when reference is made to the bitterness of spirit, 'the hatred, variance, emulations, wrath, strife, envying,' which are characteristic of the Protestant world at the present time, when every man's hand seems to be against his brother, whether he be Catholic, Romanist, or Protestant. The Romanist may fairly argue, that the spirit of a Bonner or of a Gardiner may animate the heart of a Protestant as well as of the Papist, and may be as truly exhibited in the maledictions of the press, as in the fires of Smithfield; in moral as in physical persecution.

Nor may we here forget the deep impression made upon the minds of many by the solemnity of the religious services of Rome; a man of the world observing and expressing clearly the feelings of others says, 'that not only the impressive melody of the vocal and instrumental music, but the imposing solemnity of the ceremonies, raise the character of religion, and give it an air of dignity and majesty unknown to any of the reformed Churches.' *

Here, again, I am not enquiring whether this be a right or wrong impression; I only quote the words to show that such an impression is made, and I mention the fact as one of the reasons why the cause of Romanism is gaining ground among us. These ceremonies may be ridiculed by some persons; although his heart must be radically bad who suffers himself to ridicule, however he may censure, the worship of any human being: the motive is always to be respected even when the action is wrong. But be these ceremonies ridiculous or not (which, in truth, is merely a matter of opinion), the impression they make on some devout and imaginative hearts is great. And hence to the ceremonies of religion, wherever Church principles prevail, a due importance will be attached. When men regard the prayers as only another form of preaching, and are desirous of obtaining through the Liturgy, as from the sermon, instruction or excitement

---

* 'An Analytical Enquiry into the Principles of Taste,' by Richard Payne Knight, p. 363.

for themselves; when they look upon public worship only as a useful exercise of their own minds, they will find ceremonies in their way, they will find it more useful to sit than to kneel, because they can hear better; they will wish the minister to face them, and to address them, that they may hear distinctly every word he utters; they will wish to have the prayers read to them, and they would remove all forms but those which enable the preacher of the prayers to address them, or, as the common phrase is, ' to pray to them ' the more easily. It is only consistent in latitudinarians, thinking of themselves, their feelings, and their excitements, to despise ceremonies which are to them, and under these circumstances, so much worse than useless, that one is scarcely surprised to find such persons, when not bound by traditional prejudices of education, preferring the ostentatiously unceremonious worship of the conventicle to that of the Church, in which some ceremonies are unavoidable, even by those of the clergy who, in violating the Rubric, are the most criminal. But take the Church view of public worship, and then, as I have said, their due importance will be attached to the ceremonies of divine worship. Once realize the idea that public worship is not a mere attendance at an appointed place to hear of GOD; that it is not a mere saying of prayer in public which may be nearly as well done in private; once realize the idea that it is the means vouchsafed to a privileged class, the elect of God, of offering to the King of kings, in communion with all holy creatures, cherubim and seraphim and all the hosts of heaven, the spiritual sacrifice of prayer and praise, and of making known the Church's wants to her Divine Head; once realize this sublime idea of public worship, and the value of ceremonies will be simultaneously admitted: for by ceremonies this idea is fostered; and if we approach our earthly sovereign with much of ceremony, that we may not fall into an undue familiarity, so will the same feeling influence us—a feeling of awful reverence— whenever we approach the King of kings and Lord of lords, to give outward demonstration of our internal sentiments, and, like the seraphim, with whom we worship, to veil our faces when standing before Him, who if He permits Christians to approach Him as a Father, is still the Sovereign, though the paternal Ruler of all things.

It would, indeed, be uncandid, were we to deny, when accounting for the progress of Romanism, that the prominence of late years given to Church principles must have some influence; and we should observe what that influence is, and how far it extends. On examining the Church of England through her formularies, we discover that there are many principles which we hold in common with Romanists: they, as we, regard decency and order in approaching the Almighty God; they, as we, expect to meet God where He has promised to meet us, in His Sacraments, when our hearts are prepared to receive Him. Such being the case, it is not wonderful that latitudinarian establishmentarians, when they embrace the doctrines of the One Holy Catholic and Apostolic Church, should apply to Romanism the principle upon which, before their conversion, they were accustomed to act towards Protestants. Hitherto they have been accustomed to hold a confederacy with all who agree with them in the doctrine of justification, even although they violate every principle of the Church: it is, then, as I have said, quite natural that, upon their conversion, they should incline to unite with those whose Church principles seem to coincide with theirs, although on the doctrine of justification and on other points they may differ. Into this error those who have been catholically educated in the discipline and doctrine of the Church of England are not likely to fall; though of course there may be exceptions to the rule; for they have been taught from their youth upwards to mark and avoid the promoters of schism as much on the one side as on the other; they hold their Church principles consistently, and applying those principles to every point of doctrine and practice, they do not elevate one set of principles out of their proportion and above another set of principles; and having not merely skimmed their surface, but sounded their depth, they see how the Romanist sets Episcopacy aside by the addition of Popery, how he interferes with the doctrine of the Sacraments, by placing other ordinances on an equality with the two Sacraments of justification, and how, by excess in devotional ceremonies, he renders them extravagant rather than impressive. As people come to be more generally educated in sound Church principles, the danger of regarding Romanism too favourably will wear away; for, as we have seen, the danger chiefly rests on those who are converts from latitudinarianism; it is not a danger to which persons who have been always consistent Churchmen are much exposed.

But converts from latitudinarianism are the more exposed to this danger, and the Romanists are especially aided by those who continue to be latitudinarians. Very great is the assistance which Romanists receive from these parties. As to doctrine, the object of the Romanist is to confound Catholicism with Romanism; and in this object their cause is not only supported, but most zealously advocated by latitudinarians. Latitudinarians preach Popery by their very opposition to it. Whenever the Romanists seek to confound their rule of faith with ours, because in the formation of her theological system, and in the interpretation of Scripture, the Church of England and all sound Anglican divines defer to the traditional practices of the primitive ages, although she at the same time asserts the perfection of Scripture, which 'containeth ALL things necessary to salvation; so that whatsoever is not read therein, nor may be proved thereby, is not to be required of any man that it should be believed as an article of the Faith, or thought requisite or necessary to salvation';—* when they would confound this use of tradition as an interpreter with their abuse of it, by which the perfection of Scripture is denied, and tradition is regarded as an additional rule of faith, of equal obligation with Scripture itself—when they thus confound with their unsafe and unsound doctrine a system of interpretation which must commend itself to the minds of all intelligent, if unprejudiced, men, the Ro-

* Article VI.

manists are too often aided by latitudinarian violence, which would represent, as Romanists in disguise, all who hold that true doctrine of tradition by which alone the Romanists can be successfully refuted. Precisely in the same manner are Romanists assisted by latitudinarians, when the former seek to confound those two distinct doctrines—the Scriptural doctrine of the real Presence in the Eucharist, and the doctrine of transubstantiation, which is repugnant to the plain words of Scripture: or, when proceeding on the same principle of equivocation, they would represent as identical the primitive doctrine of a representative and spiritual sacrifice in the Holy Communion, and their own 'blasphemous fable and dangerous deceit,' that in the mass there is a true, proper, and propitiatory sacrifice for the living and the dead. In these and in other similar matters, the Romanists are too often assisted by the grandiloquent ignorance of our popular preachers.

The time does not permit, nor does the occasion require, that I should direct your attention to the precise points wherein the distinction between these several doctrines consists; but since the distinction is obvious to those who have seriously considered these subjects, since many who would reject Romish innovations of a date comparatively modern, are prepared to receive what is ancient and Catholic, it is quite clear that the cause of Rome must be greatly strengthened, when, their assertions in this respect being reiterated by Protestants, they are thus permitted by those who are most violently opposed to them, to confound Romanism with Catholicism. I am at present merely stating a fact, not advocating any system of doctrine. It is a fact, that many persons, whether right or wrong, are ready to receive what is Catholic; and if large classes of persons, latitudinarians, and Romanists opposed in everything else, agree in this, that Catholicism and Romanism are one, we must not be surprised if some persons are found to believe this at last, and so to give way before the sophistry used by the advocates of Rome.

It is thus that the Romanists have been permitted at this time to place themselves on a ground more advantageous than any which they have occupied in this country since the time of the Reformation. The controversy between us and Rome is now regarded by many as one bearing chiefly on the truth of certain opinions, which must be left to the decision of each man's private judgment; and on the expediency of certain forms and practices, which must be decided by each man's taste and feeling. So that there is, as it were, a kind of sectarian warfare waged between us, and we are occupied chiefly in details; some men pointing out peculiar excellences which they suppose themselves to have discovered in the Romish system, others contending that everything connected with Rome is hopelessly and irretrievably corrupt; while not a few, both in Rome and in England, hope and believe that a re-union between the two Churches may in a short course of time be effected. In all this the gain is incalculable on the side of Rome. This is called Popery, and that is called Popery, and everything that a perverse man dislikes, or an ignorant man does not understand, he calls Popery, until men begin to think that, after all, Popery is as often right as it is wrong; and thus they keep out of view the real, besetting, withering sin of Popery. Let us concede to Rome, for the sake of argument, all that she demands; let us accept her exaggerations, whether in her own favour or to our disparagement; let us admit that in her interpretation of Scripture she is as likely to be right as the latitudinarian; let us acknowledge that in the majesty of her services, and the symbolical sublimity of her ordinances, she surpasses the Church of England; for the sake of argument, let us admit this, and more than this—still we are compelled to ask: 'In whose praise does the pealing anthem swell along your aisles? for whose honour is this high service intended?' And in nine cases out of ten the answer must be, that these things are intended, not for the sole glory of God, the Blessed Trinity, but for the honour of the creature, of one 'highly favoured,' no doubt, 'among women:' but if of creatures the most distinguished, still a creature, and merely a creature, a woman born like ourselves in sin, and saved only by the blood-shedding of her Blessed Son—they are intended for the honour of the Virgin Mary.

This is the answer—the idolatry of Rome—to be returned to all those, whether in the Church of England or in the Church of Rome, who dream of a re-union between the two Churches.

How is it possible by any concessions, by any explanations, to effect a reconciliation between two religious communities, in which the object of worship is not the same? How can there be union with Rome, while she practically elevates the Virgin Mary into an idol, and we, who hold the perfection of Scripture, are commanded to keep ourselves from idols?

We might indeed regard the Romanists as idolaters for their worship of images; but they tell us that they do not intend by this unholy practice to worship wood and stone, the work of men's hands, but the person whom the wood and stone represents. Let us then accept their explanation, with the passing observation, that if the explanation suffices, such a sin as the worship of images never existed, and the second commandment was as needless to the sons of Israel as it seems to be regarded by the Church of Rome, for the very heathens must have held this same doctrine with reference to their images; and if they thought one image more holy than another, they were only guilty of the same inconsistency as the Romanists. But, as I have said, on this point we will forbear to dwell, that we may proceed to inquire, whom does the image represent? Whose image is that which is most honoured and adorned in every Romish sanctuary? And the very stones cry out that the image which stands foremost is that of the Blessed Virgin.

It is said that supplication is only made to the Virgin that she may act as the intercessor of her worshippers. We at once may answer, that to apply to her for intercession (and what I now say has reference to the whole doctrine of the intercession of departed saints), is to interfere with one of the fundamental verities of our holy faith—one of the deepest sources of Christian consolation—the intercession of the one and only Mediator.

PERIL OF IDOLATRY. 103

Against this sin the exhortations are many in the New Testament, because into this sin 'little children' are easily led; and it is because the sin is the result of a Scriptural principle wrongly applied, that those who have been educated in it are so unwilling to renounce it. The voice of nature as well as of revelation declares that the Almighty Lord God is to the sinful creature an awful Being, a terrible Lord God, a consuming fire: this is a truth at the very foundation of all revealed religion, a truth implied in the condemnation of our race for original sin, and in man's consequent need of a Saviour. Except through the intercession of a Mediator, God is too awful to be approached by man, even in a state of redemption. But what is the glory, what the consolation of the Gospel? Is it not this: that, to provide us with a Mediator— to afford us the means of approaching the otherwise unapproachable God—the Word was made flesh, and the manhood was taken into God: so that in the Lord Jesus, perfect God though He be, we have a great High Priest that is passed into the heavens—a High Priest who can be touched with the feelings of our infirmities, and was in all points tempted like as we are, though without sin?* Although to approach God, then, in Himself were impossible, we may approach God Incarnate—in Him we may abide, and He will abide in us, if through faith we are in a state of justification; and abiding in Him who is God as well as man, we are in communion with God Himself. Having such a

* Heb. iv. 15.

Mediator, we are commanded 'to come boldly,' that is, without looking through a false humility for any other Mediator, to 'come boldly to the throne of grace, that we may obtain mercy, and find grace to help in time of need.'* Is it not an impeachment of the mercy of God Incarnate, our only Mediator, to seek any other intercessor? The Romanists seem to forget that although the Lord Jesus Christ is true God, and to be worshipped, He is also very man: were it not so, they would not, in their eagerness for another Mediator, invest their 'Virgin of the assumption' with the attributes of Deity, and so place her in the only Mediator's office. It is no answer to this to say that we ourselves employ the intercession of living saints, and that all who believe in the communion of saints believe that the holy ones in the Church triumphant unite their prayers with ours; for the question here is, as to the principle upon which the prayers of others are sought. We do not seek the prayers of others—we do not value intercessory prayer, as a means by which we may approach Him who, except for such intercession, we should not dare to approach. We seek not the prayers of our fellow-creatures as if by their own righteousness, their own entreaty, they could obtain what we cannot. But we pray for one another, because there is a mysterious efficacy in joint prayer, ordained by God, of which efficacy, through the medium of Christian friends, we would avail ourselves; even as for the general welfare the one voice of the universal Church goes up on high—the incense of prayer, grateful to the Al-

* Heb. iv. 16.

mighty Father when offered through the mediation of His only begotten Son. The word intercession is used in the two cases in a different sense.

But, my brethren, it is not as an intercessor, only or chiefly, that the Virgin Mary is worshipped in the Church of Rome. To her the Romanist flies for direct refuge and protection; to her he prays directly for strength against all his enemies, visible and invisible, and (it is an awful thought!) upon her he calls to say unto his soul, I am thy salvation—although 'there is no Saviour beside Me,'* saith the Lord of hosts. But still further: to her the Romanists ascribe the attributes of God Himself: they address her, as their patroness and deliverer; they pray to her to assist them, to guide them in their councils; they address her as able to do all things in heaven and earth. I do not deny that God, the Blessed Trinity, is also worshipped in the Roman Church; but when I speak of the idolatry of Rome, I ask whether He and He only is worshipped? I might almost ask, with reference to some foreign Churches, whether God, the Blessed Trinity, is the chief object of worship? And what is idolatry but the giving to anything created that homage, that adoration, that worship, which is due only to the Creator? † The very reason why the highest title

* Isaiah xliii. 11.
† Upon this subject I may refer the reader to the first and fifth of the Letters to Dr. Wiseman, by the Rev. William Palmer, of Worcester College—letters which have not been refuted. I may add the following extracts from the Psalter of Bonaventure.
Extract from the 'Crown of the Blessed Virgin':—
'O thou, our governor, and most benignant Lady, in right of

which the Virgin bears was conceded to her by the Universal Church in the Council of Ephesus—that of

being His mother, command your most beloved Son, our Lord Jesus Christ, that he deign to raise our minds from longing after earthly things to the contemplation of heavenly things.'

Extract from a 'Parody on the Te Deum,' by the same writer:

'We praise thee, Mother of God ; we acknowledge thee to be a virgin. All the earth doth worship thee, the spouse of the eternal Father. All the angels and archangels, all thrones and powers do faithfully serve thee. To thee all angels cry aloud, with a never-ceasing voice, Holy, holy, holy, Mary, Mother of God. . . . The whole court of heaven doth honour thee as Queen. The holy Church throughout all the world doth invoke and praise thee, the Mother of Divine Majesty. . . Thou sittest with thy Son on the right hand of the Father. . . In thee, sweet Mary, is our hope; defend us for evermore. Praise becometh thee ; empire becometh thee ; virtue and glory be unto thee for ever and ever.'

Extract from a 'Parody on the Athanasian Creed,' by the same writer :—

'Whosoever will be saved, before all things it is necessary that he hold the right faith concerning Mary ; which faith, except every-one do keep whole and undefiled, without doubt he shall perish everlastingly. . . He (Jesus Christ) sent the Holy Spirit upon his disciples, and upon his mother, and at last took her up into heaven, where she sitteth on the right hand of her Son, and never ceaseth to make intercession with Him for us.

'This is the faith concerning the Virgin Mary, which, except every one do believe faithfully and firmly, he cannot be saved.' *

Extract from a work by Alphonsus Liguori, called ' The Glories of Mary':—†

'During the pontificate of Gregory the Great the people of Rome experienced in a most striking manner the protection of the Blessed Virgin. A frightful pestilence raged in the city to such an extent

---

* 'Sancti Bonaventuræ Opera,' tom. vi. part ii., from p. 466 to 473. Fol. Moguntiæ, 1609.

† 'The Glories of Mary, Mother of God, translated from the Italian of blessed Alphonsus Liguori, and carefully revised by a Catholic Priest.' John Coyne, Dublin, 1833.

Mother of God, is a kind of protest against this sin of worshipping her. The Church worships the Lord Jesus Christ, and says, 'Son of David, have mercy upon us.' But this even we should not do unless it were our faith that the divine and human natures are united together in the one Person of the Lord Jesus

that thousands were carried off, and so suddenly, that they had not time to make the least preparation. It could not be arrested by the vows and prayers which the holy Pope caused to be offered in all quarters, until he resolved on having recourse to the Mother of God. Having commanded the clergy and people to go in procession to the church of our Lady, called St. Mary Major, carrying the picture of the Holy Virgin, painted by St. Luke, the miraculous effects of her intercession were soon experienced; in every street as they passed the plague ceased, and before the end of the procession an angel in human form was seen on the tower of Adrian, named ever since the Castle of St. Angelo, sheathing a bloody sabre. At the same moment the angels were heard singing the anthem "Regina Cœlia," "Triumph, O Queen, Hallelujah." The holy pope added "Ora pro nobis Deum," pray for us, &c. The Church has since used this anthem to salute the Blessed Virgin in Easter time.'—*True Devotion to the Blessed Virgin*, p. 21.

Extract from the Encyclical Letter of Pope Gregory XVI. :—

'Having at length taken possession of our See in the Lateran Basilica, according to the custom and institution of our predecessors, we turn to you without delay, venerable brethren ; and in testimony of our feeling towards you, we select for the date of our letter this most joyful day, on which we celebrate the solemn festival of the most Blessed Virgin's triumphant assumption into heaven; that she, who has been through every great calamity our patroness and protectress, may watch over us writing to you, and lead our mind by her heavenly influence to those counsels which may prove most salutary to Christ's flock. . . But that all may have a successful and happy issue, let us raise our eyes to the most Blessed Virgin Mary, who alone destroys heresies, who is our greatest hope, yea, the entire ground of our hope.'

For other quotations to the same purpose see the very useful and learned volume ' On Roman Fallacies and Catholic Truths,' by the Rev. H. T. Powell.

Christ, so that they impart to each other their different attributes. The two natures are so joined together that neither subsists without the other, and both together form one single Person, which cannot be separated in all eternity. Him, therefore, that was born of the Virgin we may worship as the Son of David, without idolatry, for though the Son of David He is also God Himself: and thus we find, that as in seeking the intercession of the Virgin, the Romanists dishonour the manhood of Christ, so in making her the object of prayer, they do dishonour to his Godhead.

Assuredly it was in the spirit of prophecy that St. John wrote the words of our text. He addresses himself to little children; not to angry controversialists, contending for opinions, but to persons of meek, and gentle, and child-like dispositions; and he foresees that to the sin of idolatry such persons may possibly be tempted: their deep abiding sense of the holiness of God, their reverent disposition, their solemn consciousness of their own unworthiness, will make them realize to their hearts their incessant need of a mediator; and therefore he sets before them the Lord Jesus Christ as the one prevailing Intercessor, who, though God, is also man, and may therefore be by man approached, even as an elder brother; and thus, in directing them to keep themselves from idols, he exhorts them to seek no other intercessor except that which it is the glory of Christians to possess.

Here let us pause. We have seen some of the reasons why we should expect that Romanism should at the present time be gaining ground; we have also seen what its real sin is—to which, in fact, all the peculiarities of that Church, all that is Romish and not Catholic, either directly or indirectly, tend. And since there can be no doubt that all here present, having been educated in a branch of the Catholic Church which has been purified from idolatry, hold that practice in a just abhorrence, we must all feel it to be our bounden duty to prevent 'little children' from being perverted to Romanism.

But you will have observed, from what has been already said, that idolatry is a sin which may be so veiled, that the Christian, not less than the Jew of old, may be deceived into the commission of it. By Scripture, indeed, we are warned that there is danger of idolatry among Christians; and when we look upon the largest portion of Christendom, we find the prevalence of idolatry in the Christian Church to be a fact. In the Roman Church there have been, and there are, men of enlightened minds, who have nevertheless been reconciled to the worship of the Virgin; and we are not therefore to suppose that nothing can be urged in favour of it. Viewing Mariolatry as we do, we at once pronounce Rome to be idolatrous; but against idolatry, nakedly considered, the Romanist would protest equally with ourselves. It comes to his mind, accustomed to the practice from early youth, disguised by the sophistry which seeks a distinction between Mariolatry and idolatry, although none does in reality exist. Let us not then proudly say, ' Here is idolatry; no true Christian can be perverted to it.' For the arguments, whatever they may be, which satisfy those who were born within the pale of the Romish Church, to what we, having no prejudices in her favour, regard as idolatry, may, though of course with greater difficulty, reconcile to it the most determined Protestant, if, in seeking the consolations of religion and aids to devotion, that Protestant is drawn by circumstances to hold friendly intercourse with the Romish Separatists.

Let this be borne in mind by those latitudinarians who remain in the Church of England, and who would fain drive out of it those of their brethren who, in renouncing Romish peculiarities, still retain Catholic truth, and cling with affection to the Catholic practices preserved in our Church. I would entreat and implore them to consider what it is that they propose to do. They hold the right of private judgment, and then, because the private judgment of others differs from their own in some matters of doctrine or opinion, they would drive them to idolatry. Supposing them to be right, and to have (what I believe they have not) sound knowledge—still we may ask them, 'Through thy knowledge shall the weak brother perish for whom Christ died? When ye so sin against the brethren, and wound their weak conscience, ye sin against Christ.'* I am sure they would not so act, if it were not that, without due consideration, they apply to others principles peculiar to themselves. A latitudinarian making his religion to consist in the system of theology which commends itself to his private judgment, means by a Church, an association of persons whose general opinions as to the sense of Scripture are the

* I. Cor. viii. 11, 12.

same. If circumstances were to occur to force such a one from the Church of England, he might suffer some worldly detriment, but spiritual damage, in his own estimation, he would receive none. He might unite himself to the Presbyterians or the Independents, whose opinions he may conceive to be substantially accordant with the Thirty-nine Articles; or if he prefer the Liturgy to extempore prayer, he might form a sect using it either wholly or in part, as may seem to him most expedient. But he ought to remember that, however much he may despise them, they who hold the doctrine of 'one Catholic and Apostolic Church' have a principle different from his, which, whether right or wrong in his opinion, must influence them. Contending as they must for orthodoxy of doctrine, their religion does not consist in their opinions, or in the maintenance of a peculiar system of theology; what they seek is the supernatural grace of God: this grace —be they fools for doing so or not—they seek in the appointed way, and they believe it is to be conferred on hearts prepared by penitence and faith to receive it by God the Holy Ghost, through the Sacraments of justification: but the Sacraments, to be salutary, must, as they believe, be duly administered, and to be duly administered, they must be administered by persons commissioned by God, and they therefore hold the necessity of the Apostolical succession; which succession, notwithstanding the combined efforts of the Romanists and the latitudinarians to prove the contrary, they believe to exist in the Church of England, and therefore they love her, their spiritual mother, with no ordinary love. Now these persons, for holding all these great truths of the Gospel, may be regarded by latitudinarians as weaker than little children—'we are weak, and ye are wise.' But if any party shall say to them, 'the emoluments of an Establishment should be administered to propagate the opinions of the majority, who only are competent, whether they have studied the subject or not, to pronounce on the meaning of her formularies; you happen to form the minority; we scorn you, we hate you, we despise you, but will tolerate you, if you will quit the Establishment, and form a new sect of yourselves out of the Church'— that party exhorts them to do what they have no power to do. Belonging to the Church, not because it is an Establishment, but because it is a branch of the Catholic Church, they cannot form a sect, for a sect would not supply to them what in a Church they require; and therefore if at any time they are driven by a tyrant majority from the Church of England, and in consequence from all Churches in visible communion with her, they can only go to the Church of Rome. And Rome, we know, deals gently, if not craftily, with those who thus resort to her. The Romanists in England regard themselves as missionaries, and their system of conducting missions is to act leniently as to what they consider errors in their converts, and, if there be a willing mind, to lead them gradually to what they deem to be the truth: the prejudices of their converts against worshipping the Blessed Virgin they will for a season bear with; they have even gone so far as to say, that such worship is tolerated rather than enjoined in their formularies; liberty of opinion will be granted them for a time; and only a little time will be necessary, for the mind will gradually yield its consent to what it sees practised by persons loved and respected; and so it is, that all who hold communion with Rome, whatever may be the explanations they adopt, become practical idolaters.

See, then, the sin into which the latitudinarian would drive these 'little children,' merely because their private judgment differs from his own. I say their private judgment; for even though in forming our judgment we defer to the tradition of the Church, still, since it is our judgment, we have a right to claim for it the respect which is shown to the judgment of any other person, however differently formed. It is more than private judgment—but it is private judgment also. But when I call upon latitudinarians to be consistent, and rather to tolerate a difference of opinion than to place men in a peril of idolatry, let it not be supposed that I would speak lightly of soundness of doctrine. We are never to forget that heresy is a sin, and therefore to be strongly opposed; but then we ought always to remember what heresy is. By heresy we mean a perverse adherence to any deduction of Scripture made by our private judgment, when that deduction is found to be contrary to a decision or definition of the Church. It is evident from this, that they who tell us that their religion is the Bible, and the Bible only, as interpreted by each man's private judgment for himself, can have no right to predicate heresy of any other man, for morally speaking (and heresy has reference to the morals) one man's private judgment is as good as another's; and if he errs intellectually, he may be regarded as a bad logician, but not surely as a heretic. And therefore when anyone holding these principles speaks of any other one as a heretic, he only uses a hard word to gratify his malevolent feelings, and speaks of him as a person who, under such a system, cannot have an existence. There must be a Church with power to decide, before there can be a heresy; and heresy is an offence ascertainable in any given instance by a prosecution in our ecclesiastical courts. Let the Sabellian and the Nestorian, let those who deny the grace of the Sacraments, and contradict in the pulpit the doctrine taught at the font or the altar, be duly punished—but within the limits permitted by the Church let liberty be conceded to them, and the liberty we claim for ourselves let us extend to others.

On one point, however, we must be all agreed, that idolatry is a sin; and if it be a sin practised by Rome, surely it becomes our duty, instead of doing that which may drive men to Rome, to rob Rome on the contrary of her attractions by supplying in our own Church the wants of our little children, whether it be meat or milk.

Why should we send to Rome those who, like St. Paul, would be 'in fastings often,' and who, while rejoicing in their Christian privileges, would mingle sorrow with their joy, and rejoice with trembling; who, while regarding the Lord's day as a feast, their great spiritual and weekly holiday, would seek to mortify the flesh, and more and more effectually to crucify the whole body of sin on the weekly fast, and on those other days of fasting and abstinence appointed by the Church? Are these persons to be made favourable to Rome, as they will be, if for obeying the Church of England they are reviled as semi-papists; by which it is insinuated that the papists obey their Church, while we persecute those that obey ours? Surely the difficulty here lies not with the reviled, but with the revilers; the difficulty is not to prove that we of the Church of England may fast, but that we may abstain from fasting. Let those who in this respect assume a dispensing power (and, in the present state of discipline among us, when we must each take the dispensing power upon ourselves, I wish to imply censure to no one), let those that feast while others fast be content with their liberty, and not speak harshly of others, who, in fasting, do what their accusers perhaps are unable to do; lest peradventure it be said of their revilers, that they reviled because they felt self-condemned, and desired the fame of godliness, without its self-denials.

Certainly no man need leave the Church of England in order to lead a stricter and more serious life, if he will only conform his conduct to the rules of her Prayer Book and the direction of her Canons.

By members of the Legislature, and by certain portions of the public press, a contrast is often made between the Clergy of the Church of England and the Clergy of the Church of Rome; and however indignant we may feel if the comparison is permitted to be in favour of the latter, and however unjust such a comparison may be, if it is made to the disparagement of the general zeal and activity of the present race of

English Clergy, yet, since attention having been called, attention will now be paid to this subject, we may depend upon it, that if it shall be found that in those ordinances and observances which are common to the Churches of England and Rome, the Clergy of Rome adhere piously to all the solemn arrangements of their Church, and the Clergy of England, although the ordinances and observances are strictly enjoined by the Prayer Book and the Canons, from whatever cause, evade them, or so perform them as only to render them mere forms, burdensome to themselves and unmeaning to others, the end will be that an impression will be made on the public mind in favour of the Roman, and to the prejudice of the English priests. And woe to the Clergy of England, if, by their perverseness or their carelessness, it shall be found, at the last day, that we have been the cause of sending 'little children' to Rome, stained as she is by idolatry. But let the Clergy of England, instead of despising, observe, to the very letter, as far as may be, what the Church appoints; let them be persuaded, whether Bishops, Priests, or Deacons, that the discretionary power they now assume, as to the regulations of the Church, is a very dangerous as well as a questionable power; let them humbly remember, that although they are not, or rather ought not to be, as dissenting teachers, slaves of their congregations, they are, nevertheless, the sworn servants of the Church, to whom they are to render the most dutiful obedience. Yes, the Bishops themselves, though fathers to us, are only servants of the Church; and let all the Clergy bear in mind, that the Church has been endowed, that they receive the wages of the Church, not to do good in the way their private judgment may think best, not as mere almoners to the poor, or superintendents of schools, important as these offices in addition are, but that the Church may have servants in each parish, prepared to administer not what ordinances they approve of, but all the ordinances of the Church, not in the manner they best like, but in the precise manner prescribed by the Church, to every member of the Church residing within their respective parishes, who, being qualified to participate in them, demands them at our hands. The Quaker is quite as much justified in refusing to pay the pecuniary dues of the Church, because he disapproves of a religious establishment, as the Clergyman can be who neglects or alters an ordinance because it does not happen to commend itself to his judgment; and any one parishioner has as much right to demand of his pastor the daily prayers, and a strict observance of the festivals, as the pastor has to require the payment of his tithes. The temporal demands are paltry, and beneath contempt, as compared with the spiritual; but I repeat it, the pastor has no more right to refuse daily prayers to the parishioner, than the parishioner his peculiar dues to the Clergyman. Oh! that the laity would insist upon their spiritual rights with half the zeal that latitudinarians exact their worldly hire! The question is not whether some service is rendered to the Church by those who enjoy her endowments, but whether the particular and appointed service is rendered. Let the Clergy, as honest men, consider these things, and then the daily service, the observance of saints' days, the keeping of the festivals will no longer be a mark to distinguish the stricter and more serious of the Clergy; but these things being common in the land, the laity of the Church, to whom, and not to the Clergy only, the Church belongs, since of the body they form the most considerable part, will soon see that it is not necessary to go to Rome in order that they may enjoy those high privileges which as members of the Church, they have a right to enjoy, and for their enjoyment of which the Church of England has made ample provision.

If the Clergy are afraid that, by the performance of these and of other good works,—such as charity the result of self-denial, may suggest,—men will trust in their works, which were indeed a sin; let them not be wiser than the Church itself, which, while it condemns such sin, entertains no such fears. It seems an illegitimate method of preventing men from trusting in their good works to take steps to discourage them from doing any good works at all: let the works be done, and let us charitably hope that they are done only in zeal and love for the King of kings, and not from any vain notion of purchasing that salvation which all, who are consistent Christians, are prepared to profess and proclaim, could be purchased by nothing less than the blood of God Incarnate.

And if it be by the sublimity and grandeur of her services, marking clearly that the offices of devotion are not merely another kind of preaching intended for the instruction of hearers, but the appointed mode by which elect and justified persons approach their God;

if it be by affording through her ordinances free scope to the feelings with which the piously imaginative heart is pregnant—the feelings of awe and majesty, of tenderness and devotion combined, that Rome is winning to her the hearts of 'little children,' undesigning themselves, and therefore unsuspicious of others—let us in very charity, when offering the Church's sacrifice of prayer and praise, endeavour to meet these wants, and to aid these aspirations of persons who feel themselves better qualified to worship and adore their God, than to sit in judgment upon the opinions of a preacher; especially let this be done when all that is required is to perform the services as the Rubric directs, and with such assistance from music as the Church permits; or, at all events, let this observance of the letter, and this deference to the spirit of the English Church, be tolerated in some of our sanctuaries, if it be only to save our little children from the fascinations of Rome. Enough, and more than enough, has been done by those who are political friends, rather than dutiful children of the Church, with a view to conciliate Protestant dissenters, and to render them less hostile to an establishment: old ceremonies have been neglected, and new ones introduced, the tendency of which has been to lower the services addressed to God, and to elevate the preacher's pomp: * in the shape of metrical

* I may instance the ceremonious change of dress which takes place in the middle of the service in many churches. After having said the Prayers in a surplice, the Clergyman proceeds, often with great pomp, to the vestry, where he throws off the surplice, and then comes forth in a silk gown, such as many dissenting preachers use, but which is nowhere ordered in our Prayer Book; and thus

hymns, human inventions have been adopted; and thus a very large addition has been made to that Prayer Book which we have received from our Reformers as they from their Catholic forefathers: while offices, such as that of Baptism and the Holy Communion, have been altered, abridged, parts added to them, and parts taken from them, by the Clergy, who have vowed to observe them entire, but who have seen the evil of preaching one thing at the font or the altar, and another in the pulpit, and have thought themselves right, and the Church, therefore, wrong; and these things have been sanctioned because the end seems to have justified the means, and because by means such as these, the kneelings of our sanctuaries, having been converted into pews, they have been filled by those who, dissenters at heart, have tolerated the prayers, that they may express their sympathies in the metrical hymns, and sit under the favourite orator:—enough, and more than enough, has, in this respect, been done; let something now be conceded, when the Romanists are up and busy in the land, to save 'little children' from idolatry, not by adding to, not by taking from the Prayer Book, but by an honest observance of all that the Church of England therein appoints.

And as this shall be done we shall disarm the Ro-

adorned he proceeds to the pulpit. I may also refer to the custom of late years introduced, of having two pulpits in the church, by which means much space is uselessly occupied. If it be necessary to have a pulpit that the prayers may be preached as well as the sermon, surely one pulpit would suffice. To those who wish to address the Prayers not to the people but to Almighty God, any pulpit, except for the sermon, is offensive. They desire to look *from* the people, not *to* them.

manists of one powerful weapon which they now wield against us; and while we ourselves receive the benefits, which must result from our strict attendance on the Sacraments and ordinances of the Church, and from the reverential spirit of devotion which, through her well-ordered ceremonies, we shall imbibe, Rome may become better inclined to listen to the voice which shall issue from our sanctuaries where all is done decently and in order—when that voice, as of a holy Mother, shall be addressed to loving and dutiful children, saying, 'If there arise among you a prophet or a dreamer of dreams, and giveth thee a sign or a wonder, and the sign or the wonder come to pass whereof he spake unto thee, saying: Let us go after other gods, which thou hast not known, and let us serve them—thou shalt not hearken to that dreamer of dreams, for the Lord your God proveth you, to know whether ye love the Lord your God with all your heart and all your soul; ye shall walk after the Lord your God, and fear Him, and keep His commandments, and obey His voice, and ye shall serve Him and cleave unto Him.'*—Yea, unto Him only. We shall then be able to hear with a charitable patience, and with no sectarian rancour, the praise of what is good in Rome; for we shall have no fear when we are ready to provide for our people what they now too often think can only be obtained in Rome. Our people will see that the very miracles of Rome, if proved to be true, would, on account of her idolatry, be uninfluential; and if Rome shall say, 'Behold the signs and wonders that we do,' we shall at once reply, 'Little children, keep yourselves from idols.'

* Deut. xiii. 1–4.

SERMON XXIII.*

'*But if any man seem to be contentious, we have no such custom, neither the churches of God.*'—I. Cor. xi. 16.

NOTHING can be more striking, nothing more perfect in its charity, than the manner in which, in the 8th chapter of this Epistle, and the 14th chapter to the Romans, St. Paul treats the weaker brethren, and directs that they should be treated by others. Would to God that in these days those who esteem themselves, or are accounted by others, the stronger brethren, would act on this principle and walk by this rule!

However learned, however mighty in the Scriptures, however skilful as critics or profound as metaphysicians, those persons may be who are usually denominated High Churchmen, they are regarded by many as weaker brethren, utterly ignorant of the Gospel. If it be so, if they are weaker brethren in the opinion of those who thus assume authority to decide (sometimes, it must be admitted, without any great proficiency in theology), let them receive that gentle treatment, that allowance for conscientious prejudices, that courtesy, consideration, and kindness which St. Paul recommends. If they are in error, let them be refuted by argument; if they violate the regulations or principles of the Church of England, let the fact be proved and let

* Preached in St. Andrew's Church, Manchester, 1845.

them be suspended; but admonish them affectionately as brethren in Christ: do not resort to the arts of the profane; do not misrepresent their principles, or ridicule that conduct which, however absurd it may appear to others, they believe to be pious; do not denounce them without hearing what they have to say, or without reading, with unprejudiced minds, what they may have written : do not attribute wrong motives to them : do not call them Jesuits in disguise : do not hold them up as persons desirous to deceive. For why should they wish to deceive you more than their accusers? Their principles are not those which lead to preferment: they can only maintain them because they believe them to be the truth as it is in Jesus.*

Among the heaviest of the charges which are brought against them, their regard for antiquity and

* We have certainly just cause to complain of the Religious Tract Society, although it is supported by many good and pious men, when we find it stated in a recent number of its 'Monthly Record,' entitled 'The Christian Spectator,' that those who hold the principles advocated in the present discourse are enemies to the cause of Christian truth, more formidable than the Socialists; the Socialists being atheistic sensualists. They are accused, with the papists, of 'an intense dislike of the peculiar doctrines of Scripture.' Comparing them with avowed infidels, the work referred to, says: 'It is not possible that the object of either party could be more plainly declared. The one would throw down the Christianity of the Bible, the other would dig up the foundations of Christianity altogether. These their purposes they loudly proclaim and fiercely pursue. They have declared a war of extermination, and the inscription on the banner of both is, I will overturn, overturn, overturn.' See the 'Christian Spectator' for September 18, 1839, and the Rev. Wm. Dalby's letter to the Editor of the 'British Magazine.' However much in error the supporters of that society may consider High Churchmen to be, they are surely going too far when they speak of them in such language as this.

their respect for the Fathers is the most prominent. But what does this offence amount to?

Let me state, in a few words, what their principle is. In all questions of doctrine and practice which which may arise in the Christian Church, they fully admit that the first and last appeal lies to Holy Scripture. 'To the Law and to the Testimony; if they speak not according to this word, it is because there is no light in them.' * And where both parties agree in their interpretation of the words of Scripture, this appeal will bring all controversies to the most satisfactory determination. The private Christian, looking into this true mirror, discovers the blemishes and defects in his own conduct; and the Church puts on her ornaments, and is sanctified and cleansed by the Word.

But a little observation will convince us that the controversies which arise in the Church can seldom be decided by this appeal. The records of past ages prove this, and daily experience shows it. Each party in a dispute claims Scripture for its own side, and, as the sense of Scripture, it zealously maintains its own interpretation. If there be, then, no further appeal, the question can never be decided. There is, therefore, another test, which, in the opinion of those I am defending, Scripture itself allows and sanctions—the testimony of the Church from the beginning. And to this test St. Paul, in our text, sets us an example of making an appeal. 'We have no such custom, neither the Churches of God.'

Thus these persons conceive that a way to peace is

* Is. viii. 20.

provided in harmony with the common rule of life, and the law by which society is held together; for how much of law and of the rules of society is based on precedent! They conceive that they act in the spirit of the Church of England; for it is plain to everyone who has considered the language of the Church that a deference to antiquity pervades her Articles, forms the argument of some of her most instructive Homilies, and breathes through every portion of her Prayers: they conceive that 'when they stand in the ways and see and ask for the old paths where is the good way that we may walk therein,'* they act, as I have shown, in accordance with a principle provided for us in Scripture, and in accordance with which St. Paul reasoned in the words of our text.

Now, this it is that induces them to study the writings of the primitive Fathers of the Church. There seems, however, to be a prejudice against the very name of the Fathers; a prejudice which certainly was not felt by Ridley, or by Cranmer, or any of the learned and pious confessors, and martyrs to whom we owe the Reformation of our Church. And why should it be felt now? for, let me ask, who are the Fathers? They are merely ancient writers who lived in the earlier ages of the Church. Now, one would think that there could be no great sin in our venturing to read the works of these ancient authors. It is said that we ought to refer for our divinity to the Bible and the Bible only. God knows, my brethren, that I wish the Bible were more extensively read than it is, and no one can regret

* Jer. vi. 16.

more than I do to find the Bible so generally superseded by tracts. But those very tracts are most diligently distributed by the very persons who most vehemently blame us for venturing to read the Fathers. Nay, by those persons themselves these tracts are read : in many instances they are the fountains, not always surely the purest, from which they drink in their theology. But what is a tract? It is a little treatise or sermon composed by some person or persons, not, certainly, infallible. Now, similar treatises and sermons form the works of the Fathers. Both parties, then, you will observe, are tract readers, and why should he who reads an ancient tract be blameworthy, while he who reads a modern tract is held worthy of praise? But it is said the modern tracts are sound in doctrine, the ancient tracts are not so. And, let me ask, who says this? Is it said by an infallible man? What proof do you bring from Scripture that modern tracts must be sound in doctrine, and ancient tracts not so? It is merely a matter of opinion, and when one man praises the ancient tracts to the disparagement of the modern, it is quite as probable that his opinion should be correct as that of another person who praises the modern tracts to the disparagement of the ancient ; and more probable, if it is in the nature of truth to be better understood near to the fountain head, than after its transmission through many generations. Is it said that one is Scriptural, the other not Scriptural? This is only repeating the last assertion in a different form. If the tract contain anything of doctrine more than an extract from Scripture without note or comment—and then it is

Scripture itself—it must be a deduction from or an explanation of Scripture, and we have just as much right to assert that the deduction made from Scripture in an ancient tract is Scriptural, as another person has to make the same assertion as to a modern tract. Disagree with us, if you will, in your opinion of this matter—but why object to our principle while you adopt it in another form ? We are both tract readers ; the only difference being that some of us go for these tracts to St Chrysostom, St. Basil, and St. Athanasius, to whom our Prayer Book is indebted for much of its excellence ; others to a modern Religious Tract Society, sanctioned, it may be, by what is called the religious world ; which is, nevertheless, no more infallible than the Church of Rome, though the members of both seem to rely on their traditions with undoubting confidence.*

* By the religious world I mean that conventional union of sects and parties which is formed by those who agree to merge the distinctive features of every sect (and, when Churchmen belong to it, the distinctive features of the Church itself), in order that they may insist in common upon what that world deems to be essential truth. But the question still occurs whether that world is competent to decide what part of the Revelation of God is essential and what is not. Of this proposition those who are called High Churchmen hold the negative. The difficulty of their present position consists in the religious world having assumed that all pious persons must belong to it. But there are persons whose zeal for the cause of religion, whatever may be their faults, is ardent, but who at the same time refuse to subscribe to many of the traditional doctrines and some of the practices of the religious world. The members of the religious world cannot conceive the possibility of such persons being really pious and sincere ; hence their hostility to them : their real fault being their rejection of the tradition of the religious world, the controversy of the present day having reference, in fact, to this one question: according to what tradition shall Scripture be

But it is said, 'Scripture is so plain, we will have the Bible and the Bible only: what need have we of the Fathers in addition? this is to add to the Word of God.' Surely, we may answer, 'Scripture is plain, and we, too, will have the Bible and the Bible only—what need have you of commentators? Their comment is an addition to the Word of God.' But the Bible having come down to us in a dead language we do absolutely require some commentary to elucidate its diction and phraseology—a translation is itself, to a certain extent, a commentary; it might be easily shown how ours actually is so. Again, there is allusion in Scripture to many antiquated rites and customs; and some acquaintance with the history and opinions of the age in which the New Testament was written is important; here, then, we also require a commentary. Is it said that you can get all this from a modern commentator? this is true, and one modern commentator may borrow his facts from another without reference to the original authority, and one may copy the mistakes of another, and hence false facts may become current in the world; but the first commentators must have gone to the contemporary writers, that is to say, to the Fathers. Even admitting, then, that it is a work of supererogation for us to consult the Fathers, to ascertain whether the modern commentators are correct, still there can be nothing sinful in doing so; since, for what you know of these things, you are as dependent upon the Fathers as we are, the difference being interpreted? according to the tradition of the Church of Rome? or according to the tradition of the religious world? or according to the tradition of the primitive Church?—the latter being, as we contend, embodied in the formularies of the Church of England.

that you derive your information from secondary, we from primary sources.

As to doctrine, it is said that the wisest and best plan is to make Scripture its own interpreter, by comparing spiritual things with spiritual. I have already said that this is admitted by those who are complained of; and who are more diligent than they in explaining one Scripture by another? But I have also shown that after having done this, there are still many points on which we cannot come to an agreement,— aye, and important points, too. Now, take any passages or collection of the passages of Holy Scripture, from which you and I deduce a different doctrine. What is it that any disputant does? His favourite commentator is brought down from the shelf, and to him deference is paid. Why? Because he is recognized as the organ expressing the sense, that is, the tradition of his own sect or school, just as a Romish commentator expresses the sense, that is, the tradition of the Church of Rome. Is there any sin, then, if the High Churchman (applying this conceded principle in a different manner) looks to the Fathers, not as an inspired authority, but to ascertain from their writings what was the meaning attached to the passage or passages under consideration in the first ages of the Church, before modern controversies were started? And what makes the value of these primitive writings the greater in this respect is, that the Fathers not only possessed many written documents now lost, but it was part of their religion, if I may so say, to preserve the doctrine they had received in its purity from the Apostles, and to hand it down to their children; they transmitted the once-kindled lamp from sire to son, never suffering its light to grow dim, or its heat to evaporate. And as a member of a lately founded sect can soon detect whether an interpretation of Scripture be in accordance with what *he* calls the Gospel, so did a primitive Christian understand whether such an interpretation was or was not contrary to what *he* called the Catholic faith.

But it is said that some of the Fathers were sometimes in error. Now, I certainly do protest against the manner in which it is not unfrequently attempted by not very wise men to prove this, which is thus: 'Such a Father differs from me, a modern teacher, therefore such a Father must be in error': the whole authority of which judgment depends upon an assumption, more bold than modest, that the modern teacher is infallible. Or if he defend himself by saying that his is the opinion of the religious world, again, I ask, 'Is the religious world itself infallible?' We know that the great object with the religious world is to produce not unity in the Church, but union among sects;—to do this many Scriptural principles must, on all sides, be conceded, and much regarded as non-essential, which to some persons appears to be essential. We cannot allow, then, a reference to the opinion of the religious world to be of any authority in such a case. But as a matter of fact, we do admit that many of the Fathers did err. Who ever thought them to be infallible men? Nay, the student of the Fathers can point out to you the kind of error to which any particular Father may have had a tendency, and he can probably show how that error was detected and animadverted upon by his contemporaries. But admit that they erred—what then? Are we not to read them because they were liable to error? In many of the works published by popular Tract Societies I could point out, not only errors, but if I were to use the language of those who condemn the Fathers, I should say grievous heresies: yet, are we on that account to refuse to read any modern tract? But this is what they ought to do who censure us for studying the Fathers, because the Fathers were not infallible men. What we chiefly desire in reading them is, to ascertain, not what the private opinions of individual Fathers were, but for reasons I have before assigned, what was the general system of Doctrine in their age.

But a popular argument against this use of the Fathers, and this deference to the tradition of the ancient Church, rather than to that of the modern religious world, is, that it is impossible for the mass of mankind to study writings so voluminous. But are the mass of mankind appointed to be teachers? We may fairly expect those who are ordained to the office of teaching to attend to such things, for to enable them to do so is the very reason why the Church is endowed. But in no sense will the objection hold as applicable to members of the Church of England; for it is asserted, and has never been contradicted, that on all essential points this primitive tradition is embodied in the Book of Common Prayer. It is this that gives to the Prayer Book its weight and authority as an interpreter of Scripture. As such, it is, of necessity, to a certain extent, employed by those even who endeavour to unite their duty to the Church with their duty to the religious world;—to the Church of which the object is to bind us to those very principles, which the religious world would relax. They may have their reasons for this deference to an uninspired formulary, those who are called High Churchmen may have theirs, which is the one I have assigned;—the fact, namely, of its embodying that primitive tradition, which, though not the light of the Gospel itself, for which we look to Scripture, may be serviceable to weaker brethren, when the blasts of strange doctrine are raging furiously around us, and threatening to bring down the very bulwarks of our Zion, to act as a lanthorn for the protection of that light. And if the High Churchmen provide you, my brethren, with another reason for loving your Prayer Book, forgive them this wrong.

But then comes the grand charge of all—this system of deference to antiquity must lead to Popery: an assertion which it is the more difficult to refute since it is impossible in these days to ascertain what, in the sense of the religious world, Popery is. Some persons tell us that the surplice is a rag of Popery, because the Papists in their ministrations wear a surplice in common with ourselves; others speak of the Prayer Book as Popish, because almost the whole of the Book of Common Prayer may be found in the Roman Missal and Breviary. Some religionists regard infant baptism as a remnant of Popery, while others only think it Popish to suppose that infants derive any benefit from that Sacrament: some persons think the Catechism Popish, and others that it is Popish to teach children doctrines before they can understand them : a highly respectable, though, as I think, an awfully mistaken class of religionists, who profess to be guided by the Bible only, think the doctrine of the Trinity Popish, because the Papists, amidst all their corruptions, still worship the Trinity in Unity and the Unity in Trinity. Now, the real fact is, that you may in this way prove almost any Scriptural truth to be Popish, because Popery consists in novel enlargements of old Catholic truths ; in novel additions to ancient and true doctrines. Thus the Papist holds with us that the twenty-two Books of the old Testament are canonical ; but then he adds to them other books which we affirm to be apocryphal : he agrees with us in believing that after death there is a heaven and a hell, but then he adds a purgatory. He agrees with us that sins are to be remitted by the merits of Christ ; but he adds the merits of the saints. He agrees with us that God ought to be worshipped ; but he adds again an inferior worship due to the saints, together with the Virgin and the angels. He receives Christ as a mediator ; but again he adds the mediation of the Virgin, saints, and angels. He agrees with us in believing our Lord's real presence in the Eucharist ; he adds his corporeal presence by transubstantiation. He agrees with us in believing the communion of saints ; he adds the invocation of them. He agrees with us in maintaining the divine authority of bishops and priests ; he adds the supremacy of the pope over all bishops and priests. He receives with us the three creeds ; he adds the creed of Pope Pius the IV. These additions have led to further corruptions, such as the adoration of the consecrated bread at the Lord's Supper, the worship of images, and other superstitions not needful to refer to. You perceive, then, the very great absurdity of accusing persons of being Popish merely because it may be shown that the doctrines which they happen to hold are doctrines held also by the Papists. Why, on this ground, all would be Papists who believe in the plenary inspiration of Holy Scripture; since such is the doctrine of the Church of Rome, as strongly enforced in the Vatican as in the Meeting House. The real question is not whether the Papists hold such and such doctrines in common with us; but whether we adhere to their traditions or to the Gospel truth. To accuse those of an inclination so to do, who have a respect for antiquity, is evidently absurd; they are the very last persons to sanction Popish novelties, for the moment they do so their deference for antiquity must, in the very nature of things, cease; that is, they must renounce their principle before they can countenance Popery.

How can those who have respect for antiquity acknowledge the supremacy of the See of Rome, when they remember how Polycrates and the Bishops of Asia opposed the opinion of Pope Victor and despised his excommunications?—how the same Victor was rebuked for his arrogance and indiscretion by Irenæus?* how St. Cyprian saluted the Bishop of Rome by no higher title than that of brother and colleague, and feared not to express his contempt of Pope Stephen's judgment and

* Euseb. Eccles. Hist. lib. v. c. 24.

determinations, when that prelate gave his countenance to heretics?*—when they remember how Liberius, Bishop of Rome in the fourth century, applied to the great St. Athanasius to sanction his confession of faith: 'that I may know,' said that Pope of Rome to Athanasius, 'whether I am of the same judgment with you in matters of faith,' and that I may be more certain, and readily obey your commands'?† When they learn from Gregory the Great, himself Bishop of Rome in the sixth and seventh centuries, that 'the Fathers of the Council of Chalcedon were they who first offered to his predecessors the title of universal Bishop, which they refused to accept'; ‡ as well they might, since Gregory tells us elsewhere in this epistle, that it is 'a title blasphemous to Christian ears'? When they remember that the fourth Lateran was the first of these councils which even Romanists call general, that recognised the authority of the Roman See as supreme over the Church —a Council which assembled in the year 1215—how can they ever recognise the Church of Rome as 'the mistress and mother of all churches,' when they know that the Fathers of the second general Council, that of Constantinople, in the year 381, gave that very title to the Church, not of Rome but of Jerusalem, writing in their synodical epistle: 'We acknowledge the most venerable Cyril, most beloved of God, to be the Bishop of the Church of Jerusalem, which is the mother of all churches.'§

* Cyp. ad Pomp. 74. † Athanas. Ep. ad Epictet.
‡ Greg. Epist. lib. vii. ep. 30.
§ Conc. ii. 966; Perceval's 'Roman Schism,' p. 32.

No, my brethren, whatever difficulties some persons, relying only on themselves, may have in explaining that passage in the 16th chapter of St. Matthew, 'Thou art Peter, and upon this Rock will I build my Church,' the Romish argument founded upon that text will fall harmless upon those who defer to the Fathers; since we have St. Augustine,* and St. Gregory Nazianzen,† and St. Cyril,‡ and St. Chrysostom,§ and St. Ambrose,|| and St. Hiliary¶ expounding that Scripture in the Protestant sense.

Neither are they very likely to fall down and worship the Saints departed, who know that among the Fathers one of the strongest arguments, as they deemed it, which could be brought forward in favour of our Lord's divinity, was the fact that prayer was to be made unto Him; while we are commanded to pray only to God. The injunction to pray to Him was, in their minds, an assertion of his divinity. In vain to them will the Romanists attempt to explain away the second commandment: they will not even commence an argument upon the subject—their answer being, 'We have no such custom, neither the Churches of God': they know that image worship was not sanctioned in any part of the Church, until what is called the deutero-Nicene Council, in the year 787. And the decree of that pseudo-council was immediately repudiated by the Emperor of the West, and all the great divines of the day, and among others by the clergy of the English

* Augustine de Verb. Dom. Serm. 13.
† Nazian. Test. de Vet. Testam.
‡ Cyril de Trin. lib. iv.　§ St. Chrysost. Hom. 55 in Mat.
|| Ambros. Com. in Ephes.　¶ Hilar. de Trin. lib. ii. c. 6.

Church. In vain did the Pope of Rome give his sanction to the idolatry; at a council assembled at Frankfort the decree was (to use the language of the council itself) 'rejected,' 'despised,' and 'condemned' as a wickedness and a novelty.*

Does the Romanist bring forth his specious arguments (and he can do so) for praying in a language not understood by the people: our answer is obvious: 'We have no such custom, neither the Churches of God'; for antecedently to the eighth century we can discover no nation which had not the Liturgy and Holy Scriptures in its own language known to it; Origen expressly stating that in his time every person prayed to God in his own tongue, the Greeks using the Greek, the Romans the Roman language.†

Think you those who defer to the primitive tradition of the Church will join with the Papists in enforcing the practice of auricular confession to the priest? No, my brethren, though the Church of England does recommend, in her first exhortation to the Holy Communion, that if 'any one cannot quiet his conscience, but requireth further comfort and council, he should go to some discreet and learned minister of God, and open his grief, that by the ministry of God's Holy Word he may receive the benefit of absolution, together with ghostly council and advice'; though such be the recommendation of the Church of England,‡ we know

* Canon 11 Conc. Frankf.
† Orig. Cont. Cels. lib. viii. p. 402.
‡ 'Sudden changes without substantial necessary causes and the heady setting forth of extremities I did never love. Confession to the minister which is able to instruct, comfort, and inform

that auricular confession was never imposed as necessary until the Lateran Council in 1215.

It is sometimes insinuated that those who have a respect for the practices of antiquity must be in favour of the celibacy of the clergy, and it seems in vain that such clergymen by their own marriage show practically the injustice of the insinuation. But on this point we are under no concern; we still say to the Romanists, 'We have no such custom, neither the Churches of God.' It is true that many of the Fathers felt strongly with Richard Baxter, the celebrated nonconformist, that it might often be 'inconvenient for ministers to marry who have no sort of necessity';* these are the words of that pious nonconformist, and, perhaps, he thought as the Fathers thought, that the same was taught by St. Paul, in the 7th chapter of the First Epistle to the Corinthians: they—St. Paul, the Fathers, and that pious nonconformist—thought that men were ordained not merely to make themselves comfortable, and to maintain a respectable station in society, but to devote all their energies, their body, soul, and spirit, to the service of the Saviour, who bought them with his blood: and they thought that in many instances men could do this better without the burden of a family than with it: many of the Fathers may have erred in this opinion; and those who censure that opinion may, I suppose, likewise err—some of them may have

the weak and ignorant consciences, I have ever thought might do much good in Christ's congregation, and so I assure you I do at this day.'—Bishop Ridley's Letter. Appendix to Strype's Cranmer, ii. 965.

* Life of Mrs. Margaret Baxter, chap. vi.

carried their notions on this point to an extreme, and I for one think that they did do so;* but they were not the authors of that iniquitous and demoralizing and soul-destroying rule of the Romish Church, by which priests are constrained to vow a single life: for this rule was first obtruded in the Western Church (it is not even yet the rule of the Eastern Church) by Pope Hildebrand, in the year 1074: and then the innovation was sturdily opposed by many of our English clergy.†

But we will advance yet further. There is an inclination on the part of some Protestants to the doctrine of Purgatory: for what is Hell, in the estimation of those who deny the eternity of future punishment, but a Purgatory? And to those inclined to think well of the doctrine, the Romanist has some apparent Scriptural authority to produce. He refers us to the third chapter of the 1st epistle to the Corinthians, where we read at the 13th verse: 'The fire shall try every man's work of what sort it is. If any man's work abide which he hath built thereon, he shall receive a reward. If any man's work be burned, he shall suffer

* I may add that some of the opinions advanced on this subject by some of the learned and pious writers of the Oxford Tracts appear to me to be incautious. I admit that the argument in favour of the celibacy of the clergy is strong, and such as to recommend itself to pure and holy and devoted minds. It looks well on paper. But the experiment has been made, and it has failed.

† It was not till the time of William of Corbeil, about 1129, that the marriage of secular priests was put down in England. Anselm seems to have attempted it about 1102, but Henry I. opposed him. It is plain that many Bishops in that reign and later were married men. See Collier of Geoffrey Rydal, Bishop of Ely, 117–489; Collier, i. 381.

loss, yet he himself shall be saved yet so as by fire.' By such a passage some persons may be staggered, but we can answer, 'We have no such custom, neither the Churches of God'; and for the truth of our position we can appeal to Bishop Fisher, a martyr to the Romish cause, who expressly tells us that 'the doctrine of Purgatory was rarely, if at all, heard of among the ancients; and to this very day, the Greeks believe it not'; and he adds, with reference to the doctrine of Indulgences, 'so long as men were unconcerned about Purgatory, nobody inquired after Indulgences, for on that all their worth depends.'* Yes, and we can quote passages innumerable from the Fathers to show that the ancient faith was, as the true faith is, that ' when our life in this world is brought to a close, our state of probation ceases'; aye, and we can show that the first authoritative decree concerning Purgatory was made so lately as the Council of Florence, in the year 1438.†

And be not astonished, brethren, at the admission made by Bishop Fisher;—I could produce to you similar admissions from Romish divines on almost every point. Of all vulgar errors, as you must have already perceived, none can be greater than that which would represent the Papists as appellants to antiquity. Their principle is, obedience to those who from time to time occupy the place of ecclesiastical rulers. These, in their opinion, constitute that Church which is to be heard under penalty of being accounted a heathen or a

---

* Op. p. 496, ed. 1597, art. 'Cont. Lutherum.'
† Perceval on the Roman Schism, p. 354.

publican ; consequently there is no room for an appeal to antiquity, and accordingly the attempt to appeal from the present to the ancient Church has been branded by them, as Bishop Jebb shows, with the odious stamp of heresy.*

But it is said, that those who defer to tradition hold the dogma of Transubstantiation. That the Fathers did hold the doctrine of our Lord's real presence in the Eucharist (real though spiritual, or rather the more real because spiritual) we not only do not deny, but unequivocally assert. That is to say, they held what the Church of England holds, and what our wisehearted Reformers maintained on this subject: for, as Bishop Cleaver observes, 'the great object of our Reformers was, whilst they acknowledged the doctrine of the real presence to refute that of Transubstantiation, as it was afterwards to refute the notion of Impanation or Consubstantiation': † the Fathers held with the Church of England that 'the body and blood of Christ are verily and indeed taken and received by the faithful in the Lord's Supper': they were wont to exhort their hearers, as the Church of England exhorts us, to consider the dignity of those high and holy mysteries ; ‡ of that high mystery, that heavenly feast, the banquet of that most heavenly food: all expressions of our

* Bishop Jebb, 'Peculiar Character of the Church of England,' p. 289.

† Bishop Cleaver's Sermon, Nov. 25, 1787. See also Bishop Ridley's Treatise against the Error of Transubstantiation ; Bishop Poynet's Treatise of Reconciliation, or Diallacticon, and Archbishop Cranmer's Defence of the Catholic Doctrine, b. iii.

‡ Exhortation to Communion Office.

Liturgy: they did, indeed look upon the altar to be, as our 25th Homily calls it, 'The King of King's Table:' they were wont to declare, as in that Homily is declared, 'Thus much we must be sure to hold, that in the Supper of the Lord there is no vain ceremony, no bare sign, no untrue figure of a thing absent'; but 'that the faithful receive not only the outward Sacrament, but the spiritual thing also: not the figure, but the truth; not the shadow only, but the Body.' So says the Church of England, and so said the Fathers. If some persons cannot make a distinction between the real presence of Christ in his spirit and power, and the corporeal presence, which is Transubstantiation, and so accuse us of Popish doctrine, they must blame the Church of England too; and so we err in good company. To censure the dogma of Transubstantiation too strongly is impossible, because it has not only given occasion, as our 28th Article mildly states it, to many superstitions; but it has also led to the assertion and belief of what to my mind is absolutely blasphemous, that there is in the Eucharist an expiatory sacrifice: that therein, I utter it with horror, our Blessed Lord and Saviour is each time sacrificed afresh: that there is each time a fresh immolation and death. But still, the only real question is this, Has it been revealed? Is it part of the Revelation of God to man? The Romanist affirms that it is, and he refers to our Lord's own words,—'This is my Body—This is my Blood.' He calls upon us, in humble faith, to receive these words in the literal sense. To this all Protestants demur: the Romanist has, of course, a right to demand a reason:

by some persons he is told that the doctrine of Transubstantiation, which he would build upon this passage, involves an impossibility; that it is an insult to the understanding, a contradiction to the senses, to call upon us to embrace it. Are you contented with these —what shall I call them?—arguments? or dogmatisms? It may be that you are; but when you try to convert the Romanist, he replies that he sees no more difficulty in believing the doctrine of Transubstantiation than in receiving the doctrine of the Trinity. Upon this, perhaps, you refine and you point out the difference between things above reason, and things contrary to reason, which is doubtless perfectly correct, but it is a refinement as difficult to unlearned minds as anything to be found in the writings of the Fathers. And in spite of it, when you are engaged in controversy with the Socinian, you may perhaps find some of these hard words retorted upon yourself. The Socinian will speak of impossibilities, insults to the understanding, contradiction to the senses, and so forth. But we will not quarrel with those who thus attempt to refute the dogma of Transubstantiation. All that we say is, that we do not like to elevate ourselves and to judge what the Almighty can do or cannot do. And certainly our mode of proceeding is far easier and more intelligible to the brethren at large. We tell the Romanist that we understand the passage referred to with the English Church, in a sublime and mysterious, but not in a literal sense. For, as the Catholic creeds and holy Scripture teach, we believe our holy Redeemer's body is in heaven, and will there remain, till He shall come, in like manner as He ascended, at the end of the world to judge the quick and the dead. And as to the dogma of Transubstantiation, 'We have no such custom, neither the Churches of God.' If that passage implies the doctrine of Transubstantiation, we ask how it came to pass that this doctrine was unknown to the Catholic Church for seven hundred years? We know it as an indisputable fact, that this error was first started in the eighth century; that it found its most able advocate in Pascasius Radbert, in the ninth century; and that when this error was first introduced, it was spoken of by Raban Maurus, the pupil of our countryman, Alcuin, Archbishop of Mentz, as an error broached by some individuals 'unsoundly thinking of late,' and by the contemporary divines of the Churches of England and Ireland it was strongly opposed.* We know moreover that it was not authoritatively received even by the Roman Church till the Fourth Lateran Council, in the year 1215. So, then, brethren, those who defer to primitive tradition, and study the writings of the ancients, may be thought by some persons to be the most judicious opponents of Romanism, †—but certain it is,

* See Perceval's 'Roman Schism,' 40, 56, 132, 346, 225, 372, 429.

† The question as to the proper manner of opposing Romanism is one of great importance. I can state it on high authority, that the Papists always calculate on twenty or thirty converts to their system, after a meeting in any place of the so-called Reformation Society. The declamatory violence at these meetings disgusts some persons, in others doubts are suggested, while weak arguments are used to answer them, and recourse is eventually had, under the idea of hearing both sides, to the Romish priest for their solution. To support a good cause with bad arguments is the best aid that can be given to those whose cause is bad. There are many anti-popery

that they cannot receive the Romish doctrine of Transubstantiation until they have renounced these principles. No, nor with reference to the Eucharist will they ever consent to withhold the cup from the laity, an injustice, robbery, and wrong, not sanctioned even by the Romish Church till the Council of Constance, in 1414.

sermons and speeches reported in the newspapers, which suggest a doubt to the mind whether those who delivered them were the more ignorant of the doctrines of the Church of Rome, or of the doctrines of the Church of England. And it is no new art of the Romanists to attack the Church in this way by their own emissaries in disguise. 'In the sixteenth century, one Cummin, a friar, contrived to be taken into the Puritans' pulpits, where, as he stated in the Councils, "I preached against set forms of prayer, and I called English prayers, English mass, and have persuaded several to pray spiritually and extempore: and this hath so taken with the people, that the Church of England is become as odious to that sort of people whom I instructed, as the mass is to the Church of England, and this will be a stumbling-block to that Church so long as it is a Church." For this the Pope commended him, and gave him a reward of 2,000 ducats for his good service. Are there not many at the present day of whom, if they were to apply to the Pope for a reward on the same score, all the world could witness that they have well deserved it at his hands? Surely our opponents have some reason to feel misgivings when they find themselves treading in the footsteps of the heathen revilers of Christianity, and of the Popish hireling underminers of the bulwark of Protestantism.'—*Perceval on Apostolic Succession*, pp. 64, 65. I may here remark on the craft of the Romanists of the present day. In order to cause division among Protestants, in some of their publications they are said to have spoken of the writers of the Oxford Tracts as allies. In the report, however, of one of Dr. Wiseman's Lectures to Romanists at Manchester, it appears that 'he broke out into a strain of passionate invective against the writers of the Tracts for the Times, denouncing them, and complaining that they had started a line of argument against their Popish opponents that had been left undisturbed for a century.' —*Manchester Courier*, Oct. 26, 1839. To the falsehoods of Popish priests I have traced many of the absurd stories propagated by Dissenters against consistent Churchmen.

I will refer to one other topic and then conclude. That which, in my humble opinion, makes the Church of Rome, and all Churches connected with her, by receiving the decrees of the Council of Trent, to be absolutely heretical—that which has separated them from the Catholic Church itself, that which renders all union with them utterly impossible, is this:—that to the Scriptures of God and the Creeds of the Church they have made additions. To the three Creeds which we possess in common with the whole Church, they have added the Creed of Pope Pius IV.; and they receive the Books of the Apocrypha as equally sacred and canonical with the Books of Holy Scripture. Now, I ask, how are we to prove that in so doing the Romish Church is in error? How but by consulting those very Fathers, for having a regard for whom we are too often misrepresented? How but by referring to Origen, and Eusebius, and St. Athanasius, and St. Hilary, and Epiphanius, and St. Gregory Nazianzen, and St. Jerome:* the latter of whom, after enumerating the Canonical Books of Scripture, expressly declares that 'whatever is beside these is to be reckoned among the Apocrypha'? How but by reference to the Councils of Chalcedon, and Laodicea, and Nice, and to the Apostolical canons? Perhaps those who disapprove of this are contented with the authority of some modern writer, who asserts that he has examined the subject. Be it so; and the Romanist may be perplexed to understand why he is to be

* Præf. in Librum Regum. See the quotations at length in Perceval, 420; and the Councils, pp. 41, 56, 150, 362.

blamed for placing the same confidence in his writers, who make an assertion contrary to that on which the Protestant relies. But, at all events, it cannot be sinful in us to examine the Fathers and Councils themselves, to be certain that the modern writer is correct. And so you see that the Fathers are not utterly to be despised; but some regard to antiquity may be of service to our learned men. And he who shall tell us, as we have been virtually told of late, 'if these books contain the same doctrine with the Bible they can be of no use, since the Bible contains all necessary truth, but if they contain anything contrary to the Bible they ought not to be suffered, let them, therefore, be destroyed,' will reason more like the Moslem fanatic than an enlightened Christian.

In what has now been said it has not been my wish to give unnecessary offence. My chief object has been to show that into whatever errors our respect for antiquity may lead us—and, since all things connected with man are liable to abuse, I am ready to admit that there may be some errors—it is not to Popery that it tends; nay, that armed as others may think themselves by arguments, we are doubly armed; we have their arguments, for as much as they are worth, and we have, moreover, the testimony of the primitive Church. As a very learned man of this town profoundly remarks, 'Tradition itself is the very evidence on which we convict what are called Traditions (by the Papists) of defective authority.'* If the charge of our being popishly affected be brought against us, because even

* Parkinson's Hulsean Lectures, 1838, p. 84.

to Romanists we would extend our charity, and instead of returning railing for their railing would convince them by argument, while we treat them with that courtesy which Christianity does not absolutely forbid; and, admit, what in candour must be admitted, that they have much in their system that is true, for they have much in common, not only with the Church of England, but with all Protestants except the 'Unitarians'; if on this account the charge be brought against us, to it we must plead guilty. By some persons it is not considered a breach of Christian charity to adopt towards the Romish Dissenters every species of vituperation which the arts of rhetoric and a skilful periphrasis may render not vulgar; it is not considered a breach of Christian charity to excite against them the wildest passions of the fanatic, and to exhibit, instead of the gentle persuasions of the Christian preacher, a close imitation of the vehement declamations of the heathen orator; but against Protestant Dissenters, whom the religious world (not infallible, but acting as if it were so) pronounces to be orthodox, to insinuate that they may err on any essential point, is a breach of charity which is, in the eyes of the religious world, unpardonable. Now, my brethren, the true Churchman stands fairly and boldly in the middle way: he considers both the Protestant and the Romish Dissenter to be in error—the latter by adding to, the former by detracting from, the doctrine and discipline of the Catholic Church. He conceives it to be the part both of duty and of charity to maintain that middle position in which God has placed him, and, as occasion offers, to warn either side of the errors committed on that side, and of the danger, when warned, of adhering to them. But here he remains: he advances no further; he assumes not to himself the character of judge, when our Lord commands us 'judge not.' What amount of truth it may be necessary for each individual, for his salvation, to possess, he knows not. He only knows that each man will be judged 'by that he hath, not by that he hath not'; and that our duty it is, without respect of persons, without caring for whom it may seem to condemn, to declare all the counsel of God. We treat no error with toleration; we treat no person with unkindness or disrespect. If we see the Protestant Dissenter or the Romish Dissenter surpassing us in holiness, we do not pronounce them to be free from error, nor do we represent their errors as trivial, or conceal from them our opinion, that if the means of avoiding those errors have been within their reach they will be accountable to God for not having recourse to them; but we do say in great humility, 'What a man would this have been had he been blessed with my superior advantages! And what a sinner am I, that with all my superior advantages I am in my conduct his inferior!' and this sends us to our knees and our self-denials, that we may obtain pardon for the past through the merits and intercession of an Almighty Saviour; and grace for the future, to form habits of stricter piety.

In short, we learn from Scripture, as well as from antiquity that a firm, uncompromising adherence to our principles, a calm, steady, zealous promulgation of the truth, and a fearless rebuke of error, are all parts of Christian charity; but when either Romanist or Protestant has recourse to persecution, whether physical or moral, to the horrors of the Inquisition or to railing accusations, we reply, 'We have no such custom, neither the Churches of God.'

SERMON XXIV.*

INVOCATION OF SAINTS.

'*And another angel came and stood at the altar, having a golden censer; and there was given unto him much incense, that he should offer it with the prayers of all Saints upon the golden altar which was before the throne.*'—Revelation viii. 3.

THE Invocation of Saints is a practice repudiated by the reformed Church of England; and must be repudiated by all who receive the sixth Article, 'Holy Scripture containeth all things necessary to salvation, so that whatsoever is not read therein, nor may be proved thereby, is not to be required of any man that it should be believed as an article of the Faith, or be thought requisite or necessary to salvation.' Now, where in Scripture do we read of any Invocation of Saints? How from Scripture can the lawfulness of the practice be proved? That we do not read in Scripture anything relating to the Invocation of Saints, that the lawfulness of the practice cannot be proved therefrom, is established by this simple fact, that the Church of Rome has not, as far as I can discover, in her authorized documents attempted to vindicate her conduct in this particular, by reference to the sacred volume, unless we consider as such a reference what is said by

* Preached in the Parish Church of Leeds, Jan. 31, 1847.

one of the defenders of the Church of Rome, who remarks, that St. Jacob plainly prayed unto an angel in the 48th of Genesis, when in blessing the sons of Joseph he said, 'The angel which delivered me from all evil bless those children.'* 'Whom,' says Archbishop Usher, 'for answer we remit to St. Cyril, in the first chapter of the third book of his Thesaurus, and entreat him to tell us how near of kin he is here to those heretics of whom St. Cyril there speaketh. His words be these: "That he doth not mean," in that place, Genesis xlviii. 16, "an angel, as the heretics understand it, but the Son of God, is manifest by this, that when he had said, 'The angel,' he presently addeth, 'who delivered me from all evils'"': which St. Cyril presupposeth no good Christian will ascribe to any but to God alone.' †

If this be their mode of proving their point from Scripture, we may surely conclude that they are conscious that their practice is unscriptural. On what, then, do they ground their procedure? They refer to the tradition of the Church. But, supposing, what we do not for a moment admit, that the Romanists had the tradition of the Church on their side—our reformers would still have repudiated the practice, according to their principle and the principle of the Primitive Church, on the ground that Holy Scripture containeth all things necessary to salvation, and in that volume thus containing all things necessary to salvation we read not one word about the Invocation of Saints.

* Bellar. de Sanctor. Beatitud. lib. i. cap. 19.
† 'Answer to a Jesuit,' p. 673.

Now here we see one grand point of difference between the Church of England and the Church of Rome. We contend for the faith once and once for all delivered to the saints, which faith we find in Scripture, to which we may not add, and from which we may not take. The Church of Rome adds Tradition to Scripture. In the Council of Trent it was ruled that the Christian faith is contained partly in Holy Scripture and partly in the traditions of the Church: this 'partly in the traditions of the Church' we reject; it is one of the principles against which we, in common with all Protestants, protest, and the Church of England, as I have often reminded you, is Protestant as well as Catholic, 'Protestant as opposed to the abuses and idolatries of Popery, and Catholic as opposed to the heresies of ultra-Protestantism.' *

But it may be said that to the traditions of the Church in all our formularies a certain deference is paid, and that in establishing disputable points of doctrine our Reformers referred to the received opinions of the primitive Church. † This is true. And wicked men misrepresent, while foolish men misunderstand the Church of England, by seeking to confound this principle with the Romish principle. They might just as well accuse us of adding to the laws of the country, of making an additional law, when we consult a lawyer and ask his opinion upon a particular Act of Parliament, as represent the Church of England divines as deviating from the great principle laid down in the

---

* See Preface to 'The Church of England Vindicated.'

† See 'The Three Reformations, Lutheran, Roman, and Anglican,' by the Author.

Sixth Article, because, when doubtful on any point of doctrine, they seek to ascertain from the early writers the sense in which what Scripture says of that point of doctrine was received by the early Church,—and those branches of the Church especially which were instituted by the Apostles or apostolic men. We go to a lawyer because, thinking his opinion as to the meaning of an Act of Parliament better than our own, we desire to know precisely what the law is; but to say that on this account our rule is the law of the land because the opinion of certain lawyers would be manifestly unjust and untrue. So did our Reformers take the Bible only for their rule—a principle from which they did not deviate when they sought to ascertain the early tradition of the Church—that is, the opinion of the primitive Christians —as to the meaning of Scripture on doctrines disputed either by Romanists or by ultra-Protestants.

Here is the law laid down in Scripture: Scripture only is our rule; but says the Romanist, Scripture says thus; no, says the Calvinist, it asserts the contrary; you are both wrong, exclaims the Socinian, for I understand it in another sense;—how, says some one else, are we to act when such influential parties disagree? The Church of England replies, We will consult the early writers and go by the opinion of the early Church, instituted as it was by those who were inspired to write the Scriptures of the New Testament. It is open to those who are not of our communion to question the soundness of our principle,—but it is wicked to misrepresent us as acting contrary to our Sixth Article, while it is folly to confound our principle with that of the

Church of Rome; for the Church of Rome, as I have remarked, adds the traditions of the Church to the Holy Scriptures, whereas we use them as interpretative of Scripture, but only when Scripture is doubtful. The principle is indeed not only clearly laid down in our other formularies, but is recognised in our Thirty-fourth Article, wherein it is declared that he ought to be rebuked, 'Whosoever through his private judgment, willingly and purposely, doth openly break the traditions and ceremonies of the Church, which be not repugnant to the word of God.'

And now returning to the subject of the Invocation of Saints: our Reformers would have rejected the practice, because it is founded not upon an interpretation of Scripture, but upon the authority of tradition only; and tradition, except as interpretative of Scripture, we at once reject. But this practice is yet further actually 'repugnant to God's word.' I will quote what is said by St. Athanasius on this subject, in order at the same time to show that the Church of Rome has not even the tradition of the Church in her favour, but calls that tradition which was an invention of the middle ages:—'One creature,' he says, 'does not worship another. Whence Peter the apostle hindered Cornelius when he wished to worship him, saying "I also am a man." The Angel also hindered St. John, when he wished to worship him in the Apocalypse, saying, "See thou do it not: for I am thy fellow-servant, and of thy brethren the prophets, and of them which keep the sayings of this book, worship God:" therefore, it belongs to God only,' says St. Athanasius, 'to be worshipped. And thus the

Angels themselves know, that although they excel others in glory, they are yet all creatures, and are not in the number of those who are to be worshipped, but of them who worship the Lord.'*

Now, this passage from the celebrated St. Athanasius not only shows how he and his contemporaries worshipped none other but God, but it also demolishes the defence, which is set up for this practice in the Church of Rome, that the worship offered to the Virgin Mary and other Saints is not Divine worship, because they believe that God is infinitely superior to the Saints, and that the worship they render to the Saints is of an inferior sort, in heart, even when it is not apparently so. I say when it is not apparently so, because to all appearance the Romanists are accustomed to pray to the creature, in the same way as they pray to the Creator; but allowing them the advantage of this mental reservation, even this excuse is demolished by the Scriptural references of Athanasius. For when St. Peter stood before Cornelius it could not have been the intention of Cornelius to offer him divine honours; neither could St. John have intended to pay divine honours to the Angel; what occurred, then, at these times is a condemnation of any kind of worship (using the word as applicable to a devotional act) to the creature. So exclusively is it the prerogative of a jealous God to receive prayer, that as anyone will tell you who is conversant with the writings of the primitive Christians, the early Fathers proved the

* S. Athanasii Orat. 11, Contra Arianos, t. 1. p. 491. Ed. Benedict.

Divinity of our Blessed Lord and Saviour Jesus Christ, our only Advocate and Mediator, by the fact that prayer is made to Him. They argued thus:—It is idolatry to pray to any other but God, but prayer is made to our Lord Jesus Christ; therefore the Lord Jesus Christ is God as well as man.

In disputing on this subject with a Jesuit, Archbishop Usher says:—' Whether those blessed spirits pray for us, is not the question here, but whether we are to pray unto them. That God only is to be prayed unto, is the doctrine that was once delivered unto the saints, for which we so earnestly contend; the saints praying for us doth no way cross this (for to whom should the saints pray but to the King of saints?) their being prayed unto is the only stumbling-block that lieth in this way. And therefore in those first times the former of these was admitted by some as a matter of probability, but the latter no way yielded unto, as being derogatory to the privilege of the Deity. Origen may be a witness of both, who touching the former writeth in this sort: "I do think thus, that all those Fathers who are departed this life before us do fight with us and assist us with their prayers: for so have I heard one of the elder masters saying": and in another place: "Moreover, if the saints that have left the body and be with Christ, do any thing and labour for us in like manner as the angels do, who are employed in the ministry of our salvation, let this also remain among the hidden things of God and the mysteries that are not to be committed into writing." But because he thought that the angels and saints prayed for us did he therefore hold it needful that we should direct our prayers unto them? Hear, I pray you, his own answer in his eighth book against Celsus the philosopher: "We must endeavour to please God alone, who is above all things, and labour to have Him propitious unto us, procuring His goodwill with godliness and all kind of virtue. And if Celsus will yet have us to procure the goodwill of any others after Him that is God over all, let him consider, that as when the body is moved the motion of the shadow thereof doth follow it, so in like manner having God favourable unto us who is over all it followeth that we shall have all His friends, both angels, and souls, and spirits, loving unto us. For they have a fellow-feeling with them that are thought worthy to find favour from God. Neither are they only favourable unto such as be thus worthy; but they work with them also that are willing to do service unto Him who is God over all, and are friendly to them, and pray with them, and entreat with them, so as we may be bold to say, that when men, which with resolution propose unto themselves the best things, do pray unto God, many thousands of the sacred powers pray together with them unspoken to.'"*

I will bring this part of my subject to a conclusion with the words of another celebrated Archbishop of the Church of Ireland, Archbishop Bramhall, who, addressing the Romanists, says; 'If your Invocation of Saints were not such as it is, to request of them patronage and protection, spiritual graces, and celestial joys, by their prayers, and by their merits (alas! the

* 'Answer to a Jesuit's Challenge,' p. 365.

wisest Virgins have oil in their lamps little enough for themselves); yet it is not necessary for two reasons: first, no Saint doth love us so well as Christ; no Saint hath given us such assurance of his love, or done so much for us as Christ; no Saint is so willing or able to help us as Christ: and, secondly, we have no command from God to invocate them (so much your own authors do confess, and give this reason for it, "lest the Gentiles, being converted, should believe that they were drawn back again to the worship of the creature"); but we have another command, "Call upon Me in the day of trouble, and I will hear thee." We have no promise to be heard, when we do invocate them; but we have another promise,—"Whatsoever ye shall ask the Father in My name, ye shall receive it." We have no example in Holy Scripture of any that did invocate them, but rather the contrary;—"See thou do it not;" "I am thy fellow-servant, worship God." We have no certainty that they do hear our particular prayers, especially mental prayers, yea, a thousand prayers, poured out at one instant in several parts of the world. We know what your men say of the "glass of the Trinity," and of extraordinary revelations; but these are bold conjectures without any certainty, and inconsistent the one with the other.

'We do sometimes meet in ancient authors with the intercession of Saints in general, which we also acknowledge; or an oblique invocation of them (as you term it), that is, a prayer directed to God, that He will hear the intercession of the Saints for us, which we do not condemn; or a wish, or a rhetorical apostrophe, or perhaps something more in some single ancient author: but for an ordinary invocation in particular necessities, and much more for public invocation in the Liturgies of the Church, we meet not with it for the first six hundred years, or thereabouts; all which time, and afterwards also, the common principles and traditions of the Church were against it. So far were they from obtruding it as a necessary fundamental article of Christian religion.'*

Thus, my brethren, do we of the Church of England declare that religious worship is due to God only, and not to any creature whatsoever, be it angel, spirit, man, beast, or inanimate creature. We hold that prayer ought to be offered only to God, that it is a species of sacrifice, which is only due to the Divine Nature. We think it unlawful to repose our hope, trust, or confidence in any creature. We think it needless to ask for the intercession of Saints and Angels to render us acceptable to God; and we believe that we ought boldly to approach the Throne of Grace, confiding in the intercession of the Lord Jesus Christ. Why, indeed, should we look for any other Intercessor besides Him whom we have? Is it not an insult to our Jesus to look out for any Intercessor besides Him? Is He not all-sufficient? Has He not, the Second Person of the Blessed Trinity, become Incarnate for the very purpose of being our Mediator and our Intercessor? God though He is, hath He not become, and is he not still Man also, that He might be touched with the feeling of our infirmities, and be tempted in all points like as we are?

* Archbishop Bramhall's Works, vol. i. p. 57.

Is He not our intercessor who can have compassion on the ignorant and on them that are out of the way? Surely He hath borne our griefs and carried our sorrows and in all our afflictions He was afflicted. What saint can love us as our own Jesus hath done? What saint can give us such assurance of his love as He did when He sweat for us, as it were, great drops of blood at Gethsemane—when He was smitten, and buffeted, and spit upon, and nailed to the Cross, and died for us? To invocate a saint, not the shadow of a command can be produced from Scripture—but to this Intercessor, the Lord Jesus, we are commanded to come—' Call upon me in the day of trouble and I will hear thee.' If we may call, if we are commanded to call on Thee, O Jesus: then, O Lord, to whom else should we go? Where is there a hint of a promise that we shall be heard if we ask in the name of a saint?—Why should we, indeed, when the promise of the Lord Jesus is, ' Whatsoever ye shall ask the Father in My name, ye shall receive it.' Are you timid?—He saith, ' Come unto Me, draw nigh to the Throne of Grace with boldness.' Are you weary and heavy-laden? Do you secretly weep over your sins and earnestly desire deliverance? Jesus sees what saints cannot—your secret tears: Jesus hears what saints cannot—your earnest desires; before you have asked Him He has interceded for you. Can any intercessor be so tender as He? He neither reproaches us for our sins, nor reproves us for our disobedience, when we draw near to Him in penitence and in faith; He sees nothing but our disease; He hears nothing but our distress; and knowing our wretchedness and feeling our infirmities, the voice which once interceded for His murderers, 'Father forgive them, for they know not what they do' —that voice is heard in the courts of heaven for us His servants who are desirous to serve Him. He invites us to Him, He offers to be our Intercessor. We may approach with all our burdens and weariness and weakness, with all our sins and guilt and worthlessness. As there is no sin for which the blood of Christ cannot atone, no heart which the Spirit of Christ cannot renew, so there is no sinner for whom, on his repentance, He will not intercede. In all the doubts and distresses of your earthly pilgrimage, Jesus is your Intercessor; in all the dangers and conflicts of your Christian warfare, Jesus is your Intercessor; in all the toils and trials of this mortal state, Jesus is your Intercessor. Oh! whom else can we need or desire? Mary, Paul, Peter, Michael, Angels, Archangels, all need the intercession of the Lord Jesus, and we have the same Intercessor as they. We worship not them, for such worship, if they know that it is paid to them, must grieve their righteous souls; but we, as they do, worship the only true object of worship, the Blessed Trinity, the Father, the Son, and the Holy Ghost—and as for our Intercessor, when we are asked to share the idolatries of others, let us imagine Jesus our own Intercessor, saying to us, as He once said unto the twelve: 'Will ye also go away?' And may we have grace to answer, 'Lord, to whom shall we go? Thou hast the words of eternal life: we believe and are sure that Thou art that Christ, the Son of the living God, that ever liveth to make intercession for us.'

INVOCATION OF SAINTS. 163

But although we worship God and Him only; although we thus assert in our 22nd Article, that 'The Romish Doctrine concerning Purgatory, Pardons, Worshipping and Adoration, as well of Images as of Reliques and also invocation of Saints, is a fond thing, vainly invented and grounded upon no warranty of Scripture, but rather repugnant to the Word of God'; although the Invocation of Saints be one of the practices against which we, as Protestants, protest : yet we, as Catholics, hold, and day by day profess our faith in, the Communion of Saints. We must, in counteracting error, be very careful not to damage the truth ; in repudiating Romanism, we must not renounce our Catholicism; and in guarding against superstition, we must take care not to countenance the infidelity which seeks to reject one by one the articles of the Creed.

'The Communion of Saints' is an article of the Creed. It is one of those fundamental articles of our Belief, without accepting which an adult person cannot be baptized. What is meant by this article of our faith, 'The Communion of Saints,' I now intend to state to you in the words of that great expositor of the Apostles' Creed, whose work has been considered the standard work upon the subject, by all our divines, from the day of its publication to the present hour— Bishop Pearson.

And first of those who are denominated Saints, Bishop Pearson observes : 'Those are truly and properly Saints which are sanctified in Christ Jesus : first, in respect of their holy faith, by which they are regenerated and purified; and secondly, in respect of their conversation: for as He which hath called them is holy, so are they holy in all manner of conversation. Such persons, then, as are called by a holy calling, and not disobedient unto it; such as are endued with a holy faith, and purified thereby; such as are sanctified by the Holy Spirit of God, and by virtue thereof do lead a holy life, perfecting holiness in the fear of God; such persons, I say, are really and truly saints, and being of the Church of Christ (as all such now must of necessity be), are the proper subject of this Article, The Communion of Saints.'

Having thus described the persons who are designated as saints, Bishop Pearson goes on to prove that the saints of God, living in the Church of God, have communion with God the Father, with God the Son, with God the Holy Ghost, the Holy Blessed and Glorious Trinity. He adds: 'The saints of God in the Church of Christ have communion with the holy Angels. They who did foretell the birth of John, the forerunner of Christ, they who did annunciate unto the blessed Virgin the conception of the Saviour of the world, they who sung a glorious hymn at the nativity of the Son of God, they who carried the soul of Lazarus into Abraham's bosom, they who appeared unto Christ from heaven in his agony to strengthen Him, they who opened the prison doors and brought the Apostles forth, they who at the end of the world shall sever the wicked from among the just, and gather together the elect of God, certainly they have a constant and perpetual relation to the children of God. Nay, "are they not all ministering spirits, sent forth to minister for them who shall be

INVOCATION OF SAINTS. 165

heirs of salvation ?"* They have a particular sense of our condition, for Christ hath assured us that "there is joy in the presence of the angels of God over one sinner that repenteth."† And upon this relation the angels, who are all the angels, that is, the messengers of God are yet called the angels of men, according to the admonition of Christ, "take heed that ye despise not one of these little ones; for I say unto you, That in heaven their angels do always behold the face of my Father which is in heaven."‡

'Thus far,' says Bishop Pearson, 'have we considered the Communion of Saints, with such as are distinguished from them by nature as they are men; the fellowship which they have in heaven with God, and His holy angels, while they are on earth. Our next consideration will be, what is the Communion they have with those who are of the same nature, but not partakers of the same holiness with them.

'The saints of God, while they are of the Church of Christ on earth, have some kind of communion with those men which are not truly saints. There were not hypocrites among the Jews alone, but in the Church of Christ many cry, "Lord, Lord," whom He knoweth not. The tares have the privilege of the field, as well as the wheat; and the bad fish of the net, as well as the good. The saints have communion with hypocrites in all things with which the distinction of a saint and an hypocrite can consist. They communicate in the same water, both externally baptized alike; they communicate in the same creed, both make the same open

---
* Heb. i. 14.   † St. Luke xv. 10.   ‡ St. Mat. xviii. 10.

profession of faith, both agree in the acknowledgment of the same principles of religion; they communicate in the same word, both hear the same doctrine preached; they communicate at the same table, both eat the same bread, and drink the wine, which Christ hath appointed to be received; but the hypocrite doth not communicate with the saint in the same saving grace, in the same true faith working by love, and in the same renovation of mind and spirit; for then he were not an hypocrite, but a saint: a saint doth not communicate with the hypocrite in the same sins, in the same lurking infidelity, in the same unfruitfulness under the means of grace, in the same false pretence and empty form of godliness; for then he were not a saint, but an hypocrite.

'Thus the saints may communicate with the wicked, so they communicate not with their wickedness; and may have fellowship with sinners, so they have no fellowship with that which makes them such, that is, their sins. The Apostle's command runneth thus: "Have no fellowship with the unfruitful works of darkness"; and again, "Be not partakers of other men's sins"; and a voice from Heaven spake concerning Babylon, "Come out of her, my people, that ye be not partakers of her sins." * To communicate with sin is sin, but to communicate with a sinner in that which is not sin, can be no sin; because the one defileth, and the other cannot, and that which defileth not is no sin.

'Having thus considered those who differ from the saints of God; first, in respect of their humanity, as

* Eph. v. 11; I. Tim. v. 22; Rev. xviii. 4.

they are men; secondly, in reference to their sanctity, as they are men of holiness: we are now to consider such as differ either only in person, as the saints alive; or in present condition also, as the saints departed.

'Therefore, the saints of God living in the Church of Christ have communion with all the saints living in the same Church. "If we walk in the light, we have fellowship one with another"; * we all have benefit of the same ordinances, all partake of the same promises, we are all endued with the graces of the same Spirit, all united with the same mutual love and affection, "keeping the unity of the Spirit in the bond of peace"; † all engrafted into the same stock, and so receiving life from the same root; all "holding the [same] Head, from which all the body by joints and bands having nourishment ministered, and knit together, increaseth with the increase of God." ‡ For in the philosophy of the Apostle the nerves are not only the instruments of motion and sensation, but of nutrition also, so that every member receiveth nourishment by their intervention from the head; and since the Head of the body is Christ, and all the saints are members of that body, they all partake of the same nourishment, and so have all communion among themselves.

'Lastly, the saints of God living in the Church of Christ are in communion with all the saints departed out of this life and admitted to the presence of God. Jerusalem is sometimes taken for the Church on earth, sometimes for that part of the Church which is in heaven, to shew that as both are represented in one,

* I. St. John i. 7.   † Eph. iv. 3.   ‡ Col. ii. 19.

so both are but one city of God. Wherefore thus doth the Apostle speak to such as are called to the Christian faith : " Ye are come unto Mount Sion, and unto the city of the living God, the heavenly Jerusalem, and to an innumerable company of angels, to the general assembly and Church of the first-born, which are written in heaven, and to God the Judge of all, and to the spirits of just men made perfect, and to Jesus the Mediator of the new covenant."* Indeed, the communion of the saints in the Church of Christ with those which are departed is demonstrated by their communion with the saints alive. For if I have communion with a saint of God, as such, while he liveth here, I must still have communion with him when he is departed hence; because the foundation of that communion cannot be removed by death. The mystical union between Christ and his Church, the conjunction of the members to the head, is the true foundation of that communion which one member hath with another, all the members living and increasing by the same influence which they receive from Him. But death, which is nothing else but the separation of the soul from the body, maketh no separation in the mystical union, no breach of the spiritual conjunction, because there remaineth the same foundation. Indeed, the saint departed, before his death, had some communion with the hypocrite, as hearing the word, professing the faith, receiving the sacraments together ; which being in things only external, as they were common to them both, and all such external actions ceasing in the person dead, the

* Heb. xii. 22, 23, 24.

hypocrite remaining loseth all communion with the saint departing, and the saints surviving cease to have farther fellowship with the hypocrite dying. But since the true and unfeigned holiness of man, wrought by the powerful influence of the Spirit of God, not only remaineth, but also is improved after death; since the correspondence of the internal holiness was the true communion between their persons in their life, they cannot be said to be divided by death, which had no power over that sanctity by which they were first conjoined.

'This communion of the saints in heaven and earth upon the mystical union of Christ, their head, being fundamental and internal, what acts or external operations it produceth, is not so certain. That we communicate with them in hope of that happiness which they actually enjoy, is evident; that we have the Spirit of God given us as an earnest and so a part of their felicity, is certain. But what they do in heaven in relation to us on earth particularly considered, or what we ought to perform in reference to them in heaven, besides a reverential respect and study of imitation, is not revealed unto us in the Scriptures, nor can be concluded by necessary deduction from any principles of Christianity. They which first found this part of the Article in the Creed, and delivered their exposition unto us, have made no greater enlargement of this communion, as to the saints of heaven, than the society of hope, esteem and imitation on our side, of desires and supplications on their side; and what is now taught by the Church of Rome is, as an unwarrantable, so a novitious interpretation.

'Every one,' says this great author in conclusion, 'may learn from hence what he is to understand by this part of the Article in which he professeth to believe the Communion of Saints; for thereby he is conceived to express thus much: I am fully persuaded of this as a necessary and infallible truth, that such persons as are truly sanctified in the Church of Christ, while they live among the crooked generations of men, and struggle with all the miseries of this world, have fellowship with God the Father, God the Son, and God the Holy Ghost, as dwelling with them, and taking up their habitations in them: that they partake of the care and kindness of the blessed angels, who take delight in the ministration for their benefit: that beside the external fellowship which they have in the word and sacraments with all the members of the Church, they have an intimate union and conjunction with all the Saints on earth as the living members of Christ; nor is this union separated by the death of any; but as Christ in whom they live is the Lamb slain from the foundation of the world, so have they fellowship with all the Saints which from the death of Abel have ever departed in the true faith and fear of God, and now enjoy the presence of the Father, and follow the Lamb whithersoever He goeth. And thus I believe the Communion of Saints.' *

So speaks the writer who is universally admitted to be the great authority of the Church of England, on

* Bishop Pearson on the Creed, pp. 537-543.

the Apostles' Creed. But his exposition is a learned work intended for the study of theologians; let me now point out to you the manner in which this Article is stated, for the instruction of our children, by a very prudent and unimaginative divine, Archbishop Secker, whose name is well known to you, as his work on the Church Catechism is used, as a book of instruction, in many of our schools.

He says: 'The word "saint" is of the same meaning with the word "holy"; and therefore comprehends all Christians, in the same manner as has been already explained. Having "communion" is being entitled to partake of benefits and kindnesses, and bound to make suitable returns for them. And thus Christians, or saints, have communion or "fellowship" with "the Father from whom cometh down every good and perfect gift"; "with His Son Jesus Christ,"* through whom forgiveness and mercy is conveyed to us; with the Holy Ghost, whose sanctifying graces are conferred on such as duly qualify their hearts for the reception of them. And for these blessings we owe all thankfulness, and all duty, in thought, word, and deed. Christians have also communion with the holy angels; as these "are ministering spirits sent forth to minister for them who shall be heirs of salvation,"† and undoubtedly we ought to think of what they do for us with an inward sense of gratitude and love. But, as we are unacquainted with particulars, we can make no particular acknowledgments: nor ought we to make any general ones, by outward expressions of respect;

* St. James i. 17; I. St. John i. 3.   † Heb. i. 14.

since "worshipping God alone" is commanded;* and worshipping angels condemned in Scripture.†

'With respect to those of our own nature, we are bound so far to hold communion even with the worst of unbelievers, as not only to do them every kind of justice, but sincerely to wish, and, if occasion offer, heartily endeavour their good, both in body and soul. But to all, "who have obtained the like precious faith with ourselves,"‡ we bear a still nearer relation; as being, in a peculiar sense, children of the same Father, disciples of the same Master, animated by the same Spirit, members of the same body. And these things oblige us to the utmost care of preserving, by prudent order and mutual forbearance, as much unity in the Church as possibly we can.

'Such indeed as obstinately deny the fundamental doctrines, or transgress the fundamental precepts of Christianity, ought to be rejected from Christian communion. But to renounce the communicating with any others, who are willing to admit us to it on lawful terms, is the way to cut off ourselves, not them, from the body of Christ: who yet, we doubt not, will allow those on both sides to belong to His Church, who through pardonable passions or mistakes will not allow one another to do so.

'And, as we should maintain communion with all proper persons, we should shew our disposition to it in all proper ways: attend on the public instruction, join in the public worship, sacraments, and discipline, which our Lord hath appointed; and keep the whole

* St. Matt. iv. 10.   † Col. ii. 18.   ‡ II. St. Pet. i. 1.

of them pure from all forbidden or suspicious alterations or mixtures: avoid, with great care, both giving and taking needless offence, in respect to these or any matters; and by all fit means "edify one another in love";* obeying those who are set over us; condescending to those who are beneath us; esteeming and honouring the wise and virtuous; teaching and admonishing the ignorant and faulty; bearing with the weak, relieving the poor, and comforting the afflicted.

'Nor have we "communion" only with the "saints" on earth, but are of one city and one family with such as are already got safe to heaven. Doubtless they exercise that "communion" towards us by loving and praying for their brethren, whom they have left behind them. And we are to exercise it towards them, not by addressing petitions to them, which we are neither authorized to offer, nor have any grounds to think they can hear; but by rejoicing in their happiness; thanking God for the grace which He hath bestowed on them, and the examples which they have left us; holding their memories in honour; imitating their virtues; and beseeching the Disposer of all things, that having followed them in holiness here, we may meet them in happiness hereafter; and become, in the fullest sense, "fellow-citizens with the saints and of the household of God,"† having "with all those that are departed in the true faith of His holy name, our perfect consummation and bliss, both

---

* Rom. xiv. 19; Eph. iv. 16.
† Eph. ii. 19.

in body and soul, in His eternal and everlasting glory, through Jesus Christ our Lord. Amen." ' *

Another celebrated Archbishop of the Church of England, Archbishop Wake, published a Commentary on the Church Catechism, which also has always been popular in our public schools; and I will now give you his exposition of this Article of our Creed, 'the Communion of Saints,' as it is in question and answer.

'1. *Q.* What is the first duty or privilege belonging to those who are members of Christ's Church?

A. THE COMMUNION OF SAINTS.

2. *Q.* What do you mean by Saints?

A. Though the word in our language be more restrained; yet in that, in which this creed was composed, it may indifferently denote either holy persons or holy things; and this article may very well be extended to both of them.

3. *Q.* Whom do you mean by holy persons?

A. Though all Christians in general are so called in Scripture; and we are charitably to presume that all such are holy persons; yet by saints we are most properly to understand such as answer the end of their calling, by a lively faith, and a holy conversation, in which two the Gospel Saintship does consist. (Ephes. iii. 17, 18. v. 3. Col. iii. 12.)

4. *Q.* With whom, and in what things, do you believe such persons to have communion?

---

* Secker's Lectures on the Church Catechism; Lecture xiv. pp 121, 122, in the edition published by the Society for Promoting Christian Knowledge, quoted by Bishop Mant, in his edition of the Prayer Book.

A. I believe that all the true members of Christ's Church have a right of fellowship, or communion, with God the Father, and our Lord Jesus Christ; as they are received into covenant by the one, through the death and passion of the other.

I believe that they have a fellowship with the Holy Ghost, by His dwelling in them, and sanctifying of them.

I believe that they have a fellowship with the Holy Angels; who both minister unto them in their exigencies, and have a most tender, affectionate concern for them.

I believe that they all have a fellowship with one another, as members of the same mystical body of Christ; professors of the same faith; heirs of the same promises; guided by the same spirit; and governed by the same laws. And I believe that they ought, as living members, to have a fellowship of love and charity also towards each other.

And, lastly, I believe that they have a right of communicating in all the ordinances of the Gospel; in the prayers of the Church; in the ministry of the word and sacraments; and whatsoever else hath been appointed by Christ, or established in the Church for the common good and benefit of all the members of it.

5. *Q.* Do you not, by this account of the present Article, utterly shut out those from any part in it who yet are more commonly called saints; I mean such as have departed this life in the fear of God, and the faith of Jesus Christ?

A. No, by no means; I believe them to partake in this communion also; as they are still living members of Christ's Holy Catholic Church; and therefore I believe that they have a fellowship, no less than we, with God and Christ That they are sanctified by the same Spirit; are visited by the Holy Angels; have some kind of fellowship with one another; and with us also, however separated by death from us.

6. *Q.* Wherein do you suppose their fellowship with us to consist?

A. I look upon the case to be much the same with us as it is with members of the same civil society upon earth, when they are in a foreign country, far distant from one another. We are members of the same Church; united to the same Head; sanctified by the same Spirit; heirs of the same promises; shall in a little time be in the same place and state; and when the end of the world comes, we shall all be translated to the same glory and happiness, in God's Heavenly Kingdom.

7. *Q.* To what offices of communion does this belief oblige us, at present, towards others?

A. To the members of Christ's Church, still living, it obliges us to love and charity; to mutual prayers for, and help of, each other, in all such things as may promote the salvation of us all. How the saints departed maintain communion with us we cannot tell. Probable it is, that they do, in general, pray for us, as it is certain they wish well to us. But for ourselves, who are yet here on earth, we must bless God for the grace He hath pleased to bestow upon them; and by which they were delivered from the sins and temptations of this evil world, and enabled faithfully to serve Him unto the end. We must set before us their examples and imitate their virtues. We must account of them as living members of Christ's body; and be not only ready, but desirous, to go to them, whenever it shall please God to call for us. We must take care decently to dispose of their bodies; and faithfully to fulfil, as much as in us lies, what they have left in trust with us, to be done for them after their departure.

8. *Q.* What think you of that honour which is paid to them in the Church of Rome?

A. It is not only vain, and without all warrant from God's Word; but is indeed superstitious and idolatrous. To pray to any creature and he at a vast distance from us, in the house of God, with all the outward marks of religious worship; nay, and oftentimes in the same words, and in the same breath, in which we pray to God; and that, lastly, with a confidence that the person so prayed to can hear our prayers, and answer our desires: being evidently to give to the creature the honour due to the Creator, which cannot be done without the peril of idolatry.' *

And now I will read to you what is said by another writer, a prelate who has always been held in veneration among Church of England divines, Bishop Ken. Bishop Ken, though not actually a martyr, was a confessor for the Church of England against Popery,

* Archbishop Wake's Catechism, pp. 66–69. Published by the Society for Promoting Christian Knowledge, 1832.

being one of the seven illustrious prelates who were sent to the Tower for opposing the endeavour to establish Popery, which was made by that unprincipled and infatuated monarch, James II. His work, entitled 'The Practice of Divine Love, being an Exposition of the Church Catechism,' is a standard work of divinity. In this little work he of course treats of the Apostles' Creed; but he does so devotionally, and not, like Bishop Pearson, in a learned and logical discourse. He rather applies the truths which have been proved and established by others. His exposition of that article of the creed, 'The Communion of Saints,' to which I am now calling your attention, is as follows; and you will perceive how entirely it corresponds with that of Bishop Pearson:—

'I believe, O King of Saints, that among the saints on earth, whether real or in outward profession only, there ought to be a mutual participation of all good things.

'I believe, O thou God of love, that all the saints on earth, by profession, ought to communicate one with another in evangelical worship, and the same holy sacraments, in the same divine and apostolic faith, in all offices of corporal and spiritual charity, in reciprocal delight in each other's salvation, and in tender sympathy as members of one and the same body. O God of peace, restore in Thy good time this Catholic Communion, that with one heart, and one mouth, we may all praise and love Thee.

'O my God, amidst the deplorable divisions of Thy Church, let me never widen its breaches. O deliver me from the sins and errors, from the schisms and heresies of the age. O give me grace to pray daily for the peace of Thy Church, and earnestly to seek it.

'I believe, O most holy Jesus, that Thy saints here below have communion with Thy saints above, they praying for us in heaven, we here on earth celebrating their memorials, rejoicing at their bliss, giving thee thanks for their labours of love, and imitating their examples.

'I believe, O gracious Redeemer, that Thy saints here on earth have communion with the holy Angels above: that they are ministering spirits, sent forth to minister for them who shall be heirs of salvation, and to watch over us; and we give thanks to Thee for their protection, and emulate their incessant praises, and ready obedience.

'Glory be to Thee, O goodness infinitely diffusive, for all the graces and blessings in which the saints communicate, for breathing Thy love into Thy mystical body, as the very soul that animates it, that all who believe in Thee may love one another, and all join in loving Thee.' *

* To many of my readers this passage will be familiar, because I quoted it in a little tract, entitled 'Pastoral Advice,' which I published for the use of young persons preparing for the last Confirmation. That little tract being acknowledged to be a compilation (as I did not wish to give merely my own opinions, but as I desired to lay before my readers the truths of the Christian religion, as asserted by divines of acknowledged reputation), I did not think it necessary to specify the sources from which the instruction given was drawn, but I may as well state here, that not only the passage quoted above, but the whole of 'The Creed in a Devotional Form,' is from that excellent prelate, to whom I have referred, Bishop Ken.

How Scriptural this is you have already heard from the expositions of two Archbishops of Canterbury, and of a prelate, if superior in learning to Bishop Ken, certainly not more than his equal in evangelic piety. With reference to that portion of the exposition which refers to the acts of communion, in which the saints departed are engaged, I shall sum up what has been said in the words of perhaps the most learned divine the Church of England has ever produced, that godly man, Bishop Bull. In writing against the corruptions of the Church of Rome, after commenting upon the other errors of that church, he says: 'As to what follows, "that the saints departed do offer up their prayers to God for us," if it be understood of the intercession of the saints in general, we deny it not. But this is no reason why we should pray to them to pray for us. Nay, on the contrary, if the deceased saints do of their own accord, and out of their perfect charity, pray for us, what need we be so solicitous to call upon them for their prayers, especially when our reason and Scripture also tell us, that we are out of their hearing, and that they do not, cannot know our particular wants and necessities? For, as to what the Romanists tell us of the glass of the Trinity, and extraordinary revelations, they are bold, presumptuous conjectures, destitute of any ground or colour from reason or Scripture, and indeed are inconsistent with one another.' *

And now let me show how this Scriptural doctrine, so far as the saints departed are concerned, is corrobo-

* Bull's Works, vol. ii. p. 266.

rated by our text. 'And another Angel came and stood at the altar, having a golden censer; and there was given unto him much incense, that he should offer it with the prayers of all Saints upon the golden altar which was before the throne.' That the prayers of the Church militant are included in this sacrifice is indisputable, and equally indisputable must it appear to those who have considered the subject, that the prayers of the Church triumphant are not excluded. In the sixth chapter of this same Apocalypse, we find it said : 'And when he had opened the fifth seal, I saw under the altar the souls of them that were slain for the word of God, and for the testimony which they held, and they cried with a loud voice, saying, How long, O Lord, holy and true, dost Thou not judge and avenge our blood on them that dwell on the earth ? And white robes were given unto every one of them ; and it was said unto them, that they should rest yet for a little season, until their fellow-servants also and their brethren, that should be killed as they were, should be fulfilled.'* 'If,' says a learned writer,† 'the prayers of the Blessed Martyrs, within their heavenly habitations, were thus offered and accepted for judgment on Christ's foes, think you that they could be less fervently offered, or less freely accepted, in behalf of their fellow-servants and fellow-sufferers, who, as the answer of God testifieth unto them, were successively to follow the path which they had trodden, and, like them,

---

* Rev. vi. 9–11.
† Rev. Charles Foster, in his Sermon on the death of the learned and excellent Bishop Jebb.

through much tribulation, to enter into the Kingdom of God? Think you that the prayers of the blessed saints in bliss could be permitted to go up for judgment—and yet the blessed privilege be denied them, of uniting their prayers with those of the Church militant, for the consummation of the Saviour's glory, and the coming of His kingdom?'

Not so, my brethren, for we read in the fifth chapter of the Apocalypse, that 'He (the Lamb), came and took the Book out of the right hand of Him that sat upon the Throne. And when He had taken the Book, the four Beasts and four-and-twenty Elders fell down before the Lamb, having every one of them harps, and golden vials full of odours, which are the Prayers of Saints.'*

Now, such was the faith, and such the hope, with which the most eminent of our Reformers, Bishop Ridley, one of the holy Martyrs of our Reformation, sought to console himself when preparing to bid adieu to a brother Reformer and Martyr: 'If it be not the place that sanctifieth the man, but the holy man doth, by Christ, sanctify the place, Brother Bradford, then happy and holy shall be that place wherein thou shalt suffer: and that shall be with thy ashes in Christ's cause sprinkled withal. So long as I understand thou art on thy journey, I shall call on our Heavenly Father to see thee safely home; and then, good brother, speak you and pray for the remnant which are to suffer for Christ's sake, according to that thou shalt know more clearly.'†

And such is still the faith of that Holy Church,

* Revelation v. 7, 8.   † Life of Bishop Ridley, p. 572.

INVOCATION OF SAINTS. 183

which this blessed martyr was instrumental in cleansing from the corruption of Popery. Yes, in our most sacred and solemn service, ye who are communicants know that the Church leads us on to laud and magnify the glorious name of our God, not with men only, but with angels and archangels, and all the company of Heaven. Holy is the joy, and elevated are the feelings of those among us who are communicants, when holding communion with the saints of the Church militant here on earth, with angels and archangels, and all the company of heaven, in the most solemn act of devotion, they praise our God, and say, 'Holy, holy, holy, Lord God of Hosts, heaven and earth are full of Thy glory: Glory be to Thee, O Lord Most High.' And when we commit the body of a brother to the ground, earth to earth, ashes to ashes, dust to dust, how tenderly does the Church apply this doctrine to our consolation, as she bids us pray that 'it may please God, of His gracious goodness, shortly to accomplish the number of His elect, and to hasten His Kingdom: that we, with all those that are departed in the true faith of His holy name, may have our perfect consummation and bliss in His eternal and everlasting glory.' This indeed must be the one great prayer of the Church triumphant, as well as militant, until Christ our Lord shall have come again in His glory : 'Looking for and hasting unto the coming of the day of God,'* we hold communion with one another in the supplication, 'even so, come, Lord Jesus.'†

And now, my brethren, I have stated to you the

* II. St. Pet. iii. 12. † Rev. xxii. 20.

Romish error against which we, as a Protestant Church protest, and I have reminded you of that article of the Catholic faith, which we, as holding the Apostles' Creed, profess; while I have warned you against the perversion of it, which sometimes occurs through the ignorance of foolish men. The Invocation of Saints we reject as a fond thing and repugnant to Scripture, and as leading men away from Christ, our only Mediator and Intercessor, into practical idolatry: but the Communion of Saints we hold, and it is a truth which all among us who have lost those who are dear to them, fondly cherish; not lost, indeed, for they believe that they are only gone before, and are employed in the Church triumphant, as we in the Church militant, in singing the praises of the one God, the Blessed Trinity, and in praying that His will may be done on earth, as it is in heaven. Sad, indeed, would it be to think of the souls of our dear departed friends, the saints whom we delight to imitate, and whose dear memories we affectionately cherish, as if they had perished; and a heavenly consolation it is to know, that washed by the blood of that Immaculate Lamb, that was slain to take away the sins of the world, whatsoever defilements they may have contracted in the midst of this miserable and naughty world, through the lusts of the flesh, or the wiles of Satan, being purged and done away; they are presented pure and without spot, just men made perfect, before the Throne of Glory, where they are precious in the sight of God;* whom they for ever laud and magnify,

* The Commendatory Prayer for a sick person at the point of departure.

looking for the time, and praying that it may be hastened, when their friends now militant on earth will be triumphant with them, glorying in the salvation purchased by the Redeemer's Blood, and freely given to the sinful sons of Adam.

Let us not be hurried in our dread of Popery into the worse extreme of infidelity, either as to this or as to any other article of our Creed. Superstition is a bad thing, but infidelity is worse; and some persons there are who are only zealous against Popery, because by attacking Popery they imagine that they can subvert Christianity itself, and destroy the truth while they only profess to assail the corruption. When one man accuses another of Popery, it is absolutely necessary, before you give attention to what he says, to ascertain not only what he protests against, but also what he himself holds; some there are who mean by Popery the Christian Religion. There is not an article of the Christian Religion which has not at some time or other been denounced as Popery by some or other heretic. A Socinian will regard as Popery the doctrines of the Trinity in Unity, the Incarnation of God, and the shedding of His blood as an Atonement for Sin; and so far he is right, for these doctrines are held by Papists, but then they are not Romanism but Catholicism. What, indeed, is Popery, but the corruption or the perversion of Truth? To suppress a Catholic truth because some persons think that it may be perverted to Romish heresy, is about as wise as it would be to destroy a child at its birth, because children sometimes grow up to be thieves and murderers.

Those Protestant Dissenters who denounce the Church of England divines as Papists, or semi-Papists, merely because, in the opinion of their accusers, their teaching leads to Popery, ought to remember that if this line of argument were a fair one, they might themselves be denounced as infidels, because in the opinion of the Church of England divines, the principles of ultra-Protestantism, if logically carried out, would terminate in infidelity. But, my brethren, such a charge as this we do not bring against them: even when in zeal for God's truth we oppose their principles, we never forget that men may be better than their doctrines; and in the fact that they are as zealous in opposing us, as we are firm in not yielding to them, we perceive in them, so far, the existence of a Christian spirit, and only require of them in their opposition the exhibition also of a Christian temper, and the renunciation of those artifices which worldly men in political warfare think allowable, but which Christian men must eschew. A solemn protest against error, and a zealous assertion of the opposite truth, are essential to the existence of vital Christianity in the heart, and on this account it was that our Blessed Lord declared that He came not to send peace on earth, but a sword:—'I am come,' He said, 'to set a man at variance against his father, and the daughter against her mother, and the daughter-in-law against her mother-in-law. And a man's foes shall be they of his own household.'* The careless worldling and the infidel stand astonished to see the zeal with which Christians contend for every

* St. Matt. x. 35, 36.

particle of truth, which to them is precious as gold dust to the refiner. And hence, knowing the principle He was establishing, our Lord predicted the consequence of it, in a wicked world. But, my brethren, let us remember that while Christian charity does not consist in the compromise of truth, and while we may not blame those who are zealous in their opposition to error, even though what to them appears to be error is in fact God's truth : we do expect in Christian men mutual forbearance and allowance ; we do expect that they will attribute right motives to each other, where the existence of wrong motives cannot be proved ; we do expect that evil passions should be restrained, and that while brotherly remonstrances are tolerated brotherly love should abound ; we do expect that Christians, when brought into controversy with each other, should never forget in how many things they are one ; they are one in their conviction of sin and their sense of guilt ; they feel the same disease of sin, and look to the same Physician of Souls ; they are taught by the same Holy Spirit, and are supported by the same Heavenly Grace ; they are, we trust, fellow-travellers in the same journey to the same country ; and being taught in the same Scriptures to love their enemies, they ought to look forward with holy joy to that time when those who have been most estranged upon earth shall walk together as friends in the everlasting mansions, where, with angels and archangels, they will praise for ever, and for ever, the God of Truth who is also the God of Love.

And so, my brethren, you perceive how with Archbishops and Bishops of the Protestant Church of England, we may hold that article of our Creed which relates to the Communion of Saints, at the very time that we protest against the Invocation of them; and how the realization of this article of our Creed can divest controversy of its bitterness, and render us charitable in our prayers, while we are inflexible in our principles.

SERMON XXV.[*]

'*The Mother of my Lord.*'

St. Luke i. 47.

I SHALL speak to you this day of the Virgin Mary; first describing to you her Blessedness, wherein it consists, and then animadverting upon the Mariolatry, or the worship of Mary, which is the deep degrading sin of the Romish Church.

Unenlightened men in their vehement opposition to the Romish Church, under the influence of mere party feelings, so overstate their case as to give an advantage to their adversary; and when our adversary sees that we are afraid to state the truth, he directs the attention of his disciples to that truth, which, by our fearing to assert it, he insinuates that we deny; and so by the incaution, or rather by the over-caution of his assailants, the Romish controversialist is enabled to confound in men's minds our truth with his error, and to propagate Romanism by defending Catholicism. Instead of defending his error of Transubstantiation, which he would find it impossible to do, the skilful Romanist, availing himself of the ignorant concessions of some Protestants, confounds Transubstantiation with the doctrine of the Real Presence, and so extricates himself from his diffi-

[*] Preached in the Parish Church of Leeds, Feb. 7, 1847.

culty; but perhaps this position is in no respect more powerfully illustrated than it is by reference to the worship of the Virgin Mary. The Romanists frequently apply to her the title of Mother of God. Ignorant Protestants very violently denounce this title as given to Mary. Papists are, of course, well pleased that so it should be, because they find it easy to prove by the universal consent of the Church, and by reference to Scripture, that Mary is the Mother of God.

But why do ultra-Protestants,—not the old Puritans,—refuse to give this title to the Virgin Mary? They, showing an ignorance of history, imagine that the title was given to do honour to the Virgin, and that it implies that worship ought to be paid to her; this being precisely the inference which the Papist desires to have drawn from the fact, but being precisely that inference against which we of the Church of England protest. We admit that the Virgin Mary is the Mother of God; but we protest againt the conclusion that she is on that account to be treated with peculiar honour, or to be worshipped; for this expression is used not to exalt her, but to assert unequivocally the Divinity of her Son: He whom she brought forth was God, and therefore she is the Bringer-forth or Mother of God.

The term was first brought prominently forward at the Council of Ephesus, the third of those four general Councils, the decisions of which are authoritative in the Church of England; and it was adopted as a formula against the Nestorians. The Nestorian Controversy originated thus. In the year 428 Nestorius was Bishop of Constantinople, and he had brought with him from

Antioch, where he had before resided, a priest named Anastasius, his chaplain and friend; this person preaching one day in the Church of Constantinople, said, 'Let no one call Mary Mother of God; for she was a woman, and it is impossible that God should be born of a human creature.' These words gave great offence to many both of the clergy and laity, for they had always been taught, says the historian Socrates,* 'to acknowledge Jesus Christ as God, and not to sever Him in any way from the Divinity.' Nestorius, however, declared his assent to what Anastasius had said, and became, from his high position in the Church, the Heresiarch.

When the heresy had spread into Egypt it was refuted by St. Cyril, Bishop of Alexandria, in a pastoral letter which he published for the direction of his people. 'I wonder,' he says, 'how a question can be raised as to whether the Holy Virgin should be called Mother of God; for if our Lord Jesus Christ is God, how is not the Holy Virgin, His Mother, the Mother of God? This is the faith we have been taught by the Apostles.'† He next proves that He who was born of the Virgin Mary is God in His own nature, since the Nicene Creed says that the only begotten Son of God, of the same substance with the Father, Himself came down from Heaven and was incarnate; and then he proceeds: 'You will say, perhaps, is the Virgin, then, Mother of the Divinity? We answer, It is certain that the Word is eternal, and of the substance of the Father. Now, in the order of nature, mothers, who

---

* Socrates, viii. 32. † Ep. ad Mon. n. 4.

have no part in the creation of the soul, are still called mothers of the whole man, and not of the body only : for surely it would be a hypercritical refinement to say, Elizabeth is mother of the body of John, and not of his soul. In the same way, therefore, we express ourselves in regard to the birth of Emmanuel, since the Word, having taken flesh upon him, is called Son of Man.'* In a letter to Nestorius himself he enters into a fuller explanation: 'We must admit in the same Christ two generations ; first, the eternal, by which he proceeds from His Father; second, the temporal, by which He is born of His Mother. When we say that He suffered and rose again, we do not say that God the Word suffered in His own nature, for the Divinity is impassible; but because the body which was appropriated to Him suffered, we also say that He suffered Himself. So too we say, He died. The Divine Word is in His own nature immortal, He is life itself: but because His own true body suffered death, we say that He Himself died for us. In the same way, when His flesh is raised from the dead, we attribute resurrection to Him. We do not say that we adore the Man along with the Word, lest the phrase "along with" should suggest the idea of their non-identity ; but we adore Him as one and the same person, because the Body assumed by the Word is in no degree external to or separated from the Word.'†
'It is in this sense,' he says afterwards, 'that the Fathers have ventured to call the Holy Virgin "Mother of God," not that the nature of the Word, or His

* Ep. ad Mon. n. 6.   † Conc. Eph. Pt. i. c. 8.

Divinity, did receive beginning of His existence from the Holy Virgin, but because in her was formed and animated a reasonable Soul and sacred Body, to which the Word united Himself in hypostasis, which is the reason of its being said that He was born according to the flesh.'

I have given you these quotations from the writings of St. Cyril, because he presided at the great Council of Ephesus, convened not by the Pope but by the Emperor, and his expressions were adopted by the council. The council approved of the title of Mother or Bringer-forth of God, as applied to the Virgin Mary; but, as our own Bishop Bull remarks, 'they did not first invent it, as some have ignorantly affirmed. And therefore they themselves, in their synodical epistle, say that the holy fathers before them doubted not to call the blessed Virgin θεοτόκον, Deiparam, the Mother of God. Indeed, a whole age before that council, we find Eusebius expressly giving that title to the sacred Virgin in his third book of the Life of Constantine, chap. xliii.; and Socrates, a most credible witness in this matter, in the seventh book of his Eccles. Hist. chap. xxxii., assures us that Origen, long before Eusebius, largely explained and asserted that title as applied to the Blessed Virgin. And to go yet higher, we have heard Irenæus, who was a scholar to a scholar of the Apostles, magnifying the Virgin on this account, that she did *portare Deum*, bear God within her. If she did *portare Deum* she did *parere Deum*: if she bore God she brought Him forth too, and so was θεοτόκος, the Mother of God, that is, of

Him that was God. Nay, the blessed martyr and disciple of the Apostles, Ignatius, in his Epistle to the Ephesians, Edit. Vass. p. 27, feared not to say, " our God Jesus Christ was conceived of Mary." But why need we search after human authorities, when the inspired Elizabeth, in her divine rapture, plainly gives the Virgin Mary the same title? "And whence is this to me, that the Mother of my Lord should come unto me?" Where μητὴρ τοῦ Κυρίου, the mother of our Lord, is doubtless of the same import with θεοτόκος, the Mother of God: for the title of our Lord belongs to Christ chiefly as He is our God. And we are to conceive Elizabeth, being filled with the Spirit, to have given this title of her Lord to the Babe in the Blessed Virgin's womb, not according to the poor narrow vulgar sense of the degenerate Jews, but according to the most august and highest sense of the word, namely, that He is so our Lord as to be our God also.'* To the same purpose we may quote the excellent Bishop Beveridge: 'When Nestorius had affirmed, that in Christ, as there are two natures, so there are two persons likewise; one person, as He was God begotten of the Father; the other as man, born of His Mother; and therefore that the blessed Virgin could not properly be called Θεοτόκος; the council, for the determination of this question, did not only consult the several texts in Scripture relating to our blessed Saviour, but considered likewise in what sense those places had been understood by the Catholic Church before that time; for which end they caused the

* Bishop Bull's Works, vol. i. sermon iv,

Nicene Creed, and several passages out of St. Cyprian, St. Basil, Athanasius, Gregory Nazianzen, and many others, to be read in council. And from thence they gathered, and therefore pronounced, that according to the Scriptures, as interpreted by the Catholic Church, Christ, though He have two natures, yet He is but one Person, and by consequence that the Virgin Mary might properly be called Θεοτόκος, because the same Person who was born of her is truly God as well as man: which being once determined by an universal council to be the true sense and meaning of the Scriptures in this point, hath been acknowledged by the universal Church ever since, till this time.' *

I may further quote the words of the very learned Dr. Barrow: 'Whatever any mother doth confer to the entire production of a child, is to be attributed to the blessed Virgin; whence she was truly and properly "the mother of our Lord," and is accordingly often so called in the Gospels; whence also she hath been in the Church defined to be and commonly styled Θεοτόκος, the bearer and mother of God; that is, of Him who is God; that term asserting the divinity of Christ and the unity of His person, against Nestorius and his partisans; who said that the Virgin was not properly Θεοτόκος, but χριστοτόκος; and that He who was born was not God, but ἄνθρωπος θεοφόρος, a man carrying God or divinity in hand.' †

'The Virgin Mary,' says Bishop Pearson, 'is frequently styled the Mother of Jesus in the language

---

* Bp. Beveridge's Works, vol. ii. p. 199.
† Barrow, vi. p. 58.

of the Evangelists, and by Elizabeth particularly the Mother of her Lord, as also by the general consent of the Church, because He which was so born of her was God, the Deipara; which being a compound title begun in the Greek Church, was resolved into its parts by the Latins, and so the Virgin was plainly named the Mother of God.'*

Jealousy for the Lord Jesus Christ, anxiety for the maintenance of His honour, and the assertion of His Divinity, not any especial regard to the creature through whose instrumentality He was brought into the world, —were the motives which influenced the Fathers of the Council of Ephesus. And the decisions of that council, because they can be proved to be Scriptural, our Church accepts, when in cases of heresy she refers her judges to the first four General Councils.†

Now, I have entered into this statement that you may understand clearly that the whole question in this Nestorian controversy had not reference, as men ignorant of ecclesiastical history suppose, to the honour of

* Pearson on the Creed, vol. i. p. 270.

† 'Provided always, and be it enacted by the authority aforesaid, that such person or persons, to whom your Highness, your heirs, or successors, shall hereafter, by letters patent under the great seal of England, give authority to have, or to execute any jurisdiction, power, or authority spiritual, or to visit, reform, order, or correct any errors, heresies, schisms, abuses, or enormities, by virtue of this Act, shall not in any wise have authority or power to order, determine, or adjudge any matter or cause to be heresy, but only such as have heretofore been determined, ordered, or adjudged to be heresy, by the authority of the Canonical Scriptures, or by the first four General Councils, or any of them, or by any other General Council, wherein the same was declared heresy by the express and plain words of the said Canonical Scriptures.'—*Gibson's Codex*, vol. i. p. 425; Fol. Oxford, 1713.—*Collier's Eccles. Hist.* vol. ii. p. 421.

the Virgin Mary, but to the honour of Jesus our God. The Council vindicated this title, not because it was a high title for Mary, but because to deny it is to deny that He is God whom she brought forth. The heresy of Nestorius related, you will not fail to observe, to the Incarnation, or Junction of the two natures in Christ, which he affirmed to be not a union, but merely a connection; whereas the object of the Council of Ephesus was to assert 'the real and inseparable union of the two natures in Christ, and to show that the human nature, which Christ took of the holy Virgin, never subsisted separately from the Divine Person of the Son of God.'

To the use of this term, however, though we contend for its propriety, divines of the Church of England are not partial, because, by the subtilty of the Romish controversialists, it has been so used, or rather misused, as to make it seem to confer peculiar honour and privileges upon the Virgin Mary.* The primitive Christians, like ourselves, were contented with speaking of the Virgin as 'The Mother of my Lord:' and this phrase sufficed until, as we have seen, heretics arose who understood the word Lord in an inferior sense, and then it became necessary to assert that God and Lord, as applied to our Blessed Saviour, are synonymous terms. And sound theologians will still occasionally use the term Mother of God, lest Nestorianism should be held unconsciously by persons who wish to be

* Some valuable remarks on the gradual perversion of the term may be found in Bishop Pearson, and in Heathcote on the Incarnation.

orthodox : and people forget the great truth expressed by St. Paul, that 'God purchased the Church with His own Blood ; '* and that Christ is ' over all, God blessed for ever.'†

But although it is only for our Lord's sake that we

---

* Acts xx. 28. 'What,' says Bishop Beveridge, 'with the blood of the Divine nature? No, for that hath no blood. With the blood of a man, a distinct person from God? No, for then it could not be called God's own blood. And therefore, it cannot possibly be otherwise interpreted than to signify the blood of a person who was God as well as man ; who being God and becoming man, and purchasing His Church with that blood which He Himself assumed with the human nature, may justly be said to have purchased His Church with His own blood. And hence it is, that to denote His two natures in one person, He hath a name given Him, wherein they are both joined in one word, " Immanuel," Isaiah, vii. 14, which is truly interpreted " God with us," Matt. i. 23. In the beginning of the word " Immanu," with us, there is the human, at the end " el," God, there is the Divine nature implied, and both in the same word, to show that, though they be two natures, yet one name or word is sufficient to express them both, they both making up but one and the same person. And thus we see how evidently it has pleased the Most High God to unveil this great mystery to us, clearly discovering, not only that Christ was begotten of Himself, and so very God from eternity ; and that he was born of a woman, and so very man in time; but also, that he was and is both very God and very man in the very self-same person.'—*Bishop Beveridge*, vol. ix. p. 92.

In like manner Bishop Pearson : 'We know it is not possible that the blood of bulls and goats should take away sins: and we may very well doubt how the blood of him, who hath no other nature than that of man, can take away the sins of other men ; there appearing no such difference as will show a certainty in the one, and an impossibility in the other. But since we may be bought with a price, well may we believe the blood of Christ sufficiently precious, when we are assured that it is the blood of God ; nor can we question the efficacy of it in purging our conscience from dead works, if we believe Christ offered up Himself through the eternal Spirit.'— *Bishop Pearson on the Creed*, vol. i. p. 228.

† Romans ix. 5.

speak of the Virgin Mary as the Mother of God, yet we Protestants of the Church of England, while we protest against the deadly sin of the Church of Rome by which the Virgin Mary is made an object of worship, are among the first with the early Christians to concede to her memory the honour which is most justly her due. It has been observed that 'no true son of the Reformed Church of England can speak disparagingly of the Blessed Virgin Mary. Our Church in her Liturgy, her Homilies, and her Articles, and the works of her standard divines and most approved preachers, always speaks of St. Mary the Blessed Virgin in the language of reverence and affection. She was a Holy Virgin and a Holy Mother, "highly favoured," " blessed among women." The Lord was with her, and she was the Earthly Parent of the only Saviour of the World.'*

Or, to quote one of the standard divines referred to, Bishop Bull: 'We think and speak most respectfully of her, and do not ordinarily mention her name without a preface or epithet of honour, as ".the Holy, the Blessed Virgin," and the like. We do, by the appointment of our Church, sing or rehearse in our daily service her excellent magnificat; and thereby we testify our assent to, and complacence in, those singular favours that God is therein said to have bestowed on her; and together with her, we finally return the praise and glory of all to God alone. We celebrate two annual festivals in her memorial, the feasts of her

---

* Tract viii. of an admirable series of tracts in the course of publication by the Society for Promoting Christian Knowledge, under the title, ' What is Romanism?'

Annunciation and Purification. And if we could think of any other honour that we could do her, without dishonouring God the Father and His eternal Son, we would most willingly yield it to her. Wherefore the papists are themselves egregious calumniators, when they charge us Protestants, that we are *beatæ Virginis conviciatores*, "reproachers of the blessed Virgin." We defy their charge; we honour the blessed Virgin as a most singular elect vessel of God; as one in the highest degree of all mere mortals honoured by God; but therefore we will not yield her any of that honour that is peculiar to God; for God Himself hath told us, that "He will not give his glory to another."* She saith, indeed, that "all generations shall call her blessed;" but not that any generation should call upon her to bless them. This had been a most arrogant sacrilegious speech, altogether unbeseeming the most humble, as well as holy Virgin.' †

But, as Bishop Bull in another place observes : ' We abominate the impious imposture of those who have translated the most humble and holy Virgin into an idol of pride and vanity, and have represented her as a vainglorious and aspiring creature like Lucifer; I tremble at the comparison, thirsting at the Divine worship and honour, and seeking out superstitious men and women, whom she may oblige to her more especial service, and make them her perpetual votaries. For what greater affront than this could they have offered to her humility and sanctity? How fulsome, yea, how

* Is. xlii. 8.
† Bishop Bull's Works, vol. i. sermon iv. pp. 97-98.

perfectly loathsome to us, are the tales of those who have had the assurance to tell us of those amorous addresses of the Blessed Virgin to certain persons her devout worshippers, choosing them for her husbands, bestowing her kisses liberally on them, giving them her breasts to suck, and presenting them with bracelets and rings of her hair as love tokens. The fable of the Jewish Talmudists, yea of Mahomet, may seem grave, serious, and sober histories, compared to these and other such like impudent fictions. Insomuch that wise men have thought that the authors of these romances in religion were no better than the tools and instruments of Satan, used by him to expose the Christian religion, and render it ridiculous, and thereby to introduce Atheism; and, indeed, we are sure that the wits of Italy, where these abominable deceits have been and are chiefly countenanced, were the first broachers and patrons of Infidelity and Atheism in Europe, since the time that Christianity obtained in it.

'In a word, such is the worship given to the Blessed Virgin by many in the Church of Rome, that they deserve to be called Mariani [Marians], rather than Christiani [Christians].

'My brethren, let us bless God that we yet breathe in a pure air, free from the noisome and pestilent fogs of those superstitious vanities, where none of those fooleries and impieties are obtruded on our faith or practice; that we live in a Church wherein no other name is invocated but the name of God the Father, Son, and Holy Ghost; nor divine worship given to any but the one true God, through Jesus

Christ the only Mediator. Oh! happy we if we knew and valued our own happiness! But alas! alas! many of us do not. We despise and trample on that Reformation of Religion, which, by a miracle of God's mercy, was wrought in this nation in the days of our forefathers, and run to schismatical assemblies, under pretence of seeking a better Reformation. They abandon that Church, and can hardly forbear to call it anti-Christian, and popish harlot, the foundation stones whereof were laid and cemented in the blood of God's holy martyrs, that died in defiance of the errors and superstitions of the Romish synagogue.* And yet

* Bishop Bull expresses himself more accurately in his 'Vindication of the Church of England,' where, instead of speaking of the Reformers as laying 'foundation stones,' he says: 'The authors of our Reformation dealt with our churches as they did with our temples and material church. They did not pull them down and raise new structures in their places, no, nor so much as new consecrate the old ones; but only removed the objects and occasions of idolatrous worship (at least out of the more open and conspicuous places), and took away some little superstitious trinkets, in other things leaving them as they found them, and freely and without scruple making use of them.' So also Bishop Hall: 'Be it known to all the world, that our church is only reformed or repaired, not made new. There is not a stone of a new foundation laid by us; yea, the old walls stood still, only the over casting of those ancient stones with untempered mortar of new inventions displeaseth us,—plainly set aside the corruptions, and the church is the same.' 'I would have them remember,' says Archbishop Laud, 'that we live in a church reformed, not made new; now all Reformation that is good and orderly takes away nothing from the old but what is faulty and erroneous; if anything be good, that it leaves standing.'—*Archbp. Laud, Hist. of His Trials and Troubles*, p. 113. 'Thus we may conclude with King James: 'For my part, I know not how to answer the objection of the Papists, when they charge us with novelties, but truly to tell them their abuses are new, but the things which they abused we retain in their primitive use, and forsake only the novel corruption.'—*Hampton Court Conf.*

these men call themselves Protestants, yea, the only true Protestants, and will scarcely allow us of the Church of England to share in the title. God grant that by this, the nation's horrid ingratitude, we do not provoke Him to recall that mercy which we ourselves indeed throw back in His face, as if it were not worth our acceptance, and to cause a dark night of Popery to return on us; wherein a superstitious and idolatrous worship shall be thrust upon us, yea, and we shall be compelled to forbidden and idolatrous worship, or to death; wherein our Bibles, that we now, not only with liberty, but with encouragement, carry about us, shall be snatched out of our hands, and fabulous lying legends be put in the room of them; wherein our excellent Liturgy, in a tongue we all understand, which many now loathe and call filthy pottage, yea, and Popish mass, shall be abolished, and the abominable Roman mass indeed placed in its stead; wherein the cup of blessing in the Holy Eucharist shall be sacrilegiously taken from us, which is now openly and freely held forth to us all, and that in so excellent a way of administration that the whole Christian world beside is not able at this day to show the like (but they scorn to take it, and refuse to receive it, unless it be given by an unhallowed hand in a factious conventicle). If ever these, and the other ill effects of Popery, which I cannot now mention, happen to us (which God avert), and I trust it will never come to pass; but I say if ever these things should befal us, we should then, when it is too late, clearly distinguish between light and darkness, and discern the vast difference between the established religion, which many now call Popery—and Popery itself. We should then cast back a kind and mournful eye upon our dear mother the Church of England, whose very bowels we now tear and rip up by our wicked schisms. We should then wish ourselves in the safe arms of her communion once again, and resolve never more to depart from it. Let us do that now while it is seasonable we shall then wish we had done, but cannot do.'*

Thus wrote Bishop Bull, that illustrious divine, in the seventeenth century; thus did he protest against Popery while he defended Catholicism, and that too though maligned by the Puritans of his day as being a semi-papist himself: how very nearly are the words of this great man, directed against the Puritans of his own day, applicable to the circumstances under which we are placed; then as now, there were many who in their disgust of Puritanism were hastening to Rome; and then, as now, the battle of God's truth was fought in the *via media* of the Church of England.

I will quote what is said to the same purpose by another of our standard divines, one whose learning and prudence are equal to his eloquence—Dr. Barrow. He says: 'The relation of the Blessed Virgin to our Lord, as it should beget a precious esteem and honourable memory of her (for let that mouth be cursed which will not call her blessed, let the name of him be branded with everlasting reproach of folly, who will not prefer her in dignity before any queen or empress), so it should not serve to breed in us fond opinions, or

* Bishop Bull's Works, vol. i. sermon iv. p. 106

to ground superstitious practices in regard to her, as it hath happened to do among divers sorts of Christians; especially among the adherents to Rome. For, they (out of a wanton mind, but in effect profanely and sacrilegiously) have attributed to her divers swelling and vain names, divers scandalously unsavory, some hideously blasphemous, titles and eulogies, as alluding to, so intrenching on, the incommunicable prerogatives of God Almighty and of our blessed Saviour; such as the Queen of Heaven, the Health of the World, the Mother of Mercies, the Spouse of God, Our Lady (as if, beside our *unus Dominus*, there were *una Domina* in the Church, forgotten by St. Paul), with the like.

' They ascribe to her the most sublime attributes of God, together with His most peculiar actions of providence and protection over us, yea of redemption itself.

' They yield acts of religious veneration (prayer and praise) to her, and those in a very high manner and strain; professing not only to serve her religiously (which the Holy Scripture chargeth us to do in regard to God and Him only), but ὑπερδουλεύειν, to do more than serve her, or to serve her with exceeding devotion.

' Who commonly do at the end of their works join, " Praise be to God and to the blessed Virgin; " as if she were to share with God in the glory and gratitude due for blessing or success on our performances.

' All this they do, without any plain reason, any plausible authority, any ancient example, yea manifestly enough against the best reason, the commands of God, the doctrine and practice of the primitive Church, all which do conspire in appropriating religious adoration to God alone; neither the Holy Scripture nor the first fathers excepting the blessed Virgin from the general rule, or taking notice of her as an object of our worship, but nipping the first essays of such a superstition in the Collyridians.

'Such groundless and foolish conceits, such dangerous and impious practices, we should carefully beware; the which, as they much derogate from God's honour, and prejudice His service, and thwart His commands, so they indeed do rather greatly discredit, injure, and abuse the blessed Virgin (making her name accessory to such enormous scandals), than they do bring any honour, or do any right to her.

'And I doubt not but, εἴ τις αἴσθησις, if she from her seat of bliss doth behold these perverse services, or absurd flatteries of her, she with holy regret and disdain doth distaste, loathe, disdain, and reject them; with a *Non nobis Domine*, Psal. cxv. "Not unto us, O Lord;" and with the angel in the Apocalypse, Ὅρα μή, "See thou do it not."

'Whose greater honour it was, in truth, to be a meek and humble servant, than to be the mother of her Lord and Saviour; it is the chief and truest honour we can do her, to esteem her great modesty and humility, to imitate her piety and grace, after her pattern conscientiously to reverence and obey her Son; unto whom therefore let us with hearty thankfulness render all glory and praise. Amen.' *

* Barrow, vi. 64.

What is here said must commend itself at once to the thoughtful mind: if the kind of honour paid by the Romanists to the Virgin Mary, when they give to her, as they do in the 'Litany of our Lady,' such blasphemous titles as 'The Queen of Heaven,' 'The Queen of Angels, Patriarchs, Prophets, and Apostles,' 'The Source and Fountain of Grace,' 'The Refuge of Sinners,' 'The Comfort of the Afflicted,' 'The Advocate of all Christians;' if the worship they offer to her, if even a petition for her intercession were anything but wrong, should we not find some similar expressions in Scripture, some allusion to the practice? whereas what we do find in Scripture, is a studied, I might almost use the term, a prophetic silence upon the subject. The very fact of her being so highly favoured, added to the fact that next to nothing is said of her, except when mention of her is necessary with reference to some circumstance connected with the Lord Jesus, added to the further fact, that when on one occasion she did interpose and interfere, she was rebuked by our Lord, who said, 'Woman, what have I to do with thee?'—this combination of circumstances seems to show that by the expressive silence of Scripture, the idolatry of Romanism was intended to be condemned. Our Reformers would have rejected the superstitious and idolatrous worship of the Virgin, on the principle of our Sixth Article, that of such worship we read nothing in Scripture; but in this case we should be inclined even to make the article more narrow than it is; we would not listen to a man who should attempt, by argument or induction, to prove thereby the lawfulness of such a practice; we should contend that nothing short of the most express and unequivocal command on the part of God would suffice. For what is the labour, if I may so say, of the Old Testament, what but this, to prevent man from worshipping any other being except God? Whenever this commandment was transgressed by the Israelites awful was the punishment which ensued. Not the slightest approximation to the worship of the creature was tolerated; not any kind of invocation, not any kind of subordinate worship, however indirect. Now, if this system, the system established by God Himself, and under His especial superintending Providence, persevered in for centuries, had been reversed, would not the most clear, the most explicit injunctions upon the subject have been necessary? Is not, then, the fact that there is not the slightest allusion to any kind of worship given to the Virgin Mary, in any part of Scripture, the very strongest condemnation of Romish idolatry that could be possibly produced? Suppose the Apostles to have acted towards the Virgin as the modern Papists; suppose that they had addressed her in prayer, should we not have found at least some allusion to the Virgin in the Epistles; and yet what do we find? Except in the narratives of the Evangelists, and once in the Acts of the Apostles, her name is not mentioned; there is not an allusion to her; not by St. Paul; not by St. James; not by St. Peter; no, not by St. John in any of his three Epistles, or in his Apocalypse, although we know that in obedience to our Lord's command, 'that disciple took her to his own home.' Nay, though in such case to the testimony of the Fathers we have no occasion to refer, we may use their words in assigning a reason why the Apostles did not regard the Virgin Mary as the Papists now do ;—'You are not ignorant,' said St. Hilary of Poictiers, 'that religious worship to the creature is accursed.'* 'Without doubt,' says St. Ambrose, 'the Holy Ghost is to be adored, since He also is to be adored, who, according to the Flesh was born of the Spirit. But lest anyone should desire the same adoration to the Virgin Mary, Mary was the Temple of God, but not the God of the Temple, and therefore He only is to be adored who operated in that Temple.' †

Only once after our Lord's ascension is the Virgin Mary mentioned: 'and when they were come in,' we read in the Acts of the Apostles, 'they went up into an upper room, where abode both Peter and James, and John and Andrew, Philip and Thomas, Bartholomew and Matthew, James the son of Alphæus, and Simon Zelotes, and Judas the brother of James ; these all continued with one accord in prayer and supplication with the women, and Mary the Mother of Jesus, and with His brethren.'‡ This is all that we hear of her ; though sixty years elapsed, or nearly so, before the Canon of Scripture was closed, we hear nothing more of her ; we know not even how she died, for the notion of her assumption is a pure fable, unsupported by even a shadow of authority. Nothing less, you observe, than the strongest Scriptural authority would

* Hilar. Pictai. de Trinitate, lib. viii. p. 963.
† Ambros. de Spiritu Sancto, lib. iii. c. ii. p. 681.   ‡ Acts i. 13.

justify the worship of the Virgin, and instead of this there is no authority at all, but, on the contrary, there is the injunction, 'Thou shalt worship the Lord thy God, and Him only shalt thou serve.' We read of her being the instrument through which our God became Incarnate; and when she had brought forth her God, her mission was accomplished, and little more is said of her.

If it be asked wherein consists the offence of asking her to intercede for us, in the same way as we ask the intercessions and prayers of our brethren on earth— (though this would not establish the Romish system, even if we were to concede the lawfulness of that kind of prayer, which they sometimes use when they say, *Ora pro nobis*, pray for us, for they in fact address the Virgin directly in prayer, as we pray to God)—we have to reply, would it not be presumption in the highest degree on our part to pray for or to intercede for another, we, who are unworthy to pray for ourselves, if we had not an express command to do so? Even now, when we have the command to pray for others, who does not feel that he would be presumptuous in his act, were he not encouraged by the Divine injunction? Nay, I believe that Christians have generally advanced in grace before they are very earnest in this sacred exercise. The natural man would regard the fact of our praying for another as a superstition; for, not understanding how God can be moved by prayer, regarding prayer as at best but a spiritual exercise, profitable only to the person resorting to it, he would think it impossible that my soul should be benefited by your prayers, or your soul by mine. We, however, do pray for one another—because God permits, commands it. But not one word do we find, I will not say of injunction, but even of permission, to ask the prayers of the Virgin Mary, or of any saint departed; nay, further, not one hint do we find in Scripture to lead us to suppose that the Virgin Mary or any Saint departed can hear our prayers: on the contrary, God is the only Omnipresent Being, and the Lord Jesus is present wherever two or three are gathered together in His name, because He is not man only, but God also. That without imparting to the Virgin Mary and to the saints departed the Divine attribute of Omnipresence, which must be peculiar to God, God might have given them the power of being present in more places than one at one time, we may admit to be possible, since with God all things are possible : but we certainly should not believe such an improbable and incomprehensible miracle without warranty from Scripture the most unquestionable ; and to such a miracle there is not the most distant allusion. Nor do we find that God ever works a miracle, when of miraculous interposition there is no need: in the Lord Jesus Christ we know that we have an Omnipresent Mediator; why then should a stupendous miracle be hourly wrought, a most incomprehensible fact, to do what is more effectually done by Him, who, though man, is also God? 'There is,' we are expressly instructed, ' one God and one Mediator between God and men, the man Christ Jesus.'* Why should we look for another? We are

* I. Tim. ii. 5.

told that 'He is able to save to the uttermost those who come unto God by Him, seeing He ever liveth to make intercession for them.'* His power you cannot doubt, since you believe Him to be God, and will you doubt the willingness of Him who died for your salvation? Nay, He asserts the completeness of His mediation: 'Verily, verily, I say unto you, whatsoever ye shall ask the Father in my Name, He will give it you.' †

But the real answer to this objection, that there can be no more harm in asking the intercession of Saints departed, than in asking the intercession and prayers of our living friends is this, that the practice results from a wrong principle expressly condemned in Scripture. ‡

When we pray for one another, we pray as fellow-sinners, and not under the notion that the prayers of one person, on account of his greater sanctity, will be more efficacious than those of another. All, being

* Heb. vii. 25. † St. John xvi. 29.
‡ Bishop Andrewes, in a sermon printed in Hooker's works, observes: 'Against invocation of any other than God alone, if all arguments else should fail, the number whereof is both great and forcible, yet this very bar and single challenge might suffice; that whereas God hath in Scripture delivered us so many patterns for imitation when we pray, yea, framed ready to our hands in a manner all, for suits and supplications, which our condition on earth may at any time need, there is not one, no not one to be found directed unto Angels, Saints, or any, saving God alone. So that, if in such cases as this we hold it safest to be led by the best examples that have gone before, when we see what Noah, what Abraham, what Moses, what David, what Daniel, and the rest did; what form of prayer Christ Himself taught His Church, and what His blessed Apostles did practise; who can doubt but the way for us to pray so as we may undoubtedly be accepted, is by conforming our prayers to theirs, whose supplications we know were acceptable?'

sinners, even though in another sense saints,—saints being sinners justified by faith in Jesus,—we approach the Throne of Grace, not relying upon any merits of our own, but simply in the name of Christ our only Mediator. We are told, it is true, that 'the prayers of the righteous man availeth much'; * but the righteous man here means any justified person. But on what principle do Romanists apply to the saints departed, and especially to the Virgin Mary, for their prayers? It is expressly on this very ground of their superior sanctity; they refer to the merits of sinful creatures, for so the Virgin Mary and the saints departed would still be regarded, if regard was had to any merit of their own. It is not because prayer for others is permitted to be one mode of evincing charity and brotherly love—so that as we can help one another by our actions, we can help them also by our supplications to the throne of grace, in which way the saints departed most probably do co-operate with the saints alive—it is not on this account that the Virgin Mary and the saints are invoked, but it is expressly stated that it is on the ground of their greater influence in the Court of Heaven. And while this is a principle condemned throughout the Bible, since God is no respecter of persons, it is especially, and in the most marked and prophetic manner, condemned by an incident recorded by the first three Evangelists. St. Matthew tells us, that while our Blessed Lord 'yet talked to the people, behold His mother and His brethren stood without desiring to speak with Him. Then one said unto Him,

* St. James v. 16.

Behold Thy mother and Thy brethren stand without desiring to speak with Thee. But He answered and said unto them that told Him, Who is My mother, and who are My brethren? And he stretched forth His hand and said, Behold My mother and My brethren! For whosoever shall do the will of My Father which is in Heaven, the same is My brother, and sister, and mother;'* or as St. Luke expresses it, 'He answered and said unto them, My mother and brethren are these which hear the word of God, and do it.' †

Not the slightest intention is here exhibited on the part of our Lord, when, humanly speaking, if it had been His intention, an opportunity seemed to be expressly provided, of exalting His mother above His other disciples; neither did she assume any peculiar claim on His notice; she came attended with her kinsfolks, evidently to give more effect to her request, showing thereby that she, at all events, did not regard her influence as irresistible. But those around Him acted as the Romanists do, they evidently supposed that she had a mother's claim upon Him, and that His other relatives might demand His attention; and solemnly were they rebuked. They were reminded or warned that the Messiah, being God as well as man, is no respecter of persons, that nothing is done through favour or interest, or from personal consideration. No one persevering in sin may approach Him; everyone doing the will of His Father which is in Heaven is permitted to draw nigh. All are equal—the question with respect to all is, whether theirs is the principle of

* St. Matt. xii. 46. † St. Luke viii. 21.

obedience, and if it be, then they have as much interest in Him and with Him, as His mother and His brethren, nay, they are accounted one with them :—' My mother and brethren are those who hear the word of God and do it.' No passage in condemnation of Romish invocation stronger than this need to be produced; no passage stronger to convince us that it were worse than vain to rely on the merits or intercession of others unless we are both hearers and doers of the Word; no passage which can give us greater confidence to approach the Lord Jesus at once, to draw nigh with boldness, and through Him, and Him only, to make our requests known unto God. And yet the passage is not a solitary one, for in the 11th of St. Luke we read that ' it came to pass, as He spake these things, a certain woman of the company lifted her voice and said unto Him : Blessed is the womb that bare Thee, and the paps that Thou hast sucked ; but He said—yea rather, Blessed are they that hear the Word of God and keep it.'* On this account, even because every believer

---

* St. Luke xi. 27, 28. Dr. Barrow thus alludes to this argument :
'" Whosoever," saith He, " shall do the will of my Father that is in heaven, the same is my brother, and sister, and mother; " the same in a more excellent manner and sublime degree is allied, is endeared to me, than he can be on the score of any carnal kindred : the conformity to Him in our mind and affections doth render us nearer to Him than any cognation of blood; the having Him formed in our hearts is more considerable than the bearing of Him in the womb.

' Indeed, the mother of our Lord herself, although as such she was κεχαριτωμένη, especially favoured and graced, and blessed among women; although on that account all nations must esteem and call her blessed; although worthily she did in that respect acknowledge that God had done μεγαλεῖα, magnificent and mighty things for her ; yet really, in just esteem, to have Christ born in her

may apply to himself the words of the Virgin Mary, the Church uses the Magnificat in the evening service.

Since neither in Scripture, nor in the primitive Church, there is the shadow of authority for the honour, much less for the worship paid by the Church of Rome to the Virgin Mary, we, of the Protestant and Catholic Church of England, are in no doubt, no-perplexity whatever, when we refuse to rob God of His honour, or to share it with His creature; and yet further, as lovers of the Lord Jesus Christ we feel our spirit stirred up within us, and a holy jealousy burning in our hearts when we find, without any warranty of Scripture, the Papist dividing the divine kingdom and empire, and giving one half, the better half, the kingdom of mercy, to the Virgin Mary, and leaving only the kingdom of justice to her Son. 'This is downright treason against the only universal King and Monarch of the world.'* Thine, Oh, our Jesus, Thine is the kingdom of mercy! Thou, Oh, our Jesus, Thou art the King of mercy, the Sole Fountain of Grace! the only Refuge of Sinners! the only Advocate that Christians need! Thine is the Kingdom of Mercy, Oh, Christ our

---

soul, to have participated of His divine grace and presence in her heart, the Holy Ghost's having produced a spiritual birth of holy dispositions in her, was a nobler honour and a truer happiness than that; " neither would it," as St. Chrysostom saith, "have been anywise profitable to her, if she had not been virtuous, to bear Christ in her womb, or to bring forth that admirable birth;" this our Saviour plainly declared, when as a good woman, transported by the ravishing excellency of His discourse, did cry out, " Blessed is the womb that bare Thee," He thence took occasion to say, "Yea rather, blessed are they that hear the word of God and keep it."'— *Barrow's Works*, vol. vi. p. 63.

† Bishop Bull, 104.

King, and Thou, Dear saviour, didst purchase it with Thine own most precious blood. Thou who didst love us when in us there was nothing lovely; Thou who didst love us when we loved not Thee; Thou who didst love us, when, though perishing without Thee, we neither sought nor desired Thee; Thou, oh, Merciful Saviour, art ever with those who, serving Thy heavenly Father, are as dear to Thee as Mary ever was, and who may approach Thee as boldly as she can do—it were infidelity to doubt it. Thou, Oh, merciful Saviour, art present with us by Thy sanctifying Spirit in our temptations and dangers, Thou wilt never forsake us in our sufferings, nor desert us in our conflicts, Thou wilt soothe us in our sorrows, Thou wilt not abandon us at death, nor leave us in the grave. 'The love of Christ in length, and breadth, and depth, and height, passes knowledge.' Its source is unsearchable; its extent infinite; its influence invincible; its continuance sure; its effects everlasting.

Oh, my brethren, let us determine to serve God, and Jesus will be our all-sufficient Intercessor: let the Romanist, distrusting Jesus, lean upon a broken reed and worship the creature Mary—but as for me and my house, let every member of the Church of England say, I will worship the Lord my God, even the Father, the Son, and the Holy Ghost, and Him only will I serve.

SERMON XXVI.[*]

AURICULAR CONFESSION.

'*If we confess our sins, He is faithful and just to forgive us our sins, and to cleanse us from all unrighteousness.*'—I. St. John i. 2.

So MUCH that is unsound in theory, incorrect in statement, and dangerous in a practical point of view; so much that is contrary to the principles of the Church of England, and that is plainly unscriptural, has been urged, of late, on the subject of confession; the lust of power and of meddling in some, and want of discernment and neglect of enquiry in those who confound medieval corruptions with primitive truth, have led to such confusion of ideas upon the subject, that it becomes my duty as a faithful pastor, to lay before you the doctrine of the Church of England, which is also the doctrine of the Primitive Church, which, moreover, is the doctrine of Holy Scripture, upon a practice which at one time demoralized the Christian world, obliterated the doctrine of Justification by Faith, and rendered necessary a reformation of the Church, such as restored us in this, as in other respects, to our Christian liberty.

It is said, and said too by some who appear to consider such doctrines consistent with the rule and practice of the Church of England, that Confession is a means of grace.

[*] Preached in the Parish Church of Leeds, Oct. 29, 1848.

If it be so, it is of course our duty, as ministers of the Church of England, to press the observance of it upon the members of our several congregations. Sinners as you all are, we must urge upon you the observance of all the means of grace, and bid you prepare your hearts to receive the same.

But does the Church of England command confession of sins to a priest? Where is the injunction to be found? It is, as everyone who is acquainted with our Prayer Book and our Formularies, is well aware, commanded nowhere.

Mark, then, the obvious and immediate conclusion: the Church of England does not consider confession to a priest as a means of grace. If it were a means of grace, it would be generally necessary to the salvation of sinners, and upon all sinners the Church of England would enjoin it. By not enjoining it upon anyone, the Church of England asserts her Protestantism, and declares that she differs from the Church of Rome,* as in other respects, so also in this. She does not regard confession to a priest as a means of grace.

And what saith Holy Scripture? Search the Scriptures from one end to the other; from Moses to Malachi, and from Matthew to the Apocalypse, and not one word in all the Bible will you find about confession to a priest. If confession to a priest were necessary; if, that is to say, it were a means of grace, surely we should find some express, some unequivocal injunction for the observance of it. But not only is it not enjoined; it is not even suggested.

* Note XXI.

The Church of Rome does not, in her Tridentine Council, refer us to a single passage of Scripture as containing an injunction upon the subject. She merely quotes the 23rd verse of the 20th chapter of St. John, and, assuming the very point in debate, asserts that the duties of the confessional form an essential part of the sacerdotal office; and this, their gratuitous inference, our Reformers rejected, because it is not authorized or confirmed by the practice of the Primitive Church.

This is our mode, the mode of our Reformation, of using tradition, and of deferring to the practice and teaching of the Primitive Church. The Romanists add tradition to Scripture; they take as their rule of faith —Scripture and tradition. Our rule of faith is the Bible only; but if there is a dispute as to what the meaning of the Bible is, then we take into consideration the meaning attached to the Scriptural revelation, by those to whom the Apostles preached, and by the Churches established by them.* 'If what appears but probably to be taught in Scripture,' says Dr. Waterland, one of our greatest divines, 'itself appears to have been certainly taught in the primitive and Catholic Church; such probability, so confirmed and strengthened, carries with it the force of demonstration.'†

Now, all the world knows that auricular confession was not enjoined in the Roman Church until the year 1215, and that it has never been enjoined in the Greek Church. It was established in the 13th century, being a medieval, not a primitive doctrine. As being neither

* Note XXII.
† Preface to Sermons at the Lady Moyer's Lectures.

primitive nor Scriptural, it was rejected by us at our Reformation; and it was re-established and re-enforced as one of the permanent corruptions of Romanism, in the Romish Council of Trent.*

That confession of sins to God only is sufficient, is a truth asserted at least twenty times by St. Chrysostom; and is a truth maintained universally by the Fathers of the fifth century,† as may be seen, by a reference to our great divines, Taylor, Bramhall, Usher, Bingham, and a host of others; who, while they gloried in the title of Catholic, would not repudiate the designation of Protestant.‡

But while Scripture, the Primitive Church, and the Church of England, all distinguished from the Medieval and Romish Church, declare with one voice that confession to God only is sufficient, yet what saith the Church of England? In the 'Warning for the Celebration of the Holy Communion,' the Curate is directed to say to those of whose souls he has the cure: 'Because it is requisite, that no man should come to the Holy Communion, but with a full trust in God's mercy and with a quiet conscience; therefore if there be any of you, who by this means,' namely, self-examination and self-denial, 'cannot quiet his own conscience therein, but requireth further comfort or counsel, let him come to me, or to some other discreet and learned minister of God's Word, and open his grief; that by the ministry of God's holy Word he may receive the benefit of absolution, together with ghostly counsel and advice, to the quieting of his conscience, and

* Note XXIII.   † Note XXIV.   ‡ Note XXV.

and avoiding of all scruple and doubtfulness.' In the Office for the Visitation of the Sick this rubric occurs: 'Here shall the sick person be moved to make a special Confession of his sins, if he feel his conscience troubled with any weighty matter. After which Confession, the Priest shall absolve him (if he humbly and heartily desire it) after this sort.'*

Now here, observe, is a permission, not an injunction, and the cases referred to are exceptional cases. The rule in the Church of England is to confess our sins to God only; to examine ourselves, and to be our own spiritual directors. It is a portion of our responsibility, and such responsibility we cannot in ordinary cases shift upon another. The exception is with respect to those who cannot in this way, according to the general rules, obtain a sufficient trust in God's mercy, and a quiet conscience. If you cannot do this, then select some minister of God's holy Word, not of necessity the parish priest, but some one in whose spiritual wisdom and experience you can confide, and open to him your grief. And so with respect to the sick: if a man feels his conscience troubled with any weighty matter; if he cannot, by an exercise of his own mind, obtain that confidence in the Divine mercy, which is a constituent of true faith; then, in that exceptional case, you may move him to confession. †

It is not by confession, but by faith, that we are justified; but the faith which justifies is the faith of a penitent man, and the question will occur, Am I sufficiently penitent to be justified by my faith? It is a

* Note XXVI.   † Note XXVII.

doubt upon this point, when it arises, that sends us to seek advice from another; and that other, of course, cannot give us the advice we need, unless we unburthen to him our conscience and open our grief. The Church of England, therefore, permits, and in some cases advises, confession to a minister of the Gospel; but mark the distinction; she never enjoins it as a means of grace, she only sanctions it as a means of consolation, with a special indulgence to the sick.

We go to the sick bed; we see a man wretched; unable to find comfort for himself, or to receive consolation from us;—it is clear that his conscience is troubled with some weighty matter. How can we console him? How advise him, unless we know what is the cause of his affliction and grief? We urge him, therefore, to make a special confession of his sins.

He confesses; if he were well, we should, after advising him how to test the sincerity of his repentance, direct him to go to Church, and hear God's pardon pronounced upon him, in common with others; to receive absolution in and with the congregation.

But the sick man is unable to do this; he is penitent; he believes that Jesus died for his sins; he earnestly desires to have the fact of his forgiveness authoritatively declared, and to his humble and hearty desire the Church condescends.

As a means of consolation, confession to a man is recommended or permitted, in some shape or other, by every Christian community. And it is as a means of consolation that the advice is given in the 16th verse of the 5th chapter of St. James;* the only passage in

* Note XXVIII.

Scripture, I believe, that contains a direction to us to confess our sins to any other than God Himself. St. James is speaking to the afflicted and to the sick; and he exhorts men under those circumstances to seek consolation through mutual prayer; and in order that the prayer may be mutual, he advises them to confess to one another their faults. There are persons whose consciences are not only tender, but scrupulous, full of scruples; there are others, who feel that they cannot bear the weight of sin by which they are oppressed unless they have the advice of a friend; others again there are who desire sympathy, or who are perplexed as to the proper course to be pursued in overcoming the evils which are within them, or in resisting temptations from without: all such persons are, not commanded, but recommended, to open their griefs, and tell their sorrows to some friend, in whose wisdom, experience, and piety they can confide; not commanded, as if confession were a means of grace, but recommended, because such confession may be to them a means of comfort. And these their griefs they may open to one another, not of necessity, observe, to a priest, but to any friend. Let the child seek such a friend in his parent; the wife in her husband, and the husband in his wife. In this way let friend take sweet counsel with friend, as they walk together in the House of the Lord.

The minister of the Gospel is only recommended, because such exceptional cases are likely to come frequently before him, and he therefore is most likely to be best qualified to act as an adviser when difficulties occur. If confession were a means of grace, we should be directed to have recourse to the minister of the parish, because in the administration of the means of grace the efficacy depends not upon personal character, but upon the Divine commission. But when we seek, not grace, but comfort and advice, we seek for a minister who, by his learning and discretion, is competent to afford us the intellectual assistance we require. Nor is it difficult in men of age and experience to find the qualifications needed. A minister of the Church of England is not obliged to master all the minute and sometimes disgusting details through which a confessor of the Church of Rome is obliged to wade, in order to be qualified for his office.* In the sacrament of penance, as they style it, the Romanists are commanded to unlock their hearts to the priest, and persons of all ages and both sexes, standing before him in their moral nudity, are required to submit, not only to general questions as to a state of sin and repentance, but to the most minute and searching questions as to their inmost thoughts; a system this, which renders the confessor's office fit for no man, and especially unfit for the young; a system which has given rise to hypocrisy in some, and to a reliance upon their works in others; a system which is of benefit to a few only of those who have recourse to it, and is often, as Romanist writers themselves admit, a pollution to the confessor.

Very different is it when confession is only resorted to as a means of comfort or counsel. As everyone is

* Note XXIX.

at liberty to confess or not, so, in making his confession, everyone is at liberty to decide as to what he will confess and what withhold. And he of whom we seek the comfort or the counsel, is only required to seek information as to the facts which bear upon the point upon which his opinion or advice is sought. If we withhold from him any facts which relate to the case, we are guilty, not of sin, but of folly; of folly, similar to that of a man who, in consulting a physician or a lawyer, keeps back from their knowledge a portion of the truth. And what is required in him we consult is, skill in searching out the various artifices of self-deception; a skill in which those soon become proficients who have had any spiritual experience themselves, and whose hearts are honest.

But while we say this, be it always remembered, that any kind of confession to man is an exception, not the rule.* 'If we confess our sins,' not to the priest, but to God, 'He is faithful and just to forgive us our sins, and to cleanse us from all unrighteousness.' Here, and elsewhere in Scripture, we find that to the confession which the penitent sinner makes to God alone the promise of forgiveness is annexed; 'which,' saith Archbishop Usher, 'no priest upon earth hath power to make void, upon pretence that himself or some of his fellows were not first particularly acquainted with the business.' †

To confess our sins to God, and to accustom ourselves to this duty, is absolutely necessary, if we would

* Note XXX.
† Usher's 'Answer to a Jesuit,' p. 76.

really know what sinners we are. Until we are accustomed to self-examination, until we scrutinise our motives as well as our actions, our principles as well as our conduct, we are apt to be self-complacent, to think we are not worse than our neighbours, and to imagine that all will be well with us in the end. And what is the consequence? there is no clear perception of our need of a Redeemer, a Saviour, a Divine Intercessor, at the throne of grace : there is no clinging to Christ by faith, no appropriation of His righteousness, no application of His merits: Christ is not to us all that He must be to those who feel and know that except in Him we are all but as dead men.

We should accustom ourselves to examine our conduct minutely, and in detail, and then, regarding God as a Personal God, to Him, as to a Person, confess our sins one by one, as we discover them, asking forgiveness. It is not sufficient to be conscious of our sins. No, we should soon deceive ourselves if we were content with the consciousness of sin. 'A general persuasion that thou art a sinner will neither so humble nor bridle thy soul, as the catalogue of thy sins examined severally, and continually kept in mind.' *
Just so it is with respect to mental prayer; the prayer made by the mind, when not a word is spoken, is known unto God the Searcher of hearts, and is by Him heard and accepted: nevertheless He requires more than this,—even vocal prayer. He would have us give utterance in words to what we desire; for if we did not accustom ourselves to speak in our prayer, our

* Jeremy Taylor.

prayers would soon cease to be particular, and become little more than a form of meditation. So, likewise, consciousness of sin will not suffice to make us truly penitent; we shall find it expedient to confess with our lips; to speak of our sins, and to proclaim, as it were in the presence of angels, our misery and our shame. Then it is, my brethren, that we become duly and truly sensible of the impossibility of our being saved by our works; then it is that with the strong hand of faith we grasp the Saviour, who only can rescue us from that bottomless pit, towards which the weight of our sin is pressing us.

No one who is accustomed to consult his Bible can doubt for one moment that this is a duty; that confession is, like prayer and meditation, incumbent upon everyone who names the name of Christ, and would realise the blessings of the Christian covenant. We detect sin, after self-examination, in our best actions; we confess it, we lament it, we plead the merits of Jesus, our Saviour; He intercedes for us, He pardons us, He sends His spirit to guard us against falling into the sins we have repented of; and we rejoice to hear His minister declare that those are absolved who truly repent, and unfeignedly believe His holy Gospel; and we hear him speaking the Word of God. We overcome in this way one sin or evil propensity, not at once, but by a long course of such spiritual discipline; and still we have recourse to self-examination, and we discover something further that is evil in us; we confess it, we again plead, and by faith apply to our souls, the merits of our Saviour; we seek fresh supplies of grace, through the ordinances of the sanctuary and the Sacrament of the Lord's Supper; and so we advance, continually putting away evil, and continually receiving grace, until, ripe for eternity, we are transplanted to the heaven opened to us by our Redeemer's blood.

I have described what has been experienced by those who are spiritual among us, and I have stated the course which they have pursued and are pursuing.

And now I conclude, with pointing out in one sentence the difference between ourselves and the Church of Rome. The Church of Rome regards confession to man as a means of grace; this we deny; at the same time we regard it as a means of comfort to weak minds and scrupulous consciences, and to persons in difficulties or in doubt. The Church of Rome makes it the rule —we, the exception. The Church of Rome commands it; the Church of England permits it. The Church of England, in accordance with Scripture and the Primitive Church, and the Greek Church, asserts that confession to God alone is sufficient,—is the rule—is the course which ought to be pursued in all but exceptional cases; and in this respect to the Church of England, to the primitive Church, and to the written and infallible Word of the living God, the Church of Rome stands opposed.*

* Note XXXI.

APPENDIX.

Note I., page 63.

'ALTHOUGH the word Καθολικός properly signifies universal, yet they [the ancient fathers] commonly used it in the same sense as we do the word orthodox, as opposed to an heretic, calling an orthodox man a Catholic, that is, a son of the Catholic Church ; as taking it for granted that they, and they only, which constantly adhere to the doctrine of the Catholic or Universal Church are truly orthodox; which they could not do, unless they had believed the Catholic Church to be so. And besides that, it is part of our very creed that the Catholic Church is holy, which she could not be, except free from heresy, as directly opposite to true holiness.' *

Note II., page 69.

ON DEFERENCE TO TRADITION AND RESPECT FOR THE FATHERS.

Since a charge the most preposterous, of deviating from the principles of the Reformation is brought against those of our divines who defer to tradition, and, in interpreting Scripture, have more respect for the consent of the fathers who lived in and near to the apostolic age than for such commentators as Henry, Scott, &c., when opposed to the ancient interpretation, it may be well to refer to some other documents in addition to those alluded to in the body of this

* Bp. Beveridge, Works, ii. 197.

discourse. Reference is there made to the Act of Parliament which our reformers* obtained to enable them, with the civil sanction, to condemn, as heretics, those who propounded doctrines contrary to the canonical Scriptures, and to the decisions of the first four General Councils. And we find that, on the authority here given, and with express reference to the first four General Councils, our Church anathematized Socinianism in the year 1640 : 'Whereas, much mischief is already done in the Church of God, by the spreading of the damnable and cursed heresy of Socinianism, as being a complication of many ancient heresies, condemned by the four first General Councils, and contrarient to the articles of religion now established in the Church of England—it is therefore decreed,' &c.†

How wisely our reformers made use of tradition and the fathers may be seen also by a reference to the rules laid down for the conference with the Romish priests and Jesuits, among which we find the following: 'If they should shew any ground of Scripture, and wrest it to their sense, let it be shewed by the interpretation of the old doctors, such as were before Gregory I. For that in his time began the first claim of the supremacy by the Patriarch of Constantinople, and shortly after was usurped by the Bishop of Rome, the first founder of the Papacy and supremacy of that see, by the authority of Phocas, the traitor and murderer of his Lord. And as for the testimony of the latter doctors, if they bring any, let them refuse them; for that the most part of the writers of that time, and after, yielded to the authority of the Emperor and the Bishop of Rome. If they can shew no doctor that agreed with them in their said opinion before that time, then to conclude that they have no succession in that doctrine from the time of the Apostles, and above four hundred years after (when doctrine and religion were most

* When I speak of the English reformers, I mean those great men who were publicly, and by authority, concerned in the Reformation of the Church of England, and not every private Englishman who happened to write against Popery in the sixteenth century.

† Can. IV. Sparrow's collection.

pure). For that they can shew no predecessor whom they might succeed in the same. *Quod primum verum.* If they allege any doctor of that antiquity, then to view the place; and to seek the true meaning *ex præcentibus et consequentibus*; or of other places and of the same doctor. And to oppose other doctors likewise writing of the same matter, in case the sentence of the said old doctor shall seem to make against us.'*

Well, indeed, would it be for the cause of truth, if the self-appointed disputants in favour of the Reformation, in their challenges to the Papists, would be guided by these rules. The so-called 'Reformation Society' would then be less injurious to the cause of the Reformation than it now is, and the Papists, with the worst cause, would less frequently come off triumphant.

We may now proceed to show how, in regulating her practice and defending her conduct, the Church of England, whenever she has spoken authoritatively, has followed the example of her illustrious reformers, and shown her deference to antiquity. It is well known that there were persons who were weak and foolish enough to scruple at our use of the sign of the cross. In the 30th Canon the Church of England vindicates her retention of that ceremony.

The Apology of the Church of England referred to in this canon is the celebrated work of Bishop Jewell, than which no book, excepting the Common Prayer and the Books of Homilies, has received a greater share of public sanction and authority in the English Church. The whole plan of this work is an appeal to Catholic tradition and primitive consent against the innovations of the Church of Rome, and any selection of passages rather diminishes the force of his whole train of reasoning. This is plainly seen from the outset of his work, where he states the kind of charges brought against the Reformers by the Romanists: 'That we have made a tumultuous defection from the Catholic Church; that we despise the authority of the primitive fathers and ancient

---

* Strype's Whitgift, vol. i. p. 197.

councils ; that we have imprudently and insolently abrogated the ancient ceremonies ... and by our own private authority, without the consent of a holy and General Council, we have introduced new rites into the Church ... but that they have retained all things as they were delivered to them by the Apostles, approved by the ancient fathers, and have been kept ever since, through all the intermediate ages to this day.'*

In answer to which he undertakes to prove 'that not obscurely and craftily, but *bonâ fide*, before God, truly, ingenuously, clearly, and perspicuously, we teach the most holy Gospel of God, and that the ancient fathers and the whole primitive Church are on our side, and that we have not without just cause left them, the Romish divines, and returned to the Apostles, and the ancient Catholic fathers.' † Accordingly every point of the Apology is illustrated by quotations of the words, and proofs of the practice, of the fathers. In a latter part of his work, not far from the middle, he returns to this point more specifically: 'Though they, the Papists, have not the Scriptures on their side, perhaps they will pretend they have the ancient doctors and holy fathers, for that they have ever boasted that all antiquity and the perpetual consent of all times is for them, and that all our pretences are novel, and were never heard of till within the course of a very few years last past.'

The way in which he enters upon his answer to this is very remarkable, as showing the depth of principle which he perceived to be involved in this adherence to antiquity: 'Now certainly there can nothing of more weight be said against religion than that it is new.' In what follows there are several challenges to the Romanists on this very ground, proving, as the very learned writer of 'Letters from a Reformed Catholic' ‡ says, how 'the modern Protestant and

* Translation by a Person of Quality, A.D. 1685, chap. i. sect. 5.
† Sect. xii.
‡ These plain and powerful letters were published by Messrs. Rivington. They are generally attributed to the Rev. Edward Churton, M.A., Rector of Crayke, and they are worthy of his high reputation.

Romanists have shifted positions. Our doctrine, which we may much better call the Catholic doctrine of Christ,* is not so new but that it is commended to us by the Ancient of Days, the Father of our Lord Jesus Christ, in most ancient monuments, the prophets, and gospels, and writings of the Apostles. .... But, then, as to their religion, if it be so ancient as they pretend, why do they not prove it so from the examples of the primitive Church, from the old fathers, and the ancient councils? Why doth so ancient a cause lie desolate and without a patron for so long a time? Indeed, they, the Romanists, never want fire and swords; but, then, as to the ancient fathers and councils, there is with them a deep silence.'

Again: 'Why, then, should we trust them in relation to what they pretend concerning the fathers, the ancient councils, and the Scriptures? They have not, O good God! they have not, on their side, what they pretend to have; they have neither antiquity, nor universality, nor the consent of either all times or all nations; † and of this they are not ignorant themselves, though they craftily dissemble their knowledge; yea, at times, they will not obscurely confess it; and, therefore, they—the Romanists—sometimes will allege that the sanctions of the ancient councils and fathers are such as may lawfully be changed; for different decrees, they say, will best suit the different state of the Church in different times.' What follows is most important in the present state of the Romish controversy: 'And so they hide themselves under the name of a Church, and by a wretched sham delude mankind.'

'Thus,' says Bishop Jewell, when defending the English

---

* It was not because their doctrine was Protestant, but because it was Catholic, that our Reformers and such divines as Jewell, Nowell, Hooker, and Andrews defended the doctrines of the English Reformation. And in the declaration of faith which our Reformers directed to be made by ministers they were required to say of the Book of Common Prayer, 'that it is catholic, apostolic, and most for the edifying of God's people.'—Strype's 'Annals,' vol. i. pt. i. p. 327.

† He evidently alludes here to the Rule of Vincentius.

Reformers, 'have we been taught by Christ, the Apostles, and by the holy fathers, and we do faithfully teach the children of God the same things; and for so doing are we to be called heretics by their great high priests?* Oh! immortal God! have Christ and his Apostles, and so many fathers, all erred? What, are Origen, Ambrose, Augustine, Chrysostom, Gelasius, and Theodoret apostates from the Catholic faith? Was the consent of so many bishops and learned men nothing but a conspiracy of heretics? Or that which was commendable in them, is it now blameable in us? Or that which was once true, is it now, because it displeaseth them, become false?'

He elsewhere affirms: 'When they, the Papists, have thus left nothing unsaid which can possibly be, though never so falsely and slanderously, objected against us, yet at least they cannot pretend that we have forsaken the Word of God, or the Apostles of Christ, or the primitive Church.'†

Again: 'We, the English Reformers, have approached, as nearly as possibly we could do, the Church of the Apostles, and the ancient Catholic bishops and fathers, which we know was yet a perfect, and, as Tertullian ‡ saith, an unspotted virgin, and not contaminated with any idolatry, or any great or public error. Neither have we only reformed our doctrine and made it like theirs, but we have also brought the celebration of the Sacraments and the forms of our public rites and prayers to an exact resemblance with their institutions or customs.'—Chap. vi. 15.

Nothing can be more clear than this statement of the intention of our Reformers, and of their principles of Reformation.

I need hardly remind the learned reader that all this is

* Ultra-Protestants in these days, humbly imitating the high priest of Rome, the Pope, have gone so far as to call those who do, as Jewell tells us the English Reformers did, teach the doctrine of Christ, of the Apostles, and of the holy fathers, heretics. It may be well for them to see in whose steps they are treading, while an interesting work might be published on the Popery of ultra-Protestantism.

† Chap. iv. sect. 18.

‡ It is observable that what Bishop Jewell here quotes as a dictum of Tertullian is in fact from Hegesippus apud Euseb. Hist. iii. 32.

perfectly in accordance with the memorable challenge of Bishop Jewell to the advocates of Romanism. After enumerating the chief points of difference between the friends of the Reformation and the advocates of the Romish corruptions, he boldly says: 'If any man alive were able to prove any of these articles by any one clear or plain clause or sentence, either of the Scriptures, or of the old doctors, or of any old General Council, or by any example of the primitive Church, I promised them that I would give over and subscribe unto him.' And he repeats the challenge: 'If any one of our adversaries be able to avouch any one of all these articles by any sufficient authority of Scripture, doctors or councils, as I have required, as I said before, so say I now again, I am content to yield to him and subscribe.' *

We find a similar challenge made by Archbishop Cranmer, a very short time before his death: 'Wherefore by your own description and rule of a Catholic faith, your doctrine and teaching in these four articles cannot be good and Catholic, except you can find it in plain terms in the Scripture, and old Catholic doctors, which when you do I will hold up my hand at the bar, and say guilty. And if you cannot, then it is reason that you do the like, *per legem talionis*.' †

I may observe, by the way, that the principle on which Cranmer acted was well understood by his contemporaries, as appears, for instance, by the following verses, by J. Parkhurst, prefixed to the edition of this work, published in 1580 :—

> Accipe præclarum, lector studiose, libellum,
>   Quem tibi Cranmerus scripserat ante rogos.
> Hic docta sanctam tractat ratione synaxin,
>   Insistens patres quas docuere viis.

We find our divines still influenced by the same principle in the reign of James I. when certain commissioners were appointed by the King to examine into the conduct of Antonio de Dominis, Archbishop of Spalatro. Among other things, in the course of debate, the Archbishop complained 'that we

---
* Sermon on I. Cor. at Paul's Cross, 1560.
† Answer to Gardyner, Works, iii. 42.

had made a schism, and set up a new altar against an old altar. We answered,' say the episcopal divines, in their account of what took place, 'that our altar was an old altar, conformable to that of the primitive Church, and that all innovations were from them (the Papists), and that herein we were content to be judged concerning those offices which we execute at the altar by the writings of the fathers, the first General Councils and ancient liturgies, unto which we did constantly adhere.' *

But to return to the canons. The observance of the ember days is enjoined in the 31st canon, because of 'the holy and religious example of the ancient fathers of the Church.' In the 32nd canon the office of deacon is regarded as 'a step or degree in the ministry according to the judgment of the ancient fathers and the primitive Church.'

The Homilies so abound with references to the fathers that I shall only quote from them one passage: 'Before all things this we must be sure of especially, that this Supper be done and ministered, as our Lord and Saviour did and commanded to be done, as the holy Apostles used it, and the good fathers of the primitive Church frequented it.' †

We may observe, further, that on this principle of deference to the fathers our present authorised translation of the Scripture was conducted: one of the rules laid down for the observance of the translators being: 'When any word has several significations, that which has been commonly used by the most celebrated fathers should be preferred.' ‡

Allusion has been made to the Hampton Court and Savoy Conferences. The reader has only to refer to the proceedings of the former conference in Collier, ii. 674, to see how the English Bishops, true to the principles of the English Reformation, defended all our usages before King James on the authority of the fathers and primitive practice. And in the commission for the Savoy Conference, in 1661, the commis-

* M. Ant. de Dominis, Abp. of Spalatro, his shiftings in religion, 1624.
† Hom. concerning the Sacrament, pt. iii.
‡ Collier, 'Eccles. Hist.,' ii. p. 694.

sioners are appointed 'to advise upon and revise the said Book of Common Prayer; comparing the same with the most ancient Liturgies which have been used in the Church in the primitive and purest times.'* At the conference itself, to that part of the proposal that prayers may consist of nothing doubtful, or questioned by pious, learned, and orthodox persons, the episcopal divines reply that, 'since it is not defined and ascertained who those orthodox persons are, they must either take all those for orthodox persons who have the assurance to affirm themselves such, and if so, the demand is unreasonable. For some who deny the divinity of the Son of God will style themselves orthodox, and yet there is no reason we should part with an article of our creed for their satisfaction. Besides, the proposal requires an impossibility. For there never was, nor ever will be, any prayers couched in such a manner as not to be questioned by some people who call themselves pious, learned, and orthodox. But if by orthodox is meant only those who adhere to Scripture, and the Catholic consent of antiquity, they are not of opinion that any part of the English Liturgy has been questioned by such.' —Collier, ii. p. 880.

It was from this respect for tradition that by the Puritans the Church of England was called 'The Church of the Traditioners.' Thus, in the celebrated 'Protestation of the Puritans,' in 1573, the Puritan is made to protest: 'I have now joined myself to the Church of Christ '—meaning a sect of Puritans—' which if I should now again forsake and join myself with their traditions, I should forsake the union wherein I am knit to the body of Christ, and join myself to the discipline of Antichrist. For in the Church of the Traditioners (*i.e.* the Church of England) there is no other discipline than that which hath been maintained by the Antichristian Pope of Rome, whereby the Church of God hath always been afflicted, and is until this day. For the which cause I refuse them.'†

I am well aware that some persons venture to assert that

* Ibid. ii. 877.
† Strype's Life of Parker, ii. p. 284.

the Reformers had no such deference themselves for tradition, but only employed tradition as a useful kind of argument against the Romanists. Not to mention that this is a gratuitous assertion, borne out by no single fact, and not to insist upon the proof already given that a deference to tradition and to the fathers has been always manifested in all our authorised documents and debates, I will now direct the attention of the reader to the private writings of our reformed divines. Those writings are, indeed, of no more authority than the writings of any other author not publicly recognised by the Church, but they are useful as serving to throw light on the sense in which our services were understood by them. Even Latimer and Hooper affirmed that 'they never advanced anything but what is agreeable to Holy Scripture and the Catholic faith.'* With respect to Archbishop Cranmer, the difficulty is to make a selection from his works, which abound with references to the fathers. In his celebrated answer to Smythe's preface he thus announces his rule of faith : 'As for me I ground my belief upon God's Word, wherein can be no error, having also the consent of the primitive Church.' †

These were among his last words : 'Touching my doctrine of the Sacrament, and other my doctrine, of what kind soever it be, I protest that it was never my mind to write, speak, or understand anything contrary to the most holy Word of God, or else against the holy Catholic Church of Christ, but purely and simply to imitate and teach those things only which I had learned from the sacred Scriptures, and of the holy Catholic Church of Christ from the beginning, and also according to the exposition of the most holy fathers and martyrs of the Church.

'And if anything hath peradventure chanced otherwise than I thought, I may err ; but heretic I cannot be, forasmuch as I am ready in all things to follow the judgment of the most sacred Word of God, and of the holy Church, desiring none other thing than meekly and gently to be taught, if anywhere (which God forbid) I have swerved from the truth.

* Collier, ii. 277.
† Cranmer's Works, vol. iii. p. 8.

'And I profess and openly confess, that in all my doctrine and preaching, both of the Sacrament and of other my doctrine whatsoever it be, not only I mean and judge those things, as the Catholic Church and the most holy fathers of old with one accord have meant and judged, but also I would gladly use the same words that they used, and not use any other words, but to set my hand to all and singular their speeches, phrases, ways, and forms of speech, which they do use in the treatises upon the Sacrament, and to keep still their interpretation. But in this thing I only am accused for an heretic, because I allow not the doctrine lately brought in of the Sacrament, and because I consent not to words not accustomed in Scripture and unknown to the ancient fathers, but newly invented and brought in by men, and tending to the destruction of souls, and overthrow of the old and pure religion.' *

It may indeed be shrewdly suspected that had these words been uttered in these days, by any of those High Churchmen who are the representatives of the English Reformers, they would have caused the press to groan with various anathematizing protests, and the platform to echo with eloquent declamations on the revival of Popery, deviation from the principles of the Reformation, &c., &c. But let us turn from one of our martyr-reformers to another, to that unflinching High Churchman Bishop Ridley: 'In that the Church of God is in doubt, I use herein the wise counsel of Vincentius Lirinensis, whom I am sure you will allow, who giving precepts how the Catholic Church may be in all schisms and heresies known, writeth in this manner: "When," saith he, "one part is corrupted with heresies, then prefer the whole world before that one part; but if the greatest part be infected, then prefer antiquity." In like sort now, when I perceive the greatest part of Christianity to be infected with the poison of the see of Rome, I repair to the usage of the primitive Church.' †

---

* Appeal from the Pope to the next General Council. Works, vol. iv. pp. 126, 127.

† Ridley, pp. 613, 614.

Again: 'For we have (high praise be given to God therefore) most plainly, evidently, and clearly on our side, all the prophets, all the Apostles, and undoubtedly all the ancient ecclesiastical writers which have written until of late years past (*usque ad tempora neotericorum*).'*

What indeed was it that recommended Ridley in the first instance to Cranmer? 'His well known acquaintance with Scripture and the fathers.' And 'the result of this honourable perseverance in his studies was a gradual but firm conviction that Popery was the religion neither of Scripture nor of ecclesiastical antiquity.' †

Nay, why were our reformers burnt? Let Bradford give the answer: 'To believe as the Word of God teacheth, the primitive Church believed, and all the Catholic and good holy fathers taught for five hundred years at least after Christ, will not serve, and therefore I am condemned and burned out of hand.' ‡

Mr. Churton, in his very learned and judicious Visitation Sermon, from which this quotation is taken, observes that 'similar declarations are to be found in the letters of the Martyrs, Laurence Saunders to Stephen Gardiner, pp. 202-3; Robert Glover, a layman, p. 535; and Cariless, p. 614.' §

To this I will add the following very useful remarks by Bishop Cheny, whose character was aspersed most fiercely by the Puritans, but it is defended by Strype. ‖ Cheny was one of the six reformers who, in the first Convocation of Queen Mary's reign, being then Archdeacon of Hereford, 'undertook boldly the cause of the Gospel in a disputation against almost the whole synod.' The following extracts are from a sermon delivered when he was Bishop of Gloucester and Bristol, in Bristol Cathedral: 'These new writers in matters of controversy, as Mr. Calvin and others, agree not together, but are at dissention among themselves, and are together by the

---

* Translation of a letter to his Brethren in Captivity. 'Martyrs' Letters,' pp. 29, 30.
† Soame's 'Hist. of Ref.,' iii. 28.
‡ 'Martyrs' Letters,' p. 27.
§ 'Visitation Sermon,' p. 25.   ‖ 'Annals,' I. i. 422.

ears. Therefore take heed of them. Yet read them: for in opening the text, they do pass many of the old fathers. And they are excellently well learned in the tongues; but in matters now in controversy follow them not, but follow the old fathers and doctors, although Mr. Calvin denieth some of them.' 'Scriptures, Scriptures, do you cry? Be not too hasty: for so the heretics always cried, and had the Scriptures. I would ask this question: I have to do with an heretic; I bring Scripture against him: and he will confess it to be Scripture. But he will deny the sense that I bring it for. How now? How shall this be tried? Marry, by consent of Fathers only, and not by others.' 'Good people, I must now depart shortly. Keep, therefore, this lesson with you. Believe not, neither follow this city, nor yet 2, 3, 4, 5, 6, 7; but follow you the Catholic and universal consent.' *

For preaching thus, certain Puritan aldermen of the city of Bristol complained of their Bishop, but the fact that their complaint was disregarded only serves to show that in preaching thus, he only preached, when in prosperity, the doctrines of that Reformation, which, in adversity and at peril of his life, he had maintained with such boldness.

From this circumstance we may see that the High Church English Reformers and their disciples did not in those days, any more than in these, escape the reproaches of ultra-Protestants, and what follows will show that the temper of ultra-Protestantism was not one whit more tolerant or Christian than it is now.

'There came into Bernard Gilpin' (a confessor, though not a martyr of the Reformation) 'a certaine Cambridge man, who seemed a very great scholler,' and hee dealt earnestly with Mr. Gilpin touching the discipline and reformation of the Church. † Mr. Gilpin tould him that he could not allow that an human invention should take place in the Church instead

* Strype's 'Annals,' i. pt. 2, pp. 278, 280.
† This is an instance of what will be shown in a future citation to have been the prevalent opinion of the ultra-Protestants from the time when our Reformation was completed, that the Reformation had not gone far enough.

of a divine institution. " And how ? Doe you thinke," saith the man, "that this form of discipline" (that of the ultra-Protestants or Puritans) " is a human invention ? " " I am," saith Mr. Gilpin, " altogether of that mind. And as many as shall have turned over the writings of ancient fathers will be of mine opinion. I suspect that form of discipline which appeareth not to have been received by any auncient Church." " But yet," saith the man, " latter men do see many things which those auncient fathers saw not; and the present Church seemeth better provided of many ingenious and industrious men." Mr. Gilpin seemed somewhat moved at that word, and replied : " I for my part do not hould the virtues of the latter men worthy to be compared with the infirmities of the fathers." The other man made answer that he supposed Mr. Gilpin to be in error in that point.' *

Many men may at the present time be of ' the other man's opinion,' and despise ' the auncient fathers '—of course, I mean, after deep study of them ; but they ought not to accuse, as popish, and inimical to the principles of the English Reformation, those who tread in the steps of Gilpin, and Ridley, and Cranmer, and a host of others who might be named.

So multiplied indeed being the testimonies to the principle on which our Reformation was conducted, and so easily accessible to the student, as contained in the public documents of the Church, and the most popular records and memorials of the time, it does appear somewhat astonishing that there should be found professed members of the Church of England who think that they can consistently declaim against the use of tradition, decry the appeal to antiquity, and depreciate the fathers; nay, more, that they should go the length of denouncing those who defer to the rule of primitive doctrine and primitive practice, as persons who have departed from the principles of the English Reformation. The want of information betrayed by these accusers, discreditable as it is, is still more offensive when it is found, as too frequently is the case, accompanied with a want of candour and

* ' Life of Gilpin.' Wordsworth's Biog., iv. p. 122.

a tone of insult towards those whom they cannot or will not understand. Such controversialists are well characterized in Mr. Palmer's Treatise on the Church. Strong as it is, it is not too strong a protest against the practices of which I complain; and its statements of the true position of the English Church are otherwise clear and important.*

NOTE III., page 70.

LUTHERANS.

On this subject see Palmer's 'Treatise on the Church of Christ,' p. I. ch. xii. sec. 2. Having produced a variety of proof to show the principle on which the early Lutherans acted, he says : ' All these things prove that the Lutherans did not voluntarily separate from the Church; and that, at all events, for a long time, they desired to be re-united to its full communion.' No small number of Protestants, in succeeding ages, considered them as having gone to very unjustifiable lengths, and made much too large concessions for the sake of peace; but the truth is, they were deeply and duly impressed with the evils of separation, and its contradiction to the Divine will; and felt that no obstacles, except those which arose from certain, clear, and irrefragable necessity, ought to prevent union.†

NOTE IV., p. 71.

THE PURITANS AND ULTRA-PROTESTANTS ATTACHED TO THE FOREIGN REFORMATION, AND DISCONTENTED WITH THE ENGLISH REFORMERS FOR NOT GOING FAR ENOUGH.

As it is natural to suppose, there was a party in England who, from the beginning, wished to force the English Re-

* Palmer, 'Treatise on the Church,' ii. 55, seq. See also Faber 'On the Primitive Doctrine of Election,' p. 184.
† Palmer, i. pp. 370, 371.

formers to extreme measures, especially in the Marian persecution.*

In answer to an address from the English at Frankfort Calvin wrote thus in condemnation of the English Reformers: 'I cannot always think it profitable to comply with the foolish waywardness of some few men' (*i.e.* the English Reformers), 'who are resolved to remit nothing of their ancient customs. I cannot but observe many tolerable fooleries in the English Liturgy, *tolerabiles ineptias*, such as you have described it to me. By which two words, tolerable fooleries, I mean only this, that there is not such purity and perfection as was to be desired in it; which imperfections, notwithstanding, not being to be remedied at first, were to be borne with for a time, in regard that no manifest impiety was retained in them. It was therefore so far lawful to begin with such beggarly rudiments that the learned, grave, and godly ministers of Christ might be encouraged for proceeding further in setting out somewhat which might prove more pure and perfect. If true religion had flourished till this time in the Church of England, it had been necessary that many things in that book' (the Book of Common Prayer) 'should have been omitted and others altered to the better.' He afterwards expresses his dislike of those who by being attached to the Book of Common Prayer 'are so much delighted with the dregs of Popery.'†

'Some of the English exiles, who had been friendly entertained in Switzerland and Geneva, came home prepossessed in favour of the model of these Churches; and thus being disaffected to our Book of Common Prayer, they would have gladly set up a foreign establishment.'—Collier., Eccles. Hist., ii. 417. 'Upon Queen Elizabeth's accession to the throne,

---

* See for an account of this 'Life of Jewell,' Wordsworth's Biog., iv. 37. Collier, Eccles. Hist., ii. 412, 417.

† 'The answer and judgment of that famous and excellent learned man Mr. John Calvin, the late pastor of Geneva, touching the "Book of England," after he had perused the same faithfully translated into Latin by Mr. Whittingham.' See also Heylyn's 'History of the Presbyterians,' pp. 15, 16.

the English exiles at Geneva seemed willing to make up the old difference with their brethren, and moved towards a reconciliation. But then their proposals are somewhat narrow and reflecting; they called the ceremonie trifles, they proposed the best reformed Churches, that is, Calvin's Congregation, for the measure of agreement.'—Collier, ii. 412.

'Hence arose the two parties alluded to in the sermon, whom we may designate Protestants and ultra-Protestants, meaning by Protestants those who were attached to the system of the English, and by the ultra-Protestants those who were attached to the system of the foreign or Swiss Reformers, from whom may be said to be legitimately descended the whole body of ultra-Protestants, who reject all Church authority, and put forth, on every occasion, the maxim that "the Bible only forms the religion of Protestants"; whilst, in fact, they invariably adhere to the modern interpretation of some favourite commentator; such as Calvin or Beza, or, in later times, Scott or Henry; or (what is yet more convenient) to, the exposition of Scripture by some popular preacher of the day. The Puritans continued to be supported by foreign influence, for Beza proposed to Archbishop Grindal, "that the Church of England should unite with the reformed Churches of France, Geneva, and Switzerland in a common confession of faith." But the English hierarchy thought it more advisable to stand on their own bottom, than to incorporate their belief with foreign systems, and make themselves responsible for everything defined by the reformed abroad.'*

'Beza mentions, in a letter to Bullinger, that the English Church was, according to his notions, in a lamentable condition; that, as he was informed from some of the brethren there, Popery was never thrown out, but rather transferred from his Holiness to her Majesty; he formerly hoped that the dispute had only been about caps and surplices, but now, to his great grief, he finds the controversy goes much further. 'Afterwards he takes notice that Queen Elizabeth had so

* Collier, ii. p. 512.

strong an aversion to the Geneva Church, that she received the present of his Annotations without the least sign of its being welcome.' * 'Beza was perfectly correct in stating that the dispute was more than a mere dispute about caps and surplices: the dispute in reality involved a principle—that principle being whether the Church of England should "conform to the government" of the ancient Church, or to that of the Genevan sect: that point once conceded, other alterations would follow as a matter of course. Hence the zeal on the part of the Puritans to urge, and the determination on the part of the English Reformers to resist, alteration in the ecclesiastical habits and ceremonies. This was clearly perceived at the time. In 1562 the question relating to the rites and ceremonies was debated in Convocation. Among those who voted for the retention of the old Catholic rites still in use, Strype mentions the Dean of Westminster and the chaplains of the Archbishop (our great reformer, Archbishop Parker), Peerson and Ithel, who were themselves afterwards Bishops.' †

'Hitherto I have referred to a few out of the many passages which might be quoted to shew the foreign origin and foreign partialities of the ultra-Protestants. I shall now proceed to shew, what has already been made partially apparent, that the complaint against the Church of England has been, from the beginning, that it did not go far enough —that, in other words, the English Reformers were distinguished from the foreign Reformers, by being High Churchmen. Strype asserts that the Puritans refused to conform " unless there were a further reformation." ‡ And we find the work of our illustrious Reformers thus described by the historian of the Puritans: 'The service performed in the Queen's Chapel, and in sundry cathedrals, was so splendid and showy that foreigners could not distinguish it from the

* Collier, ii. p. 503.
† See Strype's 'Annals,' vol. i. pt. I. p. 504; vol. i. pt. II. p. 349; Strype's 'Parker,' ii. 285.
‡ Strype's 'Life of Grindal,' p. 65. See also 'Annals,' vol. ii. pt. I. p. 274.

Roman, except that it was performed in the English tongue. By this method most of the Popish laity were deceived into conformity, and came regularly to church for nine or ten years, till the Pope, being out of all hopes of an accommodation, forbad them, by excommunicating the Queen, and laying the whole nation under an interdict.' *

This writer had discernment enough to see the object of the English Reformers, though he had not the wisdom to approve it, when he remarked that 'the English Reformers wished to depart no further from the Church of Rome than she from the primitive Church.' †

He was correct in this assertion for 'sodeine chaunges,' said our martyr-Reformer, Bishop Ridley, 'without substantial and necessary causes, and the heady setting forth of extremities, I did never love.' ‡

To the wisdom of the course adopted by the English Reformers ample testimony was borne by Monsieur Rognie, the French Ambassador, who declared, upon a view of our solemn service and ceremonies, 'if the reformed Churches in France had kept on the same advantage of order and decency, I am confident there would have been many thousand Protestants in that country more than there is.' But the *via media* of the English Reformers was the great cause of offence to the Genevan sect in England. For instance, in 1573 we find our great Reformer, Matthew Parker, Archbishop of Canterbury, under whose primacy our present Ritual and Liturgy were arranged and the Thirty-nine Articles drawn up, writing, in conjunction with the Bishop of London, to some absent Bishop, to this effect: '*Sal. in Christo.* These times are troublesome. The Church is sore assaulted; but not so much of open enemies, as of pretended favourers and false brethren, who under colour of reformation seek the ruin and subversion both of learning and religion.' §

---

* Neal's 'Hist. of Puritans,' i. p. 156.   † Neal, i. p. 56.
‡ 'Martyrs' Letters,' p. 40. Ed. 1564.
§ Strype's 'Life of Parker,' ii. 280.   See also 'Life of Grindal,' p. 160.

That the same feeling continued to exist till the reign of Charles I. may be seen from the letter addressed by order of the House of Commons to 'the reformed Churches' of Zealand and Holland by the assembled divines, wherein it is admitted that then 'the contest was for a more thorough Reformation.' And the adherents of the English Reformation are described as an 'anti-Christian faction who have all along made it their business to check the Reformation and cherish Popery.' They add, in order to inflame the Dutch against the exiled English: 'To make their aversion to you still more demonstrable, abundance of these men have refused to own any of you as a Christian Church, for being not prelatically constituted they conceive your ministrations want a lawful mission, which is essential to Church governors. And as for ourselves we are sadly sensible that in all these kingdoms they (*i.e.* the clergy of the Church of England) have prevailed so far in promoting Popery and discouraging religion that it would require a volume rather than a letter to relate all particulars.' *

In short, we may cite the authority of no less a person than Henderson, who, in his controversy with Charles I., asserts 'that the Laodicean lukewarmness in the English Reformation had been the constant complaint of many of the godly in this kingdom.' †

Let this suffice to show that whatever charges may be brought against those against whom, under the name of High Churchmen, an attempt is now made to raise a moral persecution, they cannot, with propriety, be accused of deviating from the principles of the English Reformation. Of the English Reformers they are, in fact, the representatives, and it is precisely on the principles of the English Reformers that they oppose the errors both of Romanists and ultra-Protestants, and uphold 'The Church of the Traditioners.'

* Rushworth's 'Collections,' pt. iii. p. 391.
† Collier, ii. 842.

NOTE V., page 71.

PROTESTANTS.

The designation of Protestant is used in England as a general term to denote all who protest against Popery. Such, however, was neither the original acceptation of the word, nor is it the sense in which it is still applied on the Continent. It was originally given to those who protested against a certain decree issued by the Emperor Charles V. and the Diet of Spires, in 1529.—Mosheim, book iv. 26. On the Continent it is applied as a term to distinguish the Lutheran communions. The Lutherans are called Protestants; the Calvinists, the Reformed. The use of the word among ourselves in a sense different from that adopted by our neighbours abroad has sometimes led to curious mistakes. The late Mr. Canning, for instance, in his zeal to support the Romanists, and not being sufficiently well instructed in the principles of the Church of England, assumed it as if it were an indisputable fact that, being Protestants, we must hold the doctrine of consubstantiation. Having consulted, probably, some foreign history of Protestantism, he found that one of the tenets which distinguishes the 'Protestant,' *i.e.* the Lutheran, from the 'Reformed,' *i.e.* the Calvinist, is that the former maintains, the latter denies, the dogma of consubstantiation.

It is evident that in our application of the word it is a mere term of negation. If a man says that he is a Protestant, he only tells us that he is not a Romanist, at the same time he may be what is worse, a Socinian, or even an infidel, for these are all united under the common principle of protesting against Popery. The appellation is not given to us, I believe, in any of our formularies, and has chiefly been employed in political warfare as a watchword to rally in one band all who, whatever may be their religious differences, are prepared to act politically against the aggressions of the Romanists. In this respect it was particularly useful at the time of the Revolution; and, as politics intrude themselves into all the considerations of an Englishman, either directly or indirectly, the term is endeared to a powerful and influential party in the State. But on the very ground that it thus keeps out of view distinguishing and vital principles, and unites in apparent agreement those who essentially differ, many of our divines object to the use of the word. They contend, with good reason, that it is quite absurd to speak of the Protestant Religion, since a religion must, of course, be distinguished not by what it renounces, but by what it professes: they apprehend that it has occasioned a kind of sceptical habit of inquiring not how much we ought to believe, but how much we may refuse to believe; of looking at what is negative instead of what is positive in our religion; of fearing to inquire after the truth lest it should lead to something which is held by the Papists in common with ourselves, and which, therefore, as some persons seem to argue, no sound Protestant can hold; forgetting that on this principle we ought to renounce the Liturgy, the Sacraments, the doctrine of the Trinity, the deity and atonement of Christ—nay, the very Bible itself. It is on these grounds that the writers of the Oxford Tracts have scrupled to use the word, and hence they have brought down upon themselves the outpourings of the vials of wrath, from all who are weak enough to prefer words to things, and especially from political divines, and men who would make religion merely an instrument to serve their political purposes. I make these observations the more freely because I differ in this respect from the writers of the Oxford Tracts. It is certainly absurd to speak of the Protestant religion—*i.e.* a negative religion—but there is no absurdity in speaking of the Church of England, or of the Church of America, as a Protestant Church—the word Church conveys a positive idea, and there can be no reason why we should not have also a negative appellation. If we admit that the Church of Rome is a true though a corrupt Church, it is well to have a term by which we may always declare that, while we hold in common with her all that she has which is Catholic, Scriptural, and pure, we protest for ever against her multiplied corruptions. Besides, the word, whether correctly or not, is in general use, and is in a certain sense applicable to the Church of England; it is surely, therefore, better to retain it, only warning our congregations, that when we call ourselves Protestants, we mean no more to profess that we hold communion with all parties who are so styled, than the Church of England, when in her creeds and formularies she designates herself not as the Protestant but as the Catholic Church of this country, intends to hold communion with those Catholic Churches abroad which have infused into their system the principles of the Council of Trent. Protestant is our negative, Catholic our definite name We tell the Papist that with respect to him we are Protestant; we tell the Protestant Dissenter that with respect to him we are Catholics; and we may be called Protestant or Protesting Catholics, or, as some of our writers describe us, Anglo-Catholics.

NOTE VI., p. 72.

THE ROMISH SCHISM.

Of this schism the following is a succinct and interesting account: 'Now at such time as Button, Billingham, and the rest of the Puritan faction had first made the schism, Harding and Sanders, and some others of the Popish fugitives, employed themselves as busily in persuading those of that religion to the like temptation. For being licensed by the Pope to exercise Episcopal jurisdiction in the realm of England, they take upon them to absolve all such in the Court of Conscience, who should return to the communion of the Church of Rome; as also to dispense in causes of irregularity, except it were incurred by wilful murther; and finally, from the like irregularities incurred by heresie, if the party who desired the benefit of the absolution, abstained from ministering at the holy altar for three years together, by means whereof, and the advantages before mentioned, which were given them by the Puritan faction, they drew many to them from the Church, both priests and people; their numbers every day increasing, as the scandal did. And finding how the sectaries enlarged their numbers by erecting a French church in London, and that they were upon the point of procuring another for the use and comfort of the Dutch, they thought it no ill piece of wisdom to attempt the like in some convenient place near England, where they might train up their disciples, and fit them for employment upon all occasions. Upon which ground a seminary is established for them at Douay, in Flanders, anno 1568; and another not long after at Rhemes, a City of Champaigne, in the realm of France. Such was the benefit which redounded to the Church of England by the perverseness of the brethren of this first separation, that it occasioned the like schism betwixt her and the Papists, who till that time had kept themselves in her communion, as before was said. For that the Papists generally did frequent the Church in these first ten years, is positively affirmed by Sir Edward Coke, in his speech at the arraignment of Garnet, the Jesuit, and afterwards at the charge which was given by him at the general assizes held in Norwich. In both of which he speaks on his own certain knowledge, not on vulgar hearsay; affirming more particularly that he had many times seen Bedenfield, Cornwallis, and some other of the leading Romanists, at the divine service of the Church, who afterwards were the first that departed from it. The like is averred by the most learned Bishop Andrews, in his book called " Tortura Torti," p. 130, and there asserted undeniably against all opposition. And which may serve instead of all, we finde the like affirmed also by the Queen herself, in her instructions given to Walsingham, then being her Resident with the French King, anno 1570. In which instructions, bearing date on August 11, it is affirmed expressly of the heads of that party, and therefore we may judge the like of the members also, that they did ordinarily resort, from the beginning of her reign, in all open places, to the Churches, and to divine service in the Church, without any contradiction or shew of misliking.

‘The parallel goes further yet. For as the Puritans were encouraged to this separation by the Missals and Decretory

Letters of Theodore Beza, whom they beheld as the chief Patriarch of their Church; so were the Papists animated to their defection by a Bull of Pope Pius V., whom they acknowledged most undoubtedly for the head of theirs. For the Pope being thrust on by the importunity of the House of Guise, in favour of the Queen of Scots, whose title they preferred before that of Elizabeth, and by the Court of France, in hatred to the Queen herself, for aiding the French Hugonots against their King, was drawn at last to issue out this Bull, against her, dated at Rome, Feb. 24, 1569. In which Bull he doth not onely excommunicate her person, deprive her of her kingdoms, and absolve all her subjects from their oaths of allegiance; but commands all her subjects, of what sort soever, not to obey her laws, injunctions, ordinances, or acts of state. The defection of the Papists had before been voluntary, but is now made necessary; the Pope's command being superadded to the scandal which had before been given them by the Puritan faction. For after this the going or not going to Church was commonly reputed by them for a sign distinctive, by which a Roman Catholic might be known from an English heretick. And this appears most plainly by the preamble to the Act of parliament against bringing or executing of Bulls from Rome—13 Eliz. 2. Where it is reckoned amongst the effects of those Bulls and writings, that those who brought them, did by their lewd practices, and subtile perswasions, work so far forth that sundry people, and ignorant persons, have been contented to be reconciled to the Church of Rome, and to have withdrawn and absented themselves from all divine service, most godlily exercised in this realm. By which it seems, that till the roaring of those Bulls, those of the Popish party did frequent the Church, though not so generally in the last five years (as our learned Andrews hath observed) as they did the first, before they were discouraged by the innovations of the Puritan faction.' *

* Heylyn's 'History of the Presbyterians,' lib. vi. p. 260.

Note VII., page 73.

ON THE CHARGE OF POPERY BROUGHT AGAINST THE ENGLISH RE-
FORMERS AND THE FRIENDS OF THE ENGLISH REFORMATION.

Against those divines who uphold the system of the English, as distinguished from the foreign Reformation, it is sought to excite the odium of the ignorant, by designating them as semi-Papists, if not actually Papists in disguise. Doubtless they will rejoice to bear the scandal of the Cross, and to escape the woe denounced upon those of whom all men speak well.* They remember our Lord's prophecy. They care little if men 'shall hate them, and separate them from their company, and reproach them, and cast out their name as evil.' They know that, 'if the world hate them, it hated their master before them,' and they 'marvel not.'† But some consolation it is to know that they share the reproaches with the English Reformers themselves, of whom some of their opponents say that they are their masters. We call no man master; but certainly, if history be not an old almanac, the persecution which persons styled High Churchmen have to undergo, is inflicted merely because they act towards both the Romish and Protestant Dissenters, precisely as the English Reformers did, seeking neither unnecessarily to offend, nor, by sacrifice of principle, to conciliate.

In notes II. and IV. many passages are adduced, which fully substantiate the assertion that the charge of Popery was brought vehemently against the English Reformers, as it is now against their representatives, the High Churchmen. We have seen how they were thus accused by Calvin, and that Beza declared that 'Popery was never thrown out of the English Church, but rather transferred from his Holiness to her Majesty.' In the same letter he remarks, 'that those few ministers who came up to the purity of the Gospel are

---

* St. Luke vi. 26. See also St. John xv. 19.
† St. John xv. 18; I. St. John iii. 13.

either thrown into prison or deprived both, unless they solemnly engage to go to the utmost lengths of conformity, and resemble Baal's priests, in their square caps, tippets, and such sort of equipages.'* The authorized version of Scripture was, as we have seen before, conducted on a principle of deference to the primitive Church. But the followers of the foreign Reformers not only translated the Scripture on different principles, but so far were they from wishing to circulate the Bible without note or comment, that they published one in the early part of Elizabeth's reign, with notes, intending to inculcate the system of Calvin instead of that of the English Reformation. In 1560, says Collier, 'the English translation of Scripture, commonly called the Geneva Bible, was published at Geneva. There are two epistles prefixed to the work; one to the Queen, the other to the reader. These addresses charged the English Reformation with remains of Popery, and endeavoured to prevail with the Queen to strike off several ceremonies.'† The fact that they omitted these addresses in a subsequent edition only shows that they found it impolitic to publish such charges, not that they intended to withdraw them: for the Popery of our Reformers was the very plea urged by the Puritans out of the Church to justify their secession, and by the Puritans in the Church for disobeying her regulations. The Protestation of the Puritans against the English Reformation thus commences: 'Being thorough persuaded in my conscience by the working and the word of the Almighty, that these relics of Antichrist be abominable before the Lord our God; and also, for that by the power, mercy, strength, and goodness of the Lord our God only I am escaped from the filthiness and pollution of these detestable traditions. . . . I have joined in prayer and hearing God's word with those that have not yielded to this idolatrous trash, notwithstanding the danger for not coming to my parish church, &c. therefore I come not back again to the preaching, &c. of them that have received these marks of the Romish beast.' 'They (the

* Collier, ii. p. 503. † Collier, ii. 471.

English Reformers) are glad to strengthen the Papists in their errors, and grieve the godly.' 'These popish garments are now become very idols indeed, because they are exalted above the word of the Almighty. . . . I come not to them (the English Reformers) because they should be ashamed, and so leave their idolatrous garment.'*

So also among the demands of the (so-called) millenary petition, one was that ' no popish opinion should be any more taught or defended ; no ministers charged to teach their people to bow at the name of Jesus.' † In ' The Plea of the Innocent,' those who adhered to the doctrines of the English Reformation, as distinguished from the Puritans, are called ' sycophantizing Papists, statizing Priests.' In the ' Prayer of the Refusers of the Habits,' they assert that ' those in power neglected that they ought to have done, to the hindrance of the course of the gospel; and that the relics of Romish idolatry was stoutly maintained.' ‡ In a work by Beale, which expressed the sentiments of the Puritans, Queen Elizabeth is spoken of as ' a defendresse of beggarly, popish, and anti-christian rites,' and the ceremonies of the church are styled ' beggarly, popish, and anti-christian.' § We may barely give the titles of some of the books which were published at the completion of the English Reformation against our English Reformers ; one was styled ' A view of Antichrist, his laws and ceremonies in our English Church unreformed ; a clear glass wherein may be seen the dangerous and desperate diseases of our English Church, being utterly ready to perish, unless she speedily have a corrosive of the wholesome words of God, his word, laid every whot to her heart, to expulse those colds and deadly infections of Popery which the tainted Poticaries of Antichrist have corrupted her withal.' In this book there is a table ' of the displaying of the Pope and Popery in our Church of England. The Pope of Rome writeth himself Father of Fathers, and Head of the

* Strype's ' Life of Parker,' ii. 283, seq.
† Strype's ' Life of Whitgift,' ii. 480.
‡ Strype's ' Annals,' vol. i. pt. II. p. 168.
§ Strype's ' Whitgift,' iii. 87.

Church. The Pope of Canterbury writeth himself, reverend Father, Matthew of Canterbury, by the sufferance of God,' &c. Another book was styled 'A brief discourse against the outward apparel and ministering garments of the Popish Church, *i.e.* the Church of England.' Another book was named 'A view of the Popish abuses yet remaining.' Thomas Cartwright seems to have set the example in thus calling the English Reformers Papists, for he and his brethren, 'in dispute of the hierarchy, now begun commonly to call these Popes, and the Archbishops of Canterbury, Popes of Lambeth.'* In 1572 a committee of the House of Commons, desirous of furthering the views of the Puritans, 'thought it advisable that some of them should repair with their bills to the Archbishop, and perhaps other of the Bishops too. . . . The Archbishop (our great Reformer Archbishop Parker) signified his dislike of it; since the ordinary course of redressing matters amiss in the Church did properly belong to the Bishops and Clergy in Convocation.' After some discussion, the Archbishop replied, 'Surely you mistook the matter: you will refer yourselves wholly to us therein.' To which Mr. Wentworth, whom Strype describes as a hot gentleman, exclaimed, 'No, by the faith I bear to God, we will pass nothing before we understand what it is. For that were to make you Popes. Make you Popes who list, for we will make you none.'† But perhaps the reader would like to know what were the deeds of Popery for which our High Church Reformers were styled, like their present representatives, Papists, and he will probably be surprised to hear that the charge of Popery was then made against almost every thing which a Churchman in these days reveres. Does the Churchman revere the Book of Common Prayer? 'It is patched for the most part out of the Pope's Portuise: it is an imperfect book, culled and picked out of the Popish dunghill, the Mass Book, full of abominations.'‡ 'The public prayers and worship of God, as it is by law in the Church of England established, is false, superstitious,

---

* Strype's 'Parker,' ii. 203. † Strype's 'Parker,' ii. 209.
‡ 'Admonition to Parliament.' Strype's 'Annals,' vol. ii. pt. II. 478.

and Popish.'* The Communion Service is spoken of in the same language; and the reading of the epistle and gospel in that office is 'utterly misliked and called a Popish introit.' 'For newly married persons to receive the communion is pronounced to be Popish, because in Popish times they had a mass.' Is confirmation valued as a holy ordinance? It was called 'superstitious, Popish, and peevish.' Are Cathedrals now supported? They come under the same category. There are no Churchmen in these days who do not consider episcopacy to be at least an apostolical ordinance. But it has been held that the names of Archbishops, Archdeacons, and Bishops, Chancellors, &c. are drawn out of the Pope's shop, together with these offices. And it was urged against our Reformers, 'that the government of the Church of England, as it is now established, is no lawful government, but Anti-christian and Popish.' †

The same charge of Popery was brought against the Church of England and her Reformers at the Hampton Court Conference. Among other marks of Popery was our retention of the sign of the cross, and the wearing of the surplice. ‡

The King, it will be seen, on reference to the account, answered to the objectors, and the mode of reasoning on this matter, adopted by his Majesty, was referred to, and has received the sanction of the Church of England in the 30th canon before mentioned.

This charge has, indeed, always been adduced to persecute into silence those of our divines who have endeavoured to uphold the principles of the English Reformers, who, they contend, are equally the principles of sound reasoning, catholicism and Scripture. Of honoured names the Church of England holds none more highly in honour than that of the judicious Hooker.

At the time when Hooker wrote, Calvinism, doctrinal as well as disciplinarian, had made considerable progress in England; and Hooker's, unhappily for his own peace of mind,

---

* Strype's 'Annals,' iv. 202. † Strype, iv. 202.
‡ See Barlow's account of the Hampton Court Conference in the 'Phenix,' i. 166.

were almost the only works of great extent which were calculated to arrest the progress of the doctrinal Calvinists. In the year 1509 a tract was published in 4to, entitled 'A Christian Letter of certain English Protestants, unfaigned favourers of the present state of religion, authorised and professed in England, unto that reverend and learned man Mr. R. Hooker, requiring resolution in certaine matters of doctrine (which seeme to overthrow the foundation of Christian religion, and of the Church among us) expresslie contained in his five books of Ecclesiasticall Polity.' This book is one of the earliest productions of those malcontents who were afterwards called doctrinal Puritans. It is the doctrines of Hooker with which they quarrel; and they profess (in contradistinction to the abettors of the Geneva discipline) an unfeigned attachment to the external establishments of the Church of England. The work is further deserving of notice as exhibiting, I believe, the earliest example, both in the matter and manner of the argument, of those numerous publications in which some Calvinistic writers have thoughtlessly and intemperately indulged themselves, from the days of this Christian letter, and from Prynne, and Hickman, downwards, to Edwards, and Toplady, and Bowman, and Sir Richard Hill, and Overton. Can it be believed, the authors of the letter in question tax the meek, the wise, the virtuous, the saint-like Richard Hooker with betraying and renouncing the doctrines to which he had solemnly subscribed? They charge him with designs of bringing back Popery. They accuse him of a wanton attack on the memory of Calvin. They condemn him of unsoundness of doctrine respecting grace and free-will, and justification and predestination, and the conditions of the Christian covenant, and the sacraments of the Christian Church. It is curious to see the Thirty-nine Articles, the Liturgy, the Homilies, Bishop Jewell's Apology, Dean Nowell's Catechism and the writings of many others of Hooker's Protestant predecessors solemnly cited against him, and confronted in due form with extracts from the Ecclesiastical Polity, for the purpose of convicting him of deserting and denying the principles of that Church of which he was a minister, in whose cause he toiled day and night, and in the defence of which, I believe, it may truly be said, that it was God's good pleasure that he should die.*

Even good Bishop Hall did not escape the charge. Sanderson, afterwards Bishop of Lincoln, in that part of the famous Preface to his Sermons, bearing date July 13, 1657, in which he shows the advantages which the Puritan writers gave to the Romish party by the unsoundness of their reasonings and their extreme intolerance, and the much greater progress which Popery was making in England towards the latter end of the Commonwealth, through their incapacity, than it had ever done before, remarks that 'They promoted the interest of Rome, and betrayed the Protestant cause, partly by mistaking the question (a very common fault among them), but especially through the necessity of some false principle or other, which, having once imbibed, they think themselves bound to maintain. Among those false principles it shall suffice for the present to have named but this one, that the Church of Rome is no true Church. The disadvantages of which assertion to our cause in the dispute about the visibility of the Church (besides the falseness and uncharitableness of it) their zeal, or prejudice rather, will not suffer them to consider. With what outcries was Bishop Hall, good man (who little dreamt of any peace with Rome), pursued by Burton and other Hotspurs for yielding it a Church! who had made the same concession over and over again before he was Bishop (as Junius, Reynolds, and our best controversy writers generally do) and no notice was taken, no noise made about it.' †

The name of Bishop Sanderson reminds me of a passage from his works applicable to this subject with which I will conclude this note. Bishop Sanderson is the author of 'The General Thanksgivings' in the Prayer Book, and therefore advice from him will be favourably received:—

'But their opinion is, that the things enjoyned are

* Wordsworth's Biog., iv. 209.
† Sanderson's 'Sermons,' pref. p. 79, edit. 1689. Wordsworth's Biog., v. 305.

Popish and superstitious, and consequently unlawful to be used: and this they render as the reason of their non-conformity. And the reason was certainly good if the opinion were true. For the Popishness first; unless we should sue out a writ *de finibus regendis* it will be hard to find out a way how to bring this controversie to an issue, much less to an end; the term hath been so strangely extended, and the limits thereof (if yet it have any) so uncertain. If they would be intreated to set bounds to what they mean by Popish and Popery, by giving us a certain definition of it, we should the sooner either come to some agreement; or, at least, understand ourselves and one another the better, wherein and how far we disagreed. In the mean time it is to me a wonder, that if reason would not heretofore, yet the sad experience of the ill consequents so visible of late time, should not have taught them all this while to consider what infinite advantage they give to the Romish party to work upon weak and wavering souls; by damning so many things under the name of Popery, which may to their understandings be sufficiently evidenced, some to have been used by the ancient Christians long before Popery was hatched, or but in the egg; and all to have nothing of Superstition or Popery in them, unless every thing that is used in the Church of Rome become thereby Popish and superstitious. Nor what great advantage they give to our newer sectaries, to extend the name yet farther; who, by the help of their new lights, can discern Popery, not only in the ceremonies formerly under debate, but even in the Churches and pulpits wherein they used to preach against Popery, and the bells wherewith they used to call the people together to hear them. These are by some of them cryed down as Popish, with other things very many, which their Presbyterian brethren do yet both allow and practise; though how long they will so do is uncertain, if they go on with the work of Reformation they have begun with as quick dispatch, and at the rate they have done these last two seven years. The having of godfathers at Baptism, churching of women, prayers at the burial of the dead, children asking their parents' blessing, &c. which whilome were held innocent, are now by very many thrown aside as rags of Popery. Nay, are not some gone so far already, as to cast into the same heap, not only the ancient hymn *Gloria Patri* (for the repeating whereof alone some have been deprived of all their livelihoods) and the Apostles' Creed; but even the use of the Lord's Prayer itself? And what will ye do in the end thereof? And what would ye have us do in the mean time, when ye call hard upon us to leave our popery, and yet you would never do us the favour to let us know what it is? It were good therefore, for your own sakes, that you may not rove *in infinitum* : and in compassion to us, that you would give us a perfect boundary of what is Popery now ; with some prognostication or ephemerides annexed (if you please) whereby to calculate what will be Popery seven years hence.' *

NOTE VIII., p. 74.

SOCINIANS.

Of a truth, the Socinian, or ' Unitarian,' as he denominates himself, meets with hard measure from his brethren among the Ultra-protestants. He protests most loudly against Popery. He takes the Bible and the Bible only for his guide. He affirms that in the Bible, interpreted according to his ability, he cannot discover those great doctrines which we of the Church of England know to be the fundamental doctrines of Christianity. He is wrong, and we of the Church of England anathematize him and refuse to regard him as a Christian. And so do many of the Ultra-protestant sects who hold, in fact, with us the great fundamentals of Christianity. But on their own principles what right can they have to do so ? Of what crime has he, on their principles, been guilty ? At the very most, he can only be guilty, as is stated above, of an obtuseness of intellect which has led to bad logic or to

---

* Sanderson's Sermons, second preface. See also first preface to his Sermons,

bad criticism. But, after all, for the Ultra-protestant to assert that the Socinian interprets Scripture wrongly is only to beg the very point in dispute. The Socinian says, 'I receive Scripture in what I believe to be the true sense, and so do you ;—we differ as to what the true sense is, but this is only a difference of opinion, and you have no more right to blame me than I have to blame you.' We of the Church of England, while we defer to Scripture only, profess to receive Scripture as the Church always understood it, and by public documents in general councils, asserted its belief. We therefore have an arbiter to decide, when two meanings can be attached to one passage of Scripture, which to adopt, our object being not to ascertain what Scripture can be made to say, but what the Lord our God actually means. But for this, Ultra-protestants denounce us as papistical and call our Church the Church of the Traditioners. They therefore are *ex hypothesi* excluded from this mode of arguing. We rejoice to find that they agree with us whenever they do agree. But we marvel when we hear them joining with us in censuring 'Unitarianism' as a heresy.

NOTE IX., p. 75.

PERSECUTION BY ULTRA-PROTESTANTS.

A violent and popular outcry has often been raised against the Church because, at the Restoration, those of the clergy who refused to conform were rejected from their benefices. But it will be well to see how the case really stands. Seven thousand English clergymen, having refused to take the Covenant at the great Rebellion, were ejected from their livings, their places being supplied by dissenting teachers. This most honourable testimony to the clergy of the Church of England at that period ought never to be forgotten. At the Restoration it was required that all those persons who thus become possessed of the property of the English Church should either conform to the regulations of the Church or resign. Of all the Puritan clergy then in possession, only two thousand thought fit to resign rather than comply. And these two thousand were ejected from what? From their rights? No, but from their usurpations. Five thousand conformed and still retained possession of the Church property, so that many of the previously ejected clergy of the Church of England, who hoped, at the Restoration, to be restored to their own, were sorely disappointed and cruelly used. The treatment of the English clergy by the Presbyterians is worthy of notice.*

The Independents, who burned some hundreds for witchcraft, and hanged the Quakers at Massachusetts, 'proposed more massacres than they executed. There was one of all the Royalists or Presbyterians in the true Marat style of taking two hundred thousand heads off at one stroke.'†

I do not refer to these things to revive angry and useless disputes; and I am perfectly aware that no Dissenters, whether Romish or Protestant, would wish to revive a spirit of persecution, now that the principle of toleration is fully understood; but when attempts are so frequently made, by stating only one side of the question, to make it appear that Dissenters were hardly used by Churchmen in times past, it becomes necessary to show that we have it in our power, by an appeal to history, to exhibit the other side of the picture, and to make it known that the little finger of an Ultra-protestant is thicker than a Churchman's loins. I believe the first declarations in favour of a toleration are to be found in Chillingworth and Jeremy Taylor.

Note X., p. 75.

THE OXFORD TRACTS.

That the simplification of our principle alluded to in the text has sometimes tended to narrow the mind, and that men have been inclined to support the Church of England on

---

* See on this subject Collier, ii. 828.
† D'Israeli's 'Charles I.' iii. 205.

grounds and with feelings purely sectarian, may be lamented but can scarcely be denied. But still, generally speaking, the simplicity of our principle has worked well, and in every controversy its tendency is to bring Churchmen to an agreement. For instance, at the commencement of the last century, the tendency of Ultra-protestantism was to Socianism. The Ultra-protestant sects in Germany, and even in Geneva, had become Socinian. Under the influence of Hoadley and the then liberal party in England, an attempt was made to gain a footing for this God-denying heresy in the English Church. To believe in the doctrine of the Trinity, to worship the Saviour, or to regard the sacraments as anything more than mere ceremonies, was represented as 'flat Popery'; to condemn those who protested against these doctrines was considered 'a renunciation of the fundamental principles of the Reformation.' But the attempt failed, for every man endowed with common honesty could understand the argument, 'You may, if you like it, leave the Church, but you cannot as an honest man continue to act therein as a minister if you deny the truth of her doctrines, and it is impossible to doubt as to what her doctrines are with reference to the Holy Trinity and the Deity of our Lord.' However liberal a man may be in the present day, he would not dare to avow Socinian opinions (knowing them to be such,) and retain any official situation in the Church.

The tendency of the principle mentioned above to promote unanimity and concord among Churchmen may be seen in another instance. In the middle of the last century it is not to be denied that a religious apathy prevailed, both in the Church and among the Sectarians, to a very considerable extent. We know, both from their writings and their biographies, that there were a vast number of orthodox clergymen steadily performing their duty in their respective cures, but from a variety of circumstances there was a vast number also too inactive. Discipline, too, had relaxed. Bishops had been appointed whose political sentiments accorded ill with those of the great body of the clergy, by whom they were regarded with suspicion and jealousy. The episcopal government is paternal, and where, from any cause, it cannot be administered with a paternal spirit, any legal powers with which our Bishops may be invested, as they cannot be exercised without harshness, can scarcely be exercised at all. At this juncture, a zeal almost amounting to enthusiasm was kindled in the bosoms of many devout and excellent men, who felt called upon to blow the trumpet in Zion, and to awaken the sleeping world around them to a sense of their spiritual wants. The movement was simultaneous, or nearly so, in the Church and among the sectarians.* But the churchmen, uniting with the sectarians, and thinking that excitement was the most thing needed, became attached to the system of the foreign rather than to that of the English Reformation. Many of the early Evangelicals, of whom it is impossible to speak without feelings of affection, veneration, and respect, were certainly guilty of many irregularities, erring only from their not having duly considered the subject of church discipline. These irregularities they gradually corrected, and the next generation of 'Evangelicals' assumed another attitude; they contended against the 'orthodox,' as the great body of the clergy were styled, that their views were strictly those of the English Church and the English Reformation. The controversy thus assumed a definite and tangible form according to the principle already alluded to. The appeal to this principle led, of course, to various explanations and various modifications of extreme opinions. The spirit of deference to the authoritative decisions of the Church of England was in his later years encouraged by Mr. Wilberforce, when that highly-gifted, amiable, and pious man had become virtually the leader of the 'Evangelical' party; and at length the moderate of that party were found to be disputing with those who professedly adhered to the principles of the English Reformers and the Catholic Church, which had been

* It is clearly shown by Mr. Venn (preface to Venn's Life) that the early 'Evangelicals' in the Church were not indebted, even indirectly, as it has been sometimes misrepresented, to the Wesleys or Whitfield for the sentiments by which they were influenced.

consistently maintained by such men as Jones of Nayland, Bishop Horne, and their successors, merely about words. At such a time, when all parties, having admitted that Church principles ought to be carried out and uniformly acted upon, were led to inquire, 'what are Church principles? is any party consistently acting upon them?'—at such a time, the celebrated Oxford Tracts made their appearance. The reputed writers of the Tracts were men of ardent piety, who had been attached to the 'Evangelical' school, and it was among the young men who had been educated in that school that they created a strong sensation. Hence, perhaps, the bitterness with which they are assailed by some of the older partisans of that section of the Church. To those who, like the present writer, had been educated strictly on the principles of the English Reformation, and belonged to the old orthodox school, they brought forward nothing new; and though we may have demurred to some of their opinions, and have thought that, in some things, they are in an extreme, we rejoiced to see right principles advocated in a manner so decided, and in a spirit so truly Christian. Against some of the pious opinions supported in these Tracts objections may occasionally be raised, for perfect coincidence of opinion is not to be expected. I do not, myself, accord with all the opinions expressed in them or always admit the deduction attempted to be drawn from the principles on which we are agreed. I think, too, that while manfully vindicating the principles of the English Reformation, in their fear lest they should appear to respect persons too highly, the writers of the Tracts did not appreciate highly enough the character of some of our leading Reformers, or make due allowance for the difficulties in which they were placed. I mention these things the rather, since I am sure the writers in question have no wish to form a party; they have no wish to check freedom of opinion within the boundaries prescribed by the Church; —their object is only to imbue the public mind with those Catholic principles by the maintenance of which the English Reformation was gloriously distinguished. This cannot be done, unless on those principles opinions are formed, and from them conclusions drawn; and at the very time that we may combat a particular opinion, if we admit the truth of the principle on which it is built, we only confirm the principle, and impress it more deeply on men's minds. I am not one of those who would say, 'Read the Oxford Tracts, and take for granted every opinion there expressed,' but I am one of those who would say, 'Read and digest those Tracts well, and you will have imbibed principles which will enable you to judge of opinions.' Their popularity will increase, since their arguments are not answered, or their statements refuted:—they are opposed simply by railing. And those who judge of such things only by second-hand reports, and garbled quotations, and anonymous misrepresentations in newspapers will, of course, rail on. May the day come when they may be awakened to a sense of the danger of thus violating the golden rule of charity! In the mean time, the wise the candid, those who are not the mere partisans of religion, but really religious, will themselves read the Tracts,—and if they do read they will commend. They may censure particular opinions, but they will commend the whole. At all events, the Scriptural Christian will be prejudiced in favour of the writers of the Oxford Tracts, on seeing the fruits of the Spirit beautifully exhibited in their conduct, love, joy, peace, long-suffering, gentleness, goodness, faith, meekness; it would be well, indeed, if their assailants, in various magazines and newspapers, would remember of what emulations, wrath, strife, seditions, are the signs. The temper manifested by their opponents is as impolitic as it is too often profane. Fully aware that it is not by reviling again that they are to maintain the cause of a reviled and crucified Master; fully aware that it is by well-doing that they are 'to put to silence the ignorance of foolish men,' the writers of the Oxford Tracts, when assailed as 'popish fanatics,' &c., when their doctrines, instead of being refuted, are declaimed against as 'figments of the darkest ages of Papal superstition,' &c., calmly reply, 'Brave words, surely. Well and good, take your fill of them, since you choose them for your portion. It does but make our spirits rise cheerily and hopefully to be thus encountered. Never were such words on one side, but deeds were on the other. We know our place and our fortunes; to give a witness and to be contemned; to be ill-used and to succeed. Such is the law which God has annexed to the promulgation of the truth; its preachers suffer, but its cause prevails. Be it so. Joyfully will we consent to this compact. And the more you attack us personally, the more, for the very omen's sake, we will exult in it.'

NOTE XI., page 80.

ON THE SACRAMENTS.

'In all ages the devil hath stirred up some light heads to esteem the sacraments but lightly, as to be empty and bare signs.' *

1. BAPTISM.—So evidently does the Church connect Baptism and Regeneration that the Puritans in Queen Elizabeth's time and the Nonconformists in the reign of Charles II. justified their secession on the ground that 'the Church clearly teaches the doctrine of real baptismal regeneration.' †

The Puritans particularly objected to our services for applying John iii. 5 to 'the baptizing in the font, that being spoken, as they said, only of the operation of the spirit. ‡ They cavilled also 'at these words used in baptism, that Jesus Christ did sanctify the flood Jordan and all other waters to the mystical washing away of sin; as though we should attribute that to the sign which is proper to the word of God in the blood of Christ; and that virtue were in the water to wash away sin.' §

Allusion is here evidently made to our baptismal service where it is expressly said that water is sanctified to the mystical washing away of sin. The Puritans also objected to the Church for teaching each baptized child to speak of himself as 'sanctified,' which is done in the catechism.

* Bp. Latimer, in Ridley's 'Life of Ridley,' p. 453.
† 'Nonconformist's Memorial.' Intro. p. 39.
‡ 'Puritan Register,' p. 97.
§ 'A View of Popish Abuses yet Remaining.' Strype's 'Annals,' vol. ii. pt. II. p. 480.

Among the eight things at the Savoy Conference charged upon the Church as 'flatly sinful and contrary to the word of God,' the fourth was 'that ministers are obliged to pronounce all baptized infants regenerate by the Holy Ghost.' The Rev. Thomas Scott observes:—

'Indeed, the Fathers, as they are called (that is, the teachers of the Christian Church during some ages after the apostles), soon began to speak on this subject in unscriptural language '—(*i.e.* according to Mr. Scott's idea of what Scriptural language is, but he is no more infallible than the Fathers, who were deep students of Scripture): 'and our pious reformers, from an undue regard to them and to the circumstances of the times, have retained a few expressions in the Liturgy which not only are inconsistent with their other doctrine, but also tend to perplex men's minds and mislead their judgment on this important subject. It is obvious, however, from their words above cited, and many other passages (particularly the articles on the sacraments), that they never supposed the mere outward administration of baptism to be regeneration, in the strict sense of the word.' †

This is certainly a curious sentence to be written by one who had subscribed his unfeigned assent and consent to the Prayer Book; and Mr. Scott's idea of piety must have been peculiar. According to his statement, our Reformers did not believe baptism to be regeneration, but yielding to 'the circumstances of the time' and 'undue regard to the Fathers,' they suffered what they did not believe to remain as the doctrine of the baptismal office, though leading, as Mr. Scott would consider, to errors the most pernicious and fatal. This, a High Churchman, who, true to the principles of the English Reformation, has a due regard for the Fathers, would, I shrewdly suspect, call impiety. From this charge I should be happy to vindicate our great reformers: and first of Cranmer. That his private views were not, as Mr. Scott suspects, different from those which he publicly avowed, may be seen from the ensuing extract from one of his last and most elaborate works, the very title of which betrays a

* Collier, ii. 885.   † Scott's Essays, No. 12, p. 137.

respect, whether due or undue, for the Fathers, sufficient to show in addition to what has before been produced, that whatever anathemas they deserve who in these days have respect to the Fathers, it is presuming rather too much on the ignorance and credulity of the public to accuse them of deviating from the principles of the Reformation.

'A Defence of the true and Catholic Doctrine of the Sacrament of the body and blood of our Saviour Christ, with a Confutation of sundry errors concerning the same, grounded and stablished upon God's Holy Word, and approved by the consent of the most ancient doctors of the Church, made by the most Reverend Father in God Thomas Archbishop of Canterbury, Primate of all England and Metropolitan.

' Although our carnal generation and our carnal nourishment be known to all men by daily experience and by our common senses; yet this our spiritual generation and our spiritual nutrition be so obscure and hid unto us, that we cannot attain to the true and perfect knowledge and feeling of them, but only by faith, which must be grounded upon God's most holy word and sacraments.

' And for this consideration our Saviour Christ hath not only set forth these things most plainly in his holy word, that we may hear them with our ears; but he hath also ordained one visible sacrament of spiritual regeneration in water, and another visible sacrament of spiritual nourishment in bread and wine, to the intent that, as much as is possible for man, we may see Christ with our eyes, smell him at our nose, taste him with our mouths, grope him with our hands, and perceive him with all our senses. For as the word of God preached putteth Christ into our ears, so likewise the elements of water, bread, and wine, joined to God's word, do after a sacramental manner put Christ into our eyes, mouths, hands, and all our senses.

' And for this cause Christ ordained Baptism in water, that as sure as we see, feel, and touch water with our bodies, and be washed with water; so assuredly ought we to believe, when we be baptized, that Christ is verily present with us, and that by him we be newly born again spiritually, and washed from our sins, and grafted in the stock of Christ's own body, and be apparelled, clothed, and harnessed with him in such wise, that as the Devil hath no power against Christ, so hath he none against us, so long as we remain grafted in that stock, and be clothed with that apparel, and harnessed with that armour.' *

Of the force of this passage we have indirect evidence in the fact that when the Religious Tract Society undertook the republication of the greater part of the 'Defence,' the passage just quoted was carefully omitted. 'Their extracts,' says Mr. Jenkyns, 'are much too imperfect to convey a full and fair view of Cranmer's tenets, especially as they do not include a remarkable passage in his first book, illustrative of his opinions on Baptism.' The passage alluded to is the one quoted above. Now, it cannot be supposed that the Religious Tract Society, &c. published the tract in question, antiquated in style and controversial in manner, as being in itself peculiarly adapted to those whom the Society is intended to benefit. The object was, of course, to insinuate that the principles of the Society are in accordance with those of the English Reformers. But on one of the most important points, the principles of the Tract Society and those of Archbishop Cranmer are very decidedly at variance. On what principle, then, can such an unnoticed omission be justified; an omission that leads the reader to infer that the Archbishop and the Society are perfectly in union? When Bishop Sanderson's advice is followed, and we have a clear definition of what Popery is, perhaps we shall find this noted as a Popish transaction. For although I am quite sure that truly pious Romanists would disdain such an artifice as this, yet of similar offences some of their most distinguished controversialists have been guilty.

But if a yet stronger passage from Archbishop Cranmer is wanted, it can easily be produced:—

'And when you say that in baptism we receive the spirit of Christ, and in the sacrament of his body and blood we receive his very flesh and blood, this your saying is no small

* Cranmer's 'Works,' ii. 302.

derogation to baptism, wherein we receive not only the spirit of Christ, but also Christ himself, whole body and soul, manhood and Godhead, unto everlasting life, as well as in the holy communion. For St. Paul saith, *Quicunque in Christo baptizati estis, Christum induistis,* As many as be baptised in Christ, put Christ upon them. Nevertheless this is done in divers respects; for in baptism it is done in respect of regeneration, and in the holy communion in respect of nourishment and augmentation.' *

That they against whom, under the name of High Churchmen, an attempt is made to excite the wrath of the irritable, and the indignation of the ignorant, are influenced by the spirit of our English Reformers no better proof can be given than their desire to circulate the authoritative documents of the Reformation. Some tracts of great importance, under the title of ' Tracts of the Anglican Fathers,' have been lately published, and ought to be widely circulated. From Archbishop Cranmer's sermon on Holy Baptism the following extracts are made:—

'And the second birth is by the water of Baptism, which Paul calleth the bath of regeneration, because our sins be forgiven us in Baptism, and the Holy Ghost is poured into us as into God's beloved children, so that by the power and working of the Holy Ghost we be born again spiritually, and made new creatures. And so by Baptism we enter into the kingdom of God, and are saved for ever, if we continue to our lives' end in the faith of Christ.

'When we are born again by Baptism, then our sins are forgiven us, and the Holy Ghost is given us, which doth make us also holy, and doth move us to all goodness.'

To this we may add the following parallel passage from one of our Homilies:—

'We must trust only in God's mercy, and that sacrifice which our High Priest and Saviour Jesus the Son of God once offered for us on the Cross, to obtain thereby God's grace and remission, as well of our original sin in Baptism,

* ' Works,' iii. 65.

as of all actual sin committed by us after our Baptism, if we truly repent and turn unfeignedly to him again.' *

But to return to Cranmer:—' Baptism is not water alone, and nothing else besides, but is the water of God, and hath his strength by the word of God, and is a seal of God's promise. Wherefore, it doth work in us all those things whereunto God hath ordained it. For our Lord Jesus Christ saith, "Go and teach all nations, and baptize them in the name of the Father, and the Son, and the Holy Ghost." This God commanded his disciples to do. Wherefore, by the virtue of this commandment, which came from heaven, even from the bosom of God, Baptism doth work in us as the work of God. For when we be baptized in the name of God, that is as much [as] to say, as God himself should baptize us. Wherefore we ought not to have an eye only to the water, but to God rather, which did ordain the Baptism of water, and commanded it to be done in his name. For he is almighty, and able to work in us by Baptism forgiveness of our sins, and all those wonderful effects and operations for the which he hath ordained the same, although man's reason is not able to conceive the same.' Therefore, consider, good children, the great treasures and benefits whereof God maketh us partakers when we are baptized, which be these. The first is, that in Baptism our sins be forgiven us, as Saint Peter witnesseth, saying, "Let every one of you be baptized for the forgiveness of his sins." The second is, that the Holy Ghost is given us, the which doth spread abroad the love of God in our hearts, whereby we may keep God's commandments according to this saying of Saint Peter, " Let every one of you be baptized in the name of Christ, and then you shall receive the gift of the Holy Ghost."

'The third is, that by Baptism the whole righteousness of Christ is given unto us that we may claim the same as our own. For so Saint Paul teacheth, saying, "As many of ye as are baptized in Christ have put upon you Christ."

'By this which I have hitherto spoken, I trust you under-

* Second part of the 'Sermon of Salvation.' See also the first 'Homily of the Passion.'

stand, good children, wherefore Baptism is called the bath of regeneration, and how in Baptism we be born again, and be made new creatures in Christ.

'But peradventure some will say, how can water work such great things? To whom I answer, that it is not the water that doeth these things, but the almighty word of God (which is knit and joined to the water) and faith which receiveth God's word and promise. For without the word of God, water is water, and not Baptism. But when the word of the living God is added and joined to the water, then it is the bath of regeneration, and Baptism water, and the lively spring of eternal salvation, and a bath that washeth our souls by the Holy Ghost, as Saint Paul calleth it, saying, "God has saved us through his mercy, by the bath of regeneration and renewing of the Holy Ghost, whom he hath poured upon us plenteously by Jesus Christ our Saviour, that we being made righteous by his grace may be heirs of everlasting life." This is a sure and true word.

'And when you shall be asked, "What availeth Baptism?" you shall answer, Baptism worketh forgiveness of sin, it delivereth from the kingdom of the devil and from death, and giveth life and everlasting salvation to all them that believe these words of Christ, and promise of God, which are written in the last chapter of Saint Mark, his Gospel: "He that will believe and be baptized shall be saved, but he that will not believe shall be damned." *

We all know that Bishop Ridley was recommended to the notice of Cranmer by certain High Church qualifications, which would in these days have had, with some parties, a very contrary effect; 'his well known acquaintance with the Scriptures and the Fathers.' † In his great and learned work against Transubstantiation we find him arguing thus : ' Now on the other side, if, after the truth shall be truly tried out, it be found that the substance of bread is the material substance of the Sacrament, although for the change of the use, office, and dignity of the bread, the bread indeed, sacramen-

* 'Tracts of the Anglican Fathers,' pp. 8, 9, 11, 12, 30.
† Soame's Reformation, iii. 28.

tally is changed into the body of Christ, as the water in baptism is sacramentally changed into the fountain of regeneration, and yet, the material substance thereof remaineth all one as before, &c.'* Indeed, all who are but slightly acquainted with the works of our Reformers must be aware that this was their favourite argument against Transubstantiation : ' There is no need to hold the dogma of Transubstantiation in order to believe that Christ is imparted in the Eucharist, because he is equally imparted in baptism, and yet no one contends that the water is transubstantiated.' This great martyr declares : ' As the body is nourished by the bread and wine at Communion, and the soul by grace and spirit with the body of Christ; even so in Baptism, the body is washed with the visible water, and the soul cleansed from all filth by the invisible Holy Ghost, and yet the water ceaseth not to be water, but keepeth the nature of water still. In like sort in the Sacrament of the Lord's Supper, the bread ceaseth not to be bread.' †

' Like as Christ was born in rags,' says Bishop Latimer, ' so the conversion of the whole world is by rags, by things which are most vile in this world. For what is so common as water ? Every foul ditch is full of it: yet we wash out remission of our sins by Baptism, for like as he was found in rags, so we must find him by Baptism. There we begin ; we are washed with water, and then the words are added ; for we are Baptized in the name of the Father, the Son, and the Holy Ghost, whereby the Baptism receiveth its strength. Now this Sacrament of Baptism is a thing of great weight: for it ascertaineth and assureth us that like as the water washeth the body and cleanseth it, so the blood of Christ our Saviour cleanseth and washeth it from all filth and uncleanness of sin.' ‡

' As therefore in Baptism,' says Bradford, ' is given to us the Holy Ghost and pardon of our sins, which yet lie not lurking in the water ; so in the Lord's Supper is given unto

* ' Enchiridion,' vol. i. p. 72.
† Wordsworth's ' Life of Ridley,' iii. p. 238 ; Ridley's ' Life of Ridley,' pp. 684, 669, 620.
‡ Latimer's ' Sermons,' ii. 779.

us the Communion of Christ's body and blood, without transubstantiation, or including the same in the bread. By Baptism the old man is put off, the new man is put on, yea Christ is put on without transubstantiating the water. And even so it is in the Lord's Supper.' *

Dr. Wordsworth gives a similar quotation from Cranmer's answer to Gardyner, one of his latest works: 'I mean that he is present in the ministration and receiving of that Holy Supper according to his own institution and ordinance, like as in Baptism, Christ and the Holy Ghost be not in the water or font, but be given in the ministration, or to them that be duly baptized in the water.' †

And now having vindicated our pious Reformers from the insinuation of Mr. Scott, that they sought the propagation of doctrines which they did not believe, and having shown what High Churchmen they are in this respect, I shall call before my reader a witness whose testimony is valuable to the facts —that baptismal regeneration is the doctrine of the Church of England, that it is the doctrine of our Reformers, that the doctrine is Scriptural, and that it is burdensome to some— but not to those who believe with the Church of England that the Scriptures teach that regeneration is the inward grace of baptism :—

'In the baptismal service, we thank God for having regenerated the baptized infant by his Holy Spirit. Now from hence it appears that in the opinion of our Reformers, regeneration and remission of sins did accompany baptism. But in what sense did they hold this sentiment? Did they maintain that there was no need for the seed then sown in the heart of the baptized person to grow up and to bring forth fruit; or that he could be saved in any other way than by a progressive renovation of his soul after the Divine image? Had they asserted any such doctrine as that, it would have been impossible for any enlightened person to concur with

* Bradford's 'Sermon on the Lord's Supper,' quoted in Wordsworth's 'Life of Latimer,' iii. 236.

† 'Cranmer's Answer to Gardyner,' p. 172. In the 'Tracts of the Anglican Fathers' quotations to the same effect are given from Bishop Hooper, p. 15.

them. But nothing can be conceived more repugnant to their sentiments than such an idea as this; so far from harbouring such a thought, they have, and that too in this very prayer, taught us to look to God for that total change both of heart and life which long since their days has begun to be expressed by the term regeneration. After thanking God for regenerating the infant by his Holy Spirit, we are taught to pray ' that he being dead unto sin and living unto righteousness may crucify the old man, and utterly abolish the whole body of sin, and then declaring the total change to be the necessary mean of his obtaining salvation, we add, " so that finally with the residue of the holy Church he may be an inheritor of thine everlasting kingdom." Is there (I would ask) any person that can require more than this ? or does God in his word require more? There are two things to be noticed in reference to this subject, the term regeneration, and the thing. The term occurs but twice in the Scriptures; in one place it refers to Baptism, and is distinguished from the renewing of the Holy Ghost; which, however, is represented as attendant on it; and in the other place it has a totally distinct meaning unconnected with the subject. Now the term they use as the Scripture uses it, and the thing they require as strongly as any person can require it. They do not give us any reason to imagine that an adult person can be saved without experiencing all that modern divines [ultra-Protestant divines] have included in the term regeneration ; on the contrary, they do both there and in the Liturgy insist upon a radical change of both heart and life. Here, then, the only question is not, " Whether a baptized person can be saved by that ordinance without sanctification," but whether God does always accompany the sign with the thing signified? Here is certainly room for difference of opinion; but it cannot be positively decided in the negative; because we cannot know or even judge respecting it in any case whatever except by the fruits that follow: and therefore in all fairness it may be considered only as a doubtful point ; and if he appeal, as he ought to do, to the holy Scriptures, they certainly do, in a very remarkable way, accord with the expressions in our

Liturgy. St. Paul says: "By one Spirit we are all baptized into one Body, whether we be Jews or Gentiles, whether we be bond or free; and have been all made to drink into one Spirit." And this he says of all the visible members of Christ's Body.* Again, speaking of the whole nation of Israel, infants as well as adults, he says: "They were all baptized unto Moses in the cloud and in the sea; and did all eat the same spiritual meat; and did all drink the same spiritual drink; for they drank of that spiritual Rock that followed them; and that Rock was Christ."† Yet, behold, in the very next verse he tells us that, "with many of them God was displeased, and over‐ threw them in the wilderness." In another place he speaks yet more strongly still: "as many of you," says he, "as are baptized into Christ, have put on Christ." Here we see what is meant by the expression "baptized into Christ": it is pre‐ cisely the same expression as that before mentioned, of the Israelites being "baptized unto Moses": the preposition εἰς is used in both places; it includes all that had been initiated into his religion by the rite of baptism; and of them univer‐ sally does the Apostle say: "they have put on Christ." Now I ask, have not the persons who scruple the use of that prayer in the baptismal service equal reason to scruple the use of these different expressions?

'Again—St. Peter says: "Repent and be Baptized every one of you for the remission of sins."‡ And in another place, "Baptism doth now save us."§ And speaking elsewhere of Baptized persons who were unfruitful in the knowledge of our Lord Jesus Christ, he says: "He hath forgotten that he was purged from his old sins."‖ Does not this very strongly counte‐ nance the idea which our Reformers entertained: That the remission of our sins, and the regeneration of our souls, is attendant on the Baptismal rite? Perhaps it will be said that the inspired writers spake of persons who had been Baptized at an adult age. But if they did so in some places, they cer‐ tainly did not in others; and where they did not, they must be understood as comprehending all, whether infants or

* I. Cor. xii. 13–27. † I. Cor. x. 1–4.
‡ Acts ii. 38, 39. § I. St. Pet. iii. 21. ‖ II. St. Pet. i. 9.

adults; and therefore the language of our Liturgy, which is not a whit stronger than theirs, may be both subscribed and used without any just occasion of offence.

'Let me, then, speak the truth before God: though I am no Arminian, I do think the refinements of Calvin have done great harm in the Church; they have driven multitudes from the plain and popular way of speaking used by the inspired writers, and have made them unreasonably and unscripturally squeamish in their modes of expression; and I conceive that the less addicted any person is to systematic accuracy, the more he will accord with the inspired writers, and the more he will approve the views of our Reformers. I do not mean, however, to say that a slight alteration in two or three instances would not be an improvement, since it would take off a burthen from many minds, and supersede the necessity of laboured explanations: but I do mean to say that there is no such objection to these expressions as to deter any conscientious person from giving his unfeigned assent and consent to the Liturgy altogether, or from using the particular expressions which we have been endeavouring to explain.' *

Whether Mr. Simeon may have written differently in other parts of his voluminous works, I am not sufficiently acquainted with those works to be able to say, but I venture to quote this as one of the most lucid expositions and one of the most Scriptural vindications of the doctrine of regeneration as held by our English Reformers, and for holding which so much abuse is heaped upon those who are designated High Churchmen, that has fallen under my notice. Mr. Simeon shows that our services do unequivocally assert that regeneration takes place at Baptism, that they are Scriptural in doing so, and that those absurd consequences which some persons would suppose to be connected with the doctrine do not of necessity follow. He tells us that some persons find this, the unquestionable doctrine of the Church, such a 'burthen' that they require some 'slight alteration in one or two places': and that in default of these alterations they are obliged to have recourse to 'laboured explanations.' Against

* Simeon's 'Works,' vol. ii. p. 259.

these persons I wish to say nothing—if they can conscientiously remain in the Church I rejoice to consider them as brethren. But they generally assume an exclusive respect for Scripture; yet, according to Mr. Simeon's showing, the expressions of Scripture, for he proves the expressions of our Baptismal Service and those of Scripture to be identical, are a burthen to them. In this instance, then, we, who want no alteration, are more Scriptural than they are. If they can conscientiously adopt their 'laboured explanations,' they are perfectly welcome. But what those persons have a right to complain of, who receive the expressions of the Liturgy in their plain and simple sense, who labour after no 'explanations,' complain of no 'burthen,' would resolutely resist any 'alteration,' is this, that an attempt is made to make it appear that they are the persons innovating in the Church; that they are opposed to the Reformers; that they are unscriptural. Mr. Simeon perceived how the quarrel commenced. By those attached to the foreign school of Reformation, regeneration is used in a sense different from that which prevails among those who are attached to the principles of the English Reformation. He would propose that we should yield to the advocates of the foreign Reformation, or ultra-Protestants. To such a proposition we shall never assent, for our phraseology is that of the Church Universal, the other that merely of a sect or party comparatively small. The distinction between regeneration and renovation is clearly preserved by those divines who are attached to the English Reformation, as may be seen from the following quotations from Bishop Bethell's work on Regeneration—a work which has long been regarded as a standard on this subject. Following and referring to Waterland, he remarks:—

'Regeneration is the joint work of water and the Spirit, or to speak more properly, of the Spirit only; renovation is the joint work of the Spirit and the man. Regeneration comes only once in or through Baptism. Renovation exists before, in, and after Baptism, and may be often repeated. Regeneration, being a single act, can have no parts, and is incapable of increase. Renovation is in its very nature progressive. Regeneration, though suspended as to its effects and benefits, cannot be totally lost in the present life. Renovation may be often repeated and totally lost.'

Afterwards he illustrates this doctrine by applying it to four separate cases:—

' 1. Grown persons coming to Baptism properly qualified receive at once the grace of Regeneration; but however well prepared, they are not regenerate with Baptism. Afterwards renovation grows more and more within them by the indwelling of the Spirit.

' 2. As to infants, their innocence and incapacity are to them instead of repentance, which they do not want, and of actual faith, which they cannot have: and they are capable of being born again, and adopted by God, because they bring no obstacle. They stipulate, and the Holy Spirit translates them out of a state of nature into a state of grace, favour, and acceptance. In their case, regeneration precedes, and renovation follows after, and they are the temple of the Spirit, till they defile themselves with sin.

' 3 As to those who fall off after regeneration, their covenant state abides, but without any saving effect, because without present renovation: but this saving effect may be repaired and recovered by repentance.

' 4. With respect to those who receive Baptism in a state of hypocrisy or impenitency, though this sacrament can only incr ease their condemnation, still pardon and grace are conditionally made over to them, and the saving virtue of regenerati on, which had been hitherto suspended, takes effect when th ey truly repent and unfeignedly believe the Gospel.

' This clear statement of the learned author contains an accurate representation of the grace conferred, and the change which takes place in Baptism; and this is what is meant by those Divines who maintain that regeneration is, in the strict sense of the word, the inward and spiritual grace of Bapti sm. The identity, if I may so express myself, of Baptism and Regeneration, is a doctrine which manifestly pervades th e writings of the Fathers. It is moreover evident that they did not imagine that Baptism produces any saving effect in adults without faith and repentance, or, in other words, without some previous renewal of the inward frame. Nor do they appear to have supposed any positive or active renewal of the soul takes place in infants. Hence it follows that they must have maintained this distinction between regeneration and renovation, or conversion, which, in the present day, has been styled, by a strange fatality, a novel contrivance. Sufficient proofs, however, of a positive kind may be collected from their own writing, that they maintained this distinction.'*

II.—In producing the opinions of our Reformers on the Sacrament of Baptism, I have accidentally brought forward their opinions on the Eucharist, and shown that as private controversialists they held in both instances the doctrines which as Reformers they propagated. The Commons in 1549 broke out into a dangerous rebellion, and to their articles of complaint Cranmer wrote the answer. To the seventh article he makes reply (showing that his notion of superstition and idolatry was somewhat different from that which now prevails in certain quarters): 'O superstition and idolatry! how they prevail among you! The very true heavenly bread, the food of everlasting life, offered to you in the Sacrament of the Holy Communion, you refuse to eat, but only at Easter! and the cup of the most holy blood, wherewith you were redeemed and washed from your sins, you refuse utterly to drink of at any other time. And yet instead of these you will eat often of the unsavoury and poisoned bread of the Bishop of Rome, and drink of his stinking puddles, which he nameth holy bread and holy water.'†

The language of Cranmer, it is admitted, is not always so strong as that of Ridley, but still it would be considered by many in these days as savouring of Popery, in their undefined use of that expression. In 1548 he published his translation of Justus Jonas's Catechism, with some alterations and corrections by himself. To the statements therein made he professed to the very last to adhere, and repudiated the

* Bishop Bethell, 'On Regeneration,' pp. 14, 16.
† Cranmer's 'Works,' ii. 26.

idea of his having deviated from the doctrine therein propounded.*

To Bishop Ridley Archbishop Cranmer was indebted for the alteration which took place in his opinions with respect to the doctrine of transubstantiation; the learned Ridley having discovered from the writings of Bertram that it was no primitive doctrine. The opinions of Ridley are therefore worthy of consideration. Of Ridley his biographer states: 'He always believed and maintained a real presence by grace to faith, and not a mere figure only: and although there were some English fanatics, such as John Webb, George Roper, and Gregory Paske, who believed that the Sacrament was only a bare sign of Christ's body, and nothing more than a remembrance of it; yet this was not the opinion of our martyrs.'†

What was the opinion of the martyr, Ridley, may be stated in his own words: 'This remembraunce thus ordeined, as the author thereof is Christ both God and man; so by the almighty power of God, farre passeth all kind of remembraunces that any other man is able to make, either of himself or of any other thing, for whosoever receiveth this holye Sacrament thus ordeyned in remembraunce of Christ, he receiveth therewith either death or lyfe. In this I doo trust we all agree. For Sainte Paule saieth of the godlie recevers in the tenth chapter of his first epistle to the Corinthians: The cuppe of blessing which we blesse, is it not the partaking or fellowship of Christes bloud? And also he saieth: The bread which we breake (and meaneth at the Lord's table), is it not the partaking or fellowshippe of Christes bodie? Now the partaking of Christes bodie and of his bloude unto the faithfull and godlie, is the partaking or fellowship of life and of immortalite.‡

'The controversie no doubt whiche at thys day troubleth the Churche (wherein anye meane learned man eitheir olde or

---

* Cranmer's 'Works,' ii. 440; iii. 13, 207, 344. See 'Tracts of Anglican Fathers,' pp. 38, 40, 43, 44.
† Wordsworth's 'Eccles. Biog.,' iii. p. 417; Ridley, iii. 147.
‡ 'Enchiridion,' p. 69.

newe doth stand in), is not whether the holie Sacrament of the bodye and bloud of Christ is no better than a piece of common breade or not? Or whether the Lord's table is no more to bee regarded than the table of any earthlye man or noe? Or whether it is but a bare signe or figure of Christ and nothing elles or noe? For all do graunt that St. Paules words do require, that the breade which we breake, is the partaking of the body of Christ. And all also doe graunt him that eateth of that breade or drinketh of that cuppe unworthilie, to be giltie of the Lordes death, and to eat and drinke his owne damnation, because he esteemeth not the Lordes bodie. All doe graunt that these words of St. Paule when he saieth (if we eate it avantageth us nothing, or if we eate not, we want nothing therebye) are not spoken of the Lordes table, but of other common meates.' *

Most clearly and unequivocally does he declare the truth as it is still held in the Church of England, at his last trial:

'My Lord, you know that where any equivocation (which is a word having two significations) is, except distinction be given, no direct answer can be made: for it is one of Aristotles fallacies containing two questions under one, the which cannot be satisfied with one answere. For both you and I agree herein, that in the Sacrament is the very true and naturall bodie and bloud of Christ, even that which was borne of the Virgine Mary, which ascended into heaven, which sitteth on the right hand of God the Father, which shall come from thence to judge the quicke and the deade, only we differ *in modo* in the way and manner of being; we confess all one thing to be in the Sacrament, and dissent in the manner of being there, I, being fully by God's word thereto perswaded, confess Christ's naturall bodie to be in the Sacrament indeede by spirit and grace, because that whotsoever receiveth worthilie that bread and wine, receiveth effectuously Christ's body and drinketh his bloud, that is, he is made effectually partaker of his passion: and you make a grosser kinde of being, enclosing a naturall, a lively, and a mooving bodie under the shape or forme of bread and wine.

* 'Enchiridion,' p. 71.

'Now this difference considered, to the question thus I answere; that in the Sacrament of the Aultar is the naturall bodie and bloude of Christ *verè et realiter*, indeed and really, if you take these tearmes in deede and really for spiritually by grace and efficacie; for so everie worthie recever receveth the verie true bodie of Christ; but if you meane really and indeed, so that thereby you would include a lively and a moveable bodie under the formes of bread and wine, then in that sense is not Christ's body in the Sacrament really and indeed.'*

Such, too, are the opinions held by those divines who have always upheld the doctrines of the English Reformation, under the conviction that they are, happily, those of the Catholic Church. ' I wish that men would more give themselves to meditate in silence what we have by the Sacrament [of the Holy Eucharist] and less to dispute of the manner how.... "This is my body," and "this is my blood," being words of promise which we all agree that by the Sacrament Christ doth really and truly in us perform his promise, why do we vainly trouble ourselves with so fierce contentions, whether by consubstantiation, or else by transubstantiation, the Sacrament itself be first possessed with Christ or no? A thing which no way can either further or hinder us howsoever it stand, because our participation of Christ in this sacrament dependeth on the co-operation of his omnipotent power, which maketh it his body and blood to us, whether with change or without alteration of the element such as they imagine, we need not greatly to care or inquire.' †

I may also here make a citation from Nowell's Catechism to show how the subject was understood by him, who, when the Reformation was completed, took what was then regarded as a very moderate, if not a low view of the subject :—

'*Master*.—It is very true that thou sayest, Now tell me the order of the Lord's supper :—

'*Scholar*.—It is even the same which the Lord Christ did institute, who, in the same night that he was betrayed,

---

* Wordsworth's Biog., iii. 237 ('Life of Bp. Latimer').

† Hooker's 'Eccl. Pol.,' book v. chap. lxvii. 3, 6; see also Bishop Cosin's 'History of Transubstantiation,' in 'Tracts for the Times.'

took bread, &c. This is the form and order of the Lord's Supper, which we ought to hold, and holily to keep, till he come.

'*Mast.*—For what use?

'*Scho.*—To celebrate and retain continually a thankful remembrance of the Lord's death, and of that most singular benefit which we have received thereby; and that as in baptism we were once born again, so with the Lord's Supper we be always fed and sustained to spiritual and everlasting life.

'*Mast.*—Thou sayest, then, that it is enough to be once baptized, as to be once born: but thou affirmest that the Lord's Supper, like as food, must be often used.

'*Scho.*—Yea, forsooth, master.

'*Mast.*—Dost thou say that there are two parts in this Sacrament also, as in Baptism?

'*Scho.*—Yea, the one part the bread and wine, the outward signs, which are seen with our eyes, handled with our hands, and felt with our taste; the other part Christ himself, with whom our souls, as with their proper food, are inwardly nourished.

'*Mast.*—And dost thou say that all ought alike to receive both parts of the Sacrament?

'*Scho.*—Yea, verily, master, for sith the Lord hath expressly so commanded, it were a most high offence in any part to abridge his commandment.

'*Mast.*—Why would the Lord have here two signs to be used?

'*Scho.*—First, he severally gave the signs both of his body and blood, that it might be the more plain express image of his death, which he suffered, his body being torn, his side pierced, and all his blood shed, and that the memory thereof so printed in our hearts should strike the deeper. And moreover, that the Lord might so provide for and help our weakness, and thereby manifestly declare, that as the bread for nourishment of our bodies, so his body hath most singular force and efficacy, spiritually to feed our souls; and as with wine men's hearts are cheered, and their strength confirmed, so with his blood our souls are relieved and refreshed; that certainly assuring ourselves that he is not only our meat, but also our drink, we do not any where else but in him alone seek any part of our spiritual nourishment and eternal life.

'*Mast.*—Is there, then, not an only figure, but the truth itself of the benefits that thou hast rehearsed, delivered in the Supper?

'*Scho.*—What else? For sith Christ is the truth itself, it is no doubt but that the thing which he testifieth in words, and representeth in signs, he performeth also in deed, and delivereth it unto us; and that he as surely maketh them that believe in him partakers of his body and blood, as they surely know that they have received the bread and wine with their mouth and stomach.' *

I may add in conclusion, that in one of our highest and holiest offices, the Communion Service of our Church, as administered to the Sovereign at the coronation, prayer is made that God would bless the bread and wine, through which the oblation is made, that by them, when thus blessed, we may be made partakers of the Body and Blood of Christ. The rubric and prayer are as follows:—

'THE QUEEN OFFERS BREAD AND WINE.

'And first the Queen offers Bread and Wine for the Communion, which being brought out of King Edward's Chapel, and delivered into her hands, the Bread upon the Paten by the Bishop that read the Epistle, and the Wine in the Chalice by the Bishop that read the Gospel, are by the Archbishop received from the Queen and reverently placed upon the altar, and decently covered with a fair linen Cloth, the Archbishop first saying this prayer:

'Bless, O Lord, we beseech thee, these thy Gifts, and sanctify them unto this holy use, that by them we may be

* Nowell's Catechism.

made partakers of the Body and Blood of thine only begotten Son Jesus Christ, and fed unto everlasting life of Soul and Body: And that thy Servant Queen Victoria may be enabled to the discharge of her weighty Office, whereunto of thy great goodness thou hast called and appointed her. Grant this, O Lord, for Jesus Christ's sake, our only Mediator and Advocate. Amen.'

That this may be wrong and Popish in the opinion of some persons is true; but then we have to bear the charge in common with the Archbishop of Canterbury and all the Bishops who took part in the service.

NOTE XII., p. 85.

The words of Cranmer are very important, and we refer our readers to his sermon on the 'Apostolic Succession and the Power of the Keys.'

To this we may add the following from Bishop Jewell:—
'Therefore, the ancient Father Irenæus giveth us this good counsel: "Eis qui sunt in ecclesia presbyteris, obaudire oportet, qui successionem ab habent apostolis, qui cum episcopatus successione, charisma veritatis certum, secundum beneplacitum Patris acceperunt": it becometh us to obey those Priests in the Church which have their succession from the Apostles, and together with the succession of their bishoprics according to the good will of God the Father have received the undoubted gift of the truth.'* Mr. Vogan, from whose able and argumentative visitation sermon I have taken this quotation, observes that ' though Bishop Jewell in his Defence sometimes appears to make little of the succession,.this was only in comparison with right faith, and under the view of the succession being unaccompanied by right faith.'

One of the falsehoods propagated in these days is, that the Reformers did not hold the divine right of episcopacy, but that this doctrine was subsequently introduced. That our Reformers were very generally of opinion, that where episco-

* 'Defence of Apology,' pt. ii. ch. 5.

pacy could not be had, ordination by Presbyters might, as a temporary measure, be tolerated—just as grace will be given to those who desire to receive the Sacraments, but from circumstances are unable to do so—is not to be denied: and I am not aware that any Churchman of the present day would disagree with them in the opinion, although, among the Protestants abroad, there is not now the same excuse for their want of episcopacy as there was in the time of the Reformation. But the episcopal succession was assumed as a necessary doctrine of the Reformed Church of England on the very first public occasion when our Reformers appeared in defence of the Reformation, after the accession of Elizabeth. At the authorised conference between the friends of the Reformation and the advocates of Romanism, to which allusion has before been made, Dean Horn, in the name of the Reformers, observes: 'The Apostles' authority is derived upon after ages, and conveyed to the Bishops, their successors.' Hence he contends for their apostolical authority to reform their Churches, without reference to the See of Rome, the Bishop of that See being only the equal of other Bishops.* The Puritans did not at first declare themselves hostile to episcopacy; but as soon as they did so, the English Reformers asserted the authority of Bishops as of divine right. Bishop Hutton maintained the doctrine, before Lord Burghley and Sir Francis Walsingham, with precisely the same arguments as those which are now employed.† Dr. Bancroft too, defended the doctrine that Bishops were, *jure divino*, superior to the other Clergy, even though the Puritans attempted to silence him by craftily bringing in political considerations, and by contending that it was inconsistent with the Queen's supremacy.‡ In short, the divine right of episcopacy was asserted before it was questioned, for men did not question at first what for 1,500 years had been undisputed; as soon as ever it was questioned, it was immediately defended on Scriptural grounds by a Bishop, and by the Archbishop's Chaplain.

* Collier, ii. 418.
† See Strype's ' Whitgift,' iii. 224.   ‡ Ibid. i. 559.

NOTE XIII., p. 89.

The use of the metrical Psalms was a concession made to the feelings of ultra-Protestants at an early period. They form no part of our appointed services according to the rubric, but, by one of Queen Elizabeth's injunctions, permission was given to those of the parishioners who chose to assemble before service commenced, or to stay after it was concluded, to sing Psalms. It is curious that we can name the precise period when the singing of a Psalm between the end of the Litany and the commencement of the Communion Service was introduced as an innovation into the parish church of Leeds. Under the date 1708, Thoresby in his Diary says:

'October 3.—Was much interrupted in family course, partly by guests and partly by a most severe cold which has so absolutely taken away my voice that I was perfectly disabled from some duties, as particularly singing, a new order of which was begun this day in the parish church, to sing a stave betwixt the daily Morning and Communion Service (as has been long done in London, &c.), and is more agreeable, making a greater distinction, as there ought to be, betwixt the several parts.' *

The innovation was noted and complained of at an early period.

'At the Reforming of this Church,' says Heylyn, 'not onely the Queen's Chappel, and all Cathedrals, but many Parochial Churches, also had preserved their Organs; to which they used to sing the appointed Hymns; that is to say, the Te Deum, the Benedictus, the Magnificat, the Nunc Dimittis, &c., performed in an Artificial and Melodious manner, with the addition of Cornets, Sackbuts, and the like on Solemn Festivals, for which as they had ground enough from the holy Scripture, if the practice and authority of David be of any credit; so were they warranted thereunto by the godly usage of the primitive times, after the Church was once restored to peace and freedom. Certain I am, that St.

* Thoresby's Diary, ii. p. 10.

Augustine imputes no small part of his conversion to that heavenly melodie which he heard very frequently in the Church of Millaine, professing that it did not only draw tears from him, though against his will, but raised his soul unto a sacred meditation on spiritual matters. But Beza having turned so many of the Psalms into metre, as had been left undone by Marot, gave an example unto Sternhold and Hopkins to attempt the like. Whose version being left unfinished, but brought unto an end by some of our English exiles which remained at Geneva, there was a purpose of imposing them upon the Church by little and little, that they might come as close as might be in all points to their mother city. At first they sung them onely in their private houses, and afterwards (as beforesaid) adventured to sing them also in the Church, as in the way of entertainment, to take up the time till the beginning of the service, and afterwards to sing them as a part of the service itself. For so I understand that passage in the Church Historian in which he tells us that Dr. Gervis being then warden of Merton Colledge, had abolished certain Latine superstitious hymns which had been used on some of the festivals, appointing the Psalms in English to be sung in their place; and that as one Leech was ready to begin the Psalm, another of the fellows called Hall, snatched the book out of his hands and told him that they could no more dance after his pipe. But whatsoever Hall thought of them, Beza and his disciples were perswaded otherwise. And that he might the better cry down that melodious harmony which was retained in the Church of England, and so make way for the Genevian fashion, even in that point also; he tells us in the same letter to Bishop Grindal, That the artificial musick then retained in the Church of England,* was fitter to be used in masks and dancings, than religious offices, and rather served to please the ear than move the affections. Which censure being passed upon it by so great a Rabby, most wonderful it was how suddenly some men of good note and quality, who otherwise deserved well enough of the Church of England, did

* Alluding to chanting and to our Cathedral Service.

bend their wits and pens against it; and with what earnestness they laboured to have their own tunes publickly introduced into all the churches, which, that they might the better do, they procured the Psalms in English metre, to be bound in the same volume with the Publick Liturgie, and sometimes with the Bible also setting them forth, as being allowed (so the title tells us), to be sung in all Churches before and after Morning and Evening Prayer, as also before and after Sermons; but with what truth and honesty, we have heard before.'*

I am not contending for the discontinuance of the metrical Psalms, for I delight in congregational singing, though I regret that, in our parochial churches, they have superseded the antiphonal chanting of the Psalms of the day. We might speak more strongly of the very novel introduction of unauthorized Hymns, which, as the present Bishop of Peterborough remarks, 'if they do not directly impugn our Liturgy and Articles, may inculcate sentiments which are at variance with every fair conclusion which may be drawn from our Liturgy and Articles': on these grounds their use may certainly be deprecated. But I intend not now to condemn the practice, but merely to notice the fact. I feel that I have no right to condemn, but I may notice an innovation, if it be only to show who are the innovators, and to request them, while living in a glass house, not to pelt so piteously, as is frequently done, those of their brethren who, in regulating the services of the sanctuary, are desirous of attending as strictly as possible to the Rubric, although they may reverence the Rubric not the less for its retention of so much of primitive usages.

NOTE XIV., page 89.

TURNING FROM THE PEOPLE IN PRAYER.

Among the things complained of by the Puritans in the Convocation of 1562 this was one. They petitioned 'that in all parish churches the minister in Common Prayer might

* Heylyn's 'Hist. of Presbyterians,' pp. 254, 255.

turn his face towards the people.'* A petition to the same effect had been previously made, and both petitions were refused. What makes this the more remarkable is, that, as will be seen in the next note, the change had been made at the end of Edward the Sixth's reign ; and, in order to please certain foreigners, orders had been given to turn towards the people in prayer. The order was reversed in Elizabeth's reign, and we see from the above quotation that the practice of turning from the people, *i.e.* towards the east, was instituted by the Reformers who completed our Reformation. Of those who petitioned that the minister might be compelled to turn to the people, Strype remarks : ' By the foregoing Articles we may plainly perceive how much biassed those divines (*i.e.* thóse who petitioned that the minister might turn his face towards the people) were (most of whom seem to have been exiles) towards those platforms which were received in the Reformed Churches where they had a little before sojourned,' thus again showing the foreign prejudices of ultra-Protestants. Other passages to the same effect might be produced if it were worth while.†

'Thirdly, and more particularly, " That in his reading of the Prayers and Psalms he (that is the priest) turn his face towards the east, and towards the people in the reading of the lessons or chapters," as appears plainly by the Rubrick which directs him thus, " That after the reading of the Psalms, the Priest shall read two lessons distinctly, that the people may hear ; the Priest that reads the two lessons standing, and turning himself, so as he may be best heard of all such as be present." The Psalms or Hymns to be indifferently said or sung at the will of the Minister ; but the Hymns for the most part sung with organs, and sometimes with other musical instruments ; both in the Royal Chapels and Cathedral Churches.'

As I have said before, the subject as to the Clergyman's position during the prayers is of very little importance. But

* Strype's 'Annals,' i. pt. I. p. 502.

† See, as relating to several points in this sermon, Heylyn's 'Cyprianus Anglicus.' In the preface to this work the customs of the Church of England before the Rebellion are described.—*Cyp. Ang.*, p. 8.

since an outcry of Popery has been raised, because one clergyman in a new church has made his arrangements so as to be able to comply with this regulation of the Church, it is as well to show that in this kind of Popery our pious Reformers were very obstinate, and that in observing this ceremony we should be following not only the Fathers, of whom some persons seem to think that they can have done nothing right, but also the Reformers, whom the same persons regard as if they had been incapable of doing wrong. The action as a significative action might be useful. When men see the officiating minister comfortably supported by his cushions on his elevated pulpit, and from his easy position, to all appearance, reading to them instead of praying to God, many of them will naturally think that if cushions be not at hand on which to kneel, they may make themselves as comfortable as they can without kneeling, attending to the words he reads to them, if he reads well, and forgetting that he is engaged in the awful duty of prayer, if he reads ill.

NOTE XV., page 90.

READING DESK.

In the royal injunctions still in force (injunct. 22, Edw. VI., and 18 of Elizabeth, A.D. 1559) it is enjoined 'that the Litany shall be sung or said in the middle of the Church, before the chancel door, at a low Desk,' commonly called the fald-stool. It is so styled in the Coronation Service.

The use of the reading pew is itself peculiar to the English Church, and was introduced, not by choice, but necessity. In the churches of the primitive Christians, it is true that the ambon, or $\beta\hat{\eta}\mu\alpha\ \gamma\nu\omega\sigma\tau\hat{\omega}\nu$, is described as a reading desk, but it corresponds rather with our pulpit, and is called *pulpitum* by St. Cyprian. The prayers were offered in the chancel; the ambon was used for the reading of the epistles and gospels, and the presbyters preached from it. The bishop generally preached from the steps of the altar. St. Chrysostom appears to have been the first bishop who mounted the pulpit, perhaps owing to the inconvenient situation of the chancel at Constantinople. The singers also used to ascend the ambon when they took their part in the service. The origin of our reading pew, or reading desk, is given in Wheatley, and I shall transcribe his account. The first book of Edward VI. ordered 'the priest, being in the choir, to begin the Lord's Prayer, called Paternoster (with which the morning and evening then began), with a loud voice. So that then it was the custom for the minister to perform divine service (*i.e.* the morning and evening prayer, as well as the communion office) at the upper end of the choir, near the altar; towards which, whether standing or kneeling, he always turned his face in the prayers: though whilst he was reading the lessons he turned to the people. Against this, Bucer, by the direction of Calvin, most grievously declaimed, urging that "it was a most antichristian practice for the priest to say prayers only in the choir, as a place peculiar to the clergy, and not in the body of the church among the people, who had as much right to divine worship as the clergy themselves!" He, therefore, strenuously insisted that "the reading divine service in the chancel was an insufferable abuse, and ought immediately to be amended, if the whole nation would not be guilty of high treason against God." This terrible outcry, however senseless and trifling, prevailed so far that when the Common Prayer Book was altered in the 5th year of King Edward, the following rubric was placed in room of the old one: viz. "the morning and evening prayers shall be used in such places of the church, chapel, or chancel, and the minister shall so turn him as the people may best hear. And if there be any controversy therein the matter shall be referred to the ordinary, and he or his deputy shall appoint the place." This alteration caused great contentions, some kneeling one way and some another, though still keeping in the chancel; while others left the accustomed place, and performed all the services in the body of the Church amongst the people. For the appeasing of this strife and diversity, it was thought fit, when the English service was again brought into the Church, at the accession of Queen Elizabeth to the throne, that the rubric should be corrected, and put into the same form in which we now have it, viz. that "the morning and evening prayers shall be used in the accustomed place of the church, chapel, or chancel"; by which, for the generality, must be meant the choir or chancel, which was the accustomed place before the second Prayer Book of King Edward. For it cannot be supposed that this second book, which lasted only one year and a half, could establish a custom. However, a dispensing power was left with the ordinary, who might determine it otherwise if he saw just cause. Pursuant to this rubric, the morning and evening service was again, as formerly, read in the chancel or choir. But because in some churches the too great distance of the chancel from the body of the church, occasioned sometimes by the interposition of a belfry, hindered the minister from being heard distinctly by the people, therefore the Bishops, at the solicitations of the inferior clergy, allowed them in several places to supersede their former practice, and to have desks or reading pews in the body of the church, where they might, with more ease to themselves, and greater convenience to the people, perform the daily morning and evening service. Which dispensation, begun first by some few ordinaries, and recommended by them to others, grew by degrees to be more general, till at last it came to be an universal practice; insomuch that the Convocation, in the beginning of King James the First's reign, ordered that in every church there should be a convenient seat made for the minister to read service in.'*

Such is the history of our reading desks. The chancels in the old churches were so inconvenient that the Bishops tolerated the use of a reading pew. But in building new churches, our care surely ought to have been so to build the chancels, that such inconvenience should no longer exist, and that we might return to our proper place. And the fact is, that, in most of the new churches, the clergyman is better heard from the chancel than from the reading desk. Why then give us a second pulpit? why not send us back to the

* Wheatley 'On Common Prayer,' p. 113.

chancel? I believe that the answer will be found to be nothing more than that the Papists, who still retain a portion of our Liturgy, officiate always at the altar, and that consequently we should be accused of symbolizing with Popery—an argument as valid against the use of the Scripture.

Let it not be said that this is a subject of no importance. I have already remarked that, confined in a narrow box, the officiating minister cannot perform his various offices as he ought to do. With his face always turned to the people—most of the people, listlessly lolling in their seats, seem to think he is reading to them. Our Liturgy (including under that designation the morning and evening service) is regarded as one long prayer, to be read by the clergyman, whereas it really consists of a great variety of services. If considered as one long prayer, such as dissenting teachers utter before they deliver their discourses, many faults may be found with our Prayer Book; but when regarded as a divine service of praise as well as of prayer, of exhortation on the part of the minister and of acclamation on the part of the people, it is equally instructive and sublime. That it is, however, in fact, if not in theory, regarded as merely one long prayer, may be inferred from the circumstance, that we are accustomed to speak, not of a clergyman's solemnizing divine service, but of his reading prayers. And, indeed, in the new rival pulpits a clergyman does appear rather to be reading prayers than praying.

NOTE XVI., p. 90.

BOWING AT THE NAME OF JESUS.

The following is our 18th Canon:—

'A Reverence and attention to be used in the church in time of Divine Service.

'In the time of Divine Service, and of every part thereof, all due reverence is to be used; for it is according to the Apostle's rule, Let all things be done decently, and according to order; answerably to which decency and order, we judge these our directions following: No man shall cover his head in the Church or Chapel, in the time of Divine Service, except he have some infirmity; in which case let him wear a night cap or coif. All manner of persons then present shall reverently kneel upon their knees, when the General Confession, Litany and other prayers are read; and shall stand up at the saying of the Belief, according to the rules in that behalf prescribed in the Book of Common Prayer: And likewise when in time of Divine Service the Lord Jesus shall be mentioned, due and lowly reverence shall be done by all persons present as it hath been accustomed; testifying, by these outward ceremonies and gestures, their inward humility, Christian resolution, and due acknowledgement that the Lord Jesus Christ, the true eternal Son of God, is the only Saviour of the world, in whom alone all the mercies, graces, and promises of God to mankind, for this life, and the life to come, are fully and wholly comprised. None, either man, woman, or child, of what calling soever shall be otherwise at such times busied in the Church, than in quiet attendance, to hear, mark, and understand that which is read, preached, or ministered; saying in their due places audibly with the Minister, the Confession, the Lord's Prayer, and the Creed; and making such other answers to the Public prayers, as are appointed in the Book of Common Prayer: neither shall they disturb the Service or Sermon, by walking or talking, or any other way; nor depart out of Church during the time of Service or Sermon, without some urgent or reasonable cause.'

So does the Church of England authoritatively decide, and that her decision is strictly in accordance with that of her Reformers is evident, because the Canon is based on the following Injunction, which our pious Reformers advised Queen Elizabeth to issue in this behalf:—

'Although Almighty God is all times to be honored with all manner of reverence that may be devised; yet of all other times in time of Common Prayer the same is to be most regarded. Therefore it is to be necessarily received that in time of the Litany, and all other Collects and Common Supplications to Almighty God, all manner of people shall devoutly and humbly kneel upon their knees and give ear thereunto, and that whensoever the name of Jesus shall be in any Lesson, Sermon, or otherwise in the Church pronounced, that due reverence be made of all persons, young and old, with lowness of courtesy and uncovering the heads of mankind' (alluding to sermons out of doors at Paul's Cross, &c.) 'as thereunto doth necessarily belong and heretofore hath been accustomed.'*

To kneel in prayer, and to bow at the name of Jesus, is not, therefore, Popish, unless our Martyr-Reformers were Papists.

NOTE XVII., p. 90.

CANDLES ON THE ALTAR.

'And here it is to be noted that such ornaments of the Church and of the Ministers thereof at all times of their ministration shall be retained and be in use, as were in this Church of England, by authority of Parliament, in the second year of the Reign of Edward VI.'†

Upon this Bishop Mant, in a note taken from Bishop Cosins and Wheatley, remarks:—

'As to the "ornaments of the Church," mentioned in this rubrick, it may be observed, that among others then in use, there were "two lights" injoined by the injunctions of King Edward the Sixth, which injunctions were also ratified by the Act of Uniformity that passed soon after the Reformation, to be set upon the Altar, as a significant ceremony to represent the light which Christ's Gospel brought into the world. And this, too, was ordered by the very same injunction which prohibited all other lights and tapers that used to be superstitiously set before images or shrines, &c. And these lights, used time out of mind in the Church, are still continued in most if not all Cathedral and Collegiate Churches and Chapels, so often as divine service is performed by candle light; and

---

* Injunction by Queen Elizabeth, 1559. Bp. Sparrow's Coll., 81.

† Rubric in Common Prayer Book.

ought also, by this rubrick, to be used in all Parish Churches and Chapels at the same times.'

Some Clergymen have due regard for these ancient and decent ornaments of the altar, in the hope that they may lead the people to look with more reverence on the Sacrament of the altar, and excite a spirit of thankfulness for the glorious and heavenly light of which they are emblematical. They may be in error, but they can hardly be charged with Popery, except by those ultra-Protestants who regard the English Reformers, who inserted this rubric, as Papistical, and a true son of the Church of England will gladly bear the charge if it be applied equally to our Martyr-Reformers.

I speak of the Communion Table as an Altar, finding that it is repeatedly so spoken of in the Coronation Office, which, having been sanctioned by the Archbishop of Canterbury and his suffragans, will not be considered Papistical by any true members of the Church of England. It appears from the following passage that our great Reformers did not foresee the revival of Popery by the retention of this word:—

'The Sacrament of the Lord's Supper, they (the Reformers) called the Sacrament of the Altar, as appears plainly by the statute 1, Edward VI., intituled "An Act against such as speak unreverently against the Sacrament of the body and blood of Christ, commonly called the Sacrament of the Altar": for which consult the body of the Act itself; or, secondly, by Bishop Ridley, one of the chief compilers of the Common Prayer Book, who doth not only call it the Sacrament of the Altar, affirming thus, that in the Sacrament of the Altar, is the natural body and blood of Christ, &c., but in his reply to an argument of the Bishop of Lincoln, taken out of St. Cyril, he doth resolve it thus, viz.: "The word Altar in Scripture signifieth as well the altar whereon the Jews were wont to offer their burnt sacrifice as the table of the Lord's Supper; and that St. Cyril meaneth by this word altar, not the Jewish altar, but the table of the Lord, &c. (*Acts and Mon.*, part iii. pp. 492, 497.) Thirdly, by Bishop Latimer, his fellow-martyr, who plainly grants "that the Lord's table may be called an Altar, and that the Doctors called it so in many places, though there be no propitiatory sacrifice but only Christ " (part ii. p. 85). Fourthly, by several affirmations of John Lambert and John Philpot, two learned and religious men, whereof the one suffered death for religion, in the reign of Henry VIII., and the other in the fiery time of Queen Mary. This sacrament being called by both the Sacrament of the Altar, in their several times; for which consult the Acts and Monuments, commonly called the Book of Martyrs.' *

NOTE XVIII., p. 90.

CLERICAL HABILIMENTS.

In the advertisements of Queen Elizabeth we find that our Reformers applied to the civil authority to enforce the regulation of the Church thus : ' In the ministration of the Holy Communion in Cathedral and Collegiate Churches, the principal Minister shall use a Cope with Gospeller and Epistoler agreeably.' †

And thus it is ordained in the 24th Canon :—

' Copes to be worn in Cathedral Churches by those that administer the Communion. In all Cathedral and Collegiate Churches, the Holy Communion shall be administered upon principal feast days, sometimes by the Bishop, if he be present, and sometimes by the Dean, and at sometimes by a Canon or Prebendary, the principal Minister using a decent Cope, being assisted with the Gospeller and Epistoler agreeably, according to the advertisements published Anno 7 Eliz.'

The use of the cope would doubtless now be considered ' flat Popery '—why more so than that of the surplice, it is difficult to say. Both were placed under the same category in the days of our Reformers, and the surplice equally with the cope was declared to be a ' patch of Papistry.' ‡

Our Reformers contended for and insisted on the use of

* ' Cyp. Ang.,' pref.
† Queen Elizabeth's Advertisements. Bp. Sparrow's Coll., p. 124.
‡ Strype's ' Parker,' i. 330.

both—'the cope in the ministration of the Lord's Supper, and the surplice in all other ministrations.'* When these habits fell into disuse I know not, but so late as the year 1681, we find the following entry in Thoresby's Diary, Thoresby being then a Nonconformist:—'Die Dom. In the forenoon went to the Minster (Durham); was somewhat amazed at their ornaments, tapers, rich embroidered copes, vestments &c.'† I need scarcely remark that if in other minsters and cathedrals this canon is transgressed, it was strictly observed at Westminster by the Archbishop of Canterbury, the officiating Bishops, and the Prebendaries, at the coronation. Why they should offend against the canon by not using their copes, on ordinary occasions, it is difficult to say, for it cannot be more popish or superstitious to use them at one time than at another. But my object in alluding to the circumstance is not to advocate the revival of what might offend weaker brethren, but to show that a due attention to the decent and orderly ceremonies of the sanctuary, as it is, certainly, not unscriptural, so it is strictly in accordance with the principles and practice of our Church and her Reformers.

It is, indeed, very evident to the student of ecclesiastical history that there were many ceremonies, of which there was a traditional observance in the Church, though enforced by no rubrical directions, from the period of the Reformation to that of the Rebellion, which, because merely traditional observances, could not be revived at the restoration, the ceremonies of the Church having been suspended for so many years. I do not know that the revival of them was to be desired, but I am only speaking of the fact. For instance, at the Hampton Court Conference, the Bishop of Winton alludes to certain common practices, such as 'kneeling on the ground, and lifting up of our hands, the knocking of our breasts,' which he says are 'ceremonies significant, the first of our humility coming before the mighty God; the second of our confidence and hope; the other of our sorrow and

* Strype's 'Annals,' i. pt. I. p. 320. † Diary, i. 75.

detestation of our sins.' * When young Prince Charles was going to Madrid the decencies of religion were carefully attended to, and the directions given to the chaplains, even at a time when Abbot was Archbishop, who was inclined to Puritanism, were as follows:—' 1. That there be one convenient room appointed for prayer, the said room to be employed, during their abode, to no other use.

'2. That it be decently adorned Chapel-wise, with an Altar, Fonts, Palls, Linen Coverings, Demy-Carpets, Four Surplices, Candlesticks, Tapers, Chalices, Pattens, a fine Towel for the Prince, other Towels for the Household, a Traverse of Waters for the Communion, a Bason and Flaggons, two Copes.

'3. That Prayers be duly kept twice a day. That all reverence be used by every one present, being uncovered, kneeling at due time, standing up at the Creeds and Gospel, bowing at the name of Jesus.

'4. That the Communion be celebrated in due form, with an oblation of every communicant, and admixing water with the wine, the Communion to be as often used as it shall please the Prince to set down: smooth wafers to be used for the Bread.

'5. That in the Sermons there be no polemical preachings to inveigh against them, or to confute them, but only to confirm the doctrine and tenets of the Church of England by all possible arguments either in fundamental or moral points; and especially to apply themselves in moral lessons to preach Christ Jesus crucify'd.

'6. That they give no occasions (or rashly entertain any) of conference or dispute (for fear of dishonour to the Prince, if upon any offence taken he should be required to send away one of them): But if the Lord Ambassador or Mr. Secretary wish them to hear any that desire some information, then they may safely do it.

'7. That they carry the Articles of our Religion in many copies, the Books of Common Prayer in several languages, store of English Service Books, &c.'†

    * 'Phenix,' i. 165.   † Collier, ii. 726.

I merely quote this passage in confirmation of what I have said, that there were many traditional observances received from our Reformers, which, after the restoration, fell into disuse. It is certain that if a young prince were in these days to go into foreign parts, no such directions for divine worship among his household would be given, and perhaps some may think that such splendour is better omitted. There is no doubt but that attention to outward circumstances may often render men mere formalists. And it is lamentable when such is the case. But sometimes, too, it happens that, by the neglect of externals, principles are themselves forgotten. It is not quite certain in these days if a young prince went abroad he would be attended by any chaplain, or be directed to worship God at all. Neither the English Reformers nor the Lutherans (the Protestants strictly so-called) were hostile to the ancient ceremonies, or to the ancient ornaments of the Church. Of the Lutherans it has been remarked that 'all their Churches, and especially their Cathedrals, are not to be distinguished from many in the midst of Rome, on account of their various paintings, exalted crucifixes, and frequent images. All veneration, however, is absolutely forbidden to be paid to them, which they strictly observe, though they own that they look upon them as convenient for notices and remembrances of our Saviour's Passion and of the devotion of his saints; and, in short, use them no otherwise than we do our prints and pictures, in our Bibles and Common Prayer Books.'* It is, indeed, notorious that although the mob at our Reformation, instigated by religious demagogues, did much injury to our churches, the images of the saints were removed from them, not by our English Reformers, but by Cromwell and his partisans. This sort of fanaticism is to be traced entirely to the Calvinists, Anabaptists, and sectaries of that class. 'It is a matter of fact,' saith a late ingenious author, 'that crosses and pictures of our Saviour were left standing when there was no such apparent hazard of their being abused; as appears from the paintings

* Northleigh's 'Topograph. Descript.,' p. 128.

of our windows in many of our Churches. We are not against the historical use but the idolatrous abuse of images.' —*Britons no Converts to Popery*. Even at the present time, in many Lutheran churches, candles are lighted, and a crucifix placed on the altar. Queen Elizabeth retained a silver crucifix on the communion table, in her chapel, until, at the instigation of Sir Francis Knollys, it was broken by Peach, her fool. Against her retention of this ornament several of our Reformers, in my opinion wisely, protested. The use of the crucifix is not of ancient date, and it is very easily abused to the purposes of superstition; I am glad, therefore, that we are well rid of it,—but this was not entirely effected before the great Rebellion. Archbishop Williams was the bitter opponent of Laud, and yet of his chapel we find the following description:—'Besides his altar, most richly furnished, there are to be seen goodly pictures, which cannot but strike the beholders with thoughts of piety and devotion at their entrance; as the picture of the Passion, and likewise of the Holy Apostles, together with a fair crucifix set up in painted glass, in the East window, just over the holy table.'[*] To these facts I simply refer to show that when men in these days declaim against, not the erection of a crucifix, but even the ornament of a cross, as proofs of a spirit hostile to that of our Reformers, and of an inclination to Popery, they speak in utter ignorance of history. All these things may be wrong, and let them so be proved, but against them the authority of our Reformers cannot be quoted--no, nor even that of the Lutheran Reformers.

NOTE XIX., p. 95.

The 53rd Canon runs thus:—

'If any preacher shall, in the pulpit particularly, or namely of purpose, impugn or confute any doctrine delivered by any other preacher in the same Church, or in any Church near adjoining, before he hath acquainted the Bishop of the

[*] Pocklington's 'Altar, Christ.,' p. 83.

Diocese therewith, and received order from him what to do in that case, because upon such public dissenting and contradicting there may grow much offence and disquietness unto the people; the churchwardens or party grieved, shall forthwith signify the same to the said Bishop, and not suffer the said preacher any more to occupy that place which he hath once abused, except he faithfully promise to forbear all such matter of contention in the Church, until the Bishop hath taken further order therein; who shall with all convenient speed so proceed therein, that public satisfaction may be made in the congregation where the offence was given. Provided, that if either of the parties offending do appeal he shall not be suffered to preach *pendente lite*.'

Here I wish to observe that my intention has not been to bring charges against those who may differ from me in opinion, and yet are united with me in a desire to adhere to the principles of the Church. But I have been desirous of pointing out the erroneous position in which we are at present placed by those who would divide us into High Churchmen and Low Churchmen. I have shown that the English Reformers contended for the principles, and resolutely maintained the practices, for defending and maintaining which those who are now styled High Churchmen are assailed as Papists. If they, then, were to assail their opponents as persons hostile to the spirit and principles of the English Reformation, as persons who, with respect to baptism especially, are wont to use a language which they acknowledge to be different from the language of the Prayer Book, however much we might regret the circumstance, it would not be a matter of much surprise to anyone. But it is notorious that such, at the present time, is not the case. Those who are called Low Churchmen are the assailants, and in assailing High Churchmen they are in fact assailing our High Church Reformers, and fighting the battles against them in favour of their old enemies, the Puritans. Surely, then, it is not much to ask, for the sake of peace, that if those who are on the strong side refrain from attacking, those who are, confessedly, so far as the Church and the English Reformers are concerned, on the weak side, should be equally forbearing. There are among them many pious and good men, whose only fault is that they take without examination the premises afforded them in the falsehoods invented by certain newspapers and magazines, and then hastily draw conclusions which would not be false were the premises correct. But with whom are these persons uniting in order to defame the representatives of our very High Church Reformers? Let them look to the cold, worldly theologians, who are seeking to inflame their passions, merely to further the party purposes of worldly policy. I will not name them. But it is notorious that against those whom they are pleased to denominate High Churchmen, are joined in one band the most cold and calculating of our divines, who regard the Church as little more than a state engine, together with others whose truly evangelical views ought to unite them with the very men to whom they are opposed, even though on some points of opinion they may differ. With respect to such combinations we may truly say with an old writer, 'if such public mischiefs be presaged by astrologers from the conjunction of Jupiter and Saturn, though the first of these be a planet of most sweet and gentle influence, what dangers, what calamities may not be feared from these political conjunctions!'

For my part, I hate party names, which often make a distinction between persons where there is no difference. I believe that, in real principle, a more united body of men never existed than the Clergy of England at the present time, and the attempt to make them suppose themselves at variance cannot certainly be of God. But if men will divide us—be it so. And if I am ranked among the High Churchmen, I shall be perfectly contented. I am content to be what the Fathers of the Church Universal were; I am content to be what our pious Reformers were; and if the opprobrious epithets which were applied to them be applied to us, we shall glory in the tribulation, and rejoice to bear the scandal of the cross. Only let it be clearly understood what a High

Churchman, according to the present signification of the term, is; let it be understood that while the Low Churchman is contending for the temporalities of an Establishment, the High Churchman looks to the spiritualities of the Church; that while the Low Churchman is a mere Establishment-man, the High Churchman is prepared to sacrifice all the advantages of an Establishment, rather than compromise an iota of God's truth; that while the Low Churchman defers to Acts of the English Parliament,* the High Churchman defers to the Church in Council; that while the Low Churchman interprets Scripture according to the tradition of men—a tradition which can be traced back only to a Calvin or an Arminius, the High Churchman interprets Scripture according to the tradition which may be traced back to the Apostles themselves, which the Church Universal has regarded as, in its origin, divine, and for adhering to which our Church was called, in the time of our Reformers, the Church of the Traditioners.

NOTE XX., page 212.

'Although the word Catholic properly signifies universal, they (the ancient Fathers) used it in the same sense that we do orthodox as opposed to heretic, calling an orthodox man a Catholic.'* Thus it was said by Pacian: 'Christianus mihi nomen, Catholicus cognomen: by the former I am distinguished from the heathen, by the latter from the heretic.' In confirmation of this, the following passages from Suicer may be adduced: 'καθολικοί, Catholici, si ad ipsa vocis hujus incunabula, et antiquissimum ascendamus usum, vocantur *Christiani orthodoxi*, atque ita.'

But it is here necessary, in order to understand the full meaning of the word, to remember who were considered heretics; and for answer we may refer to the sixth canon of the Council of Constantinople, one of the Councils to which the Church of England directs us to refer in our judgment of

* Bp. Beveridge, ii. 197 (Horne's edit.).

heresy; where it is said: 'We call them heretics who have formerly been abdicated by the Church and afterwards anathematized by us; and further, them who prefer a sound faith, but have made a schism, and gathered congregations in opposition to the canonical bishops.' Thus the Novatians, who were both Trinitarians and Episcopalians, were not considered Catholics, and were regarded as heretics, because they were opposed to their canonical bishops. In short, by a heretic was anciently meant one who dissented from the Catholic and Apostolic Church of the place in which he resided. The term is now considered opprobrious by so many parties (although that of dissenter, which in truth means nearly the same thing, is gloried in), that to use it generally would only be to give unnecessary offence; but the true member of the Church of England will resolutely maintain his claim to the title of Catholic, whether against the Papists, who set up their bishops against those canonical bishops of this country, who alone can prove their mission here, or against other dissenters, who know not, or acknowledge not, the divine right of the Church.

NOTE XXI., vol. ii. page 219.

The sixth canon of the Council of Trent, on what that Council styles the 'most holy sacrament of repentance,' stands thus: 'If any shall deny, that sacramental confession was instituted and is necessary for salvation by divine right, or shall say that the custom of confessing secretly to the priest alone, which the Catholic Church has always observed from the beginning, and continues to observe, is foreign to the institution and command of Christ, and is of human invention; let him be accursed.'

'Here sacramental confession is affirmed to be of divine institution, and auricular confession likewise, and he is accursed who shall deny it. This is bravely said; yet the Fathers might have recollected that in the Latin Church as late as 813 it was matter of dispute whether there was need to confess to a priest at all, as appears from the thirty-third canon of the Council of Caballlon, which is as follows: "Quidam Deo solummodo confiteri debere dicunt peccata, quidam vero sacerdotibus confitenda esse percensent: quod utrumque non sine magno fructu intra sanctam fit Ecclesiam. Ita dumtaxat nt et Deo, qui remissor est peccatorum, confiteamur peccata nostra, et cum David dicamus, Delictum meum cognitum tibi feci, &c. et secundum institutionem Apostoli, confiteamur alterutrum peccata nostra, et oremus pro invicem ut salvemur. Confessio itaque quæ Deo fit, purgat peccata, ea vero quæ sacerdoti fit, docet qualiter ipsa purgentur peccata," &c.— *Conc.*, vii. 1279. Was Leo the Third asleep, that he could suffer such heresy to be broached and not denounced? But all the world knows that, till 1215, no decree of Pope or council can be adduced enjoining the necessary observance of such a custom. Then, at the Council of Lateran, Innocent III. commanded it. As the Latin Church affords no sanction to the assertion of the Tridentine Fathers, so is it in vain to look for it among the Greeks, for there, as Socrates, "Hist. Eccles.," v. 19, and Sozomen, "Hist. Eccles.," vii. 16, inform us, the whole confessional was abolished by Nectarius, the Archbishop of Constantinople, in the fourth century, by reason of an indecency which was committed on a female penitent, when pursuing her penance ; which, surely, he would not have ventured to have done had he deemed it a divine institution. Sozomen, in his account of the confessional, says, that the public confession in the presence of all the people, which formerly obtained, having been found grievous $\phi o \rho \tau \iota \kappa \grave{o} \nu$ $\dot{\omega}s$ $\epsilon \iota \kappa \grave{o}s$, a well-bred, silent, and prudent presbyter was set in charge of it; thus plainly denoting the change from public to auricular confessions.'—*Perceval's 'Romish Schism.'*

To this I would add that, according to Sozomen, this system of private confession was not yet introduced at Rome, when it had been used for some time at Constantinople : for he says that in the West, and Rome especially, the penitents had no other practice than that of mourning in public classes.

NOTE XXII., page 220.

When we speak of tradition or the Fathers being authorities in the interpretation of Scripture, we do not mean to say that any person may, after studying the Fathers, and placing his own private interpretation upon them, assert that the opinion he so forms is a doctrine of the Church of England. We only assert the principles of our Reformation. It is asked why we should defer to our Prayer Book and Formularies? are they infallible? We answer, No; but the probability is that they are right; a probability amounting to a moral certainty on all important points, because of the principle upon which our Reformers acted. The Romanists at the Council of Trent took for their guidance the Christian principle developed, and, as we see from Scripture, corrupted, in the medieval Church. We, on the contrary, took for our guidance at our Reformation the Bible interpreted by the doctrine and practice of the Primitive Church : hence our Prayer Book and our Formularies. The Prayer Book, the Articles, and the Formularies were reformed or compiled by men who adopted this principle; and a private divine, even if he thinks that on some minor points a mistake has been made, ought, in modesty, to presume that he is more likely to have been mistaken, than that many acting on the same principle were in error. In this respect, as in the interpretation of Scripture, he thinks that he is probably the erroneous party, if his private judgment differs from the judgment of many who were at least as able and as learned as himself. A man more versed in Patristics could hardly be found than Archbishop Bramhall, yet he says: 'I submit myself to the representative Church, that is, a free general Council, or so general as can be procured ; and until then, to the Church of England, wherein I was baptized, or to a national English synod: to the determination of all which and each of them respectively, according to the distinct degrees of their authority, I yield a conformity and compliance

or at the least, and to the lowest of them, an acquiescence.'
—*Bramhall's Works*, ii. p. 22.

If there were a divine of that age more learned than Bramhall in what relates to primitive Christianity, it was Bishop Bull, and what says Bishop Bull in the *Examen Censuræ?* 'Whatever I may have written, either in this or other books, most humbly and most willingly do I submit it to the judgment of our holy mother the English Church; her to whom I have hitherto devoted myself in all filial obedience, and to whom, while I live, by God's help, I will devote myself.'—*Examen Censuræ—Anglo-Catholic Library*, p. 5.

On the like principle acted the judicious Hooker:—' We make not our childish appeals, sometimes from our own to foreign Churches, sometimes from both unto Churches ancienter than both are, in effect always from all others to our own selves; but, as becometh them that follow with all humility the ways of peace, we honour, reverence, and obey, in the very next degree unto God, the voice of the Church of God wherein we live. They, whose wits are too glorious to fall to so low an ebb, they which have risen and swoln so high that the walls of ordinary rivers are unable to keep them in, they whose wanton contentions is the cause whereof we have spoken, do make all where they go a sea, even they, at their highest float, are constrained both to see and grant, that what their fancy will not yield to like, their judgment cannot with reason condemn.'—*Hooker*, book v. sec. 71.

The following words of Bishop Stillingfleet may be read with advantage at the present time: 'I cannot see why the authority of some very few persons, though of great learning, should bear sway against the constant opinion of our Church ever since the Reformation; since our Church is not now to be formed according to the singular fancies of some few (though learned men), much less to be modelled by the caprichios of superstitious fanatics, who prefer some odd opinions and ways of their own before the received doctrine and practice of the Church they live in. Such as these, we rather pity their weakness than regard their censures; and are only sorry when our adversaries make such properties of them, as by their means to beget in some a disaffection to our Church. Which I am so far from (whatever malice and peevishness may suggest to the contrary), that, upon the greatest inquiry I can make, I esteem it the best Church of the Christian world; and think my time very well employed (whatever thanks I meet with for it) in defending its cause, and preserving persons in the communion of it.'—*Preface to 'Discourse of Idolatry.' Works*, vol. v.

When we read these passages from the great divines of the Church of England, divines whose Patristics and Patrology would put to shame the most learned of our modern theologians, it excites a just indignation to hear juvenile clerics, who, in conscious ignorance, not very long ago, trembled under the mild scrutiny of a bishop's chaplain, traducing, defaming, and sneering at the Church of England, whose divines are scarcely known to them by name, while they think to show their skill or their liberality by contending that the abominations of Rome are less abominable than Hooker, and Barrow, and Usher, and all English divines, who lived before the present age, supposed them to be.

NOTE XXIII., page 221.

In this note I shall present the reader with copious extracts from some of our great divines. I do so because, while all parties admit their authority, their works are little studied; the Presbyterianizers in our Church consulting the works of nonconformist theologians, and the Romanizing extreme studying Romish writers and works of Romish devotion. The learned Archbishop Usher, the friend of Laud, whose Answer to the Jesuit is itself unanswerable, is the author I shall quote first:—

'The diverse sentences of the doctors touching this question, whether external confession were necessary or not, are at large laid down by Gratian; who in the end leaveth the matter in suspense, and concludeth in this manner: " Upon what authorities, or upon what strength of reasons both these opinions are grounded, I have briefly laid open. But whether of them we should rather cleave to, is reserved to the judgment of the reader. For both of them have for their favourers both wise and religious men." And so the matter rested undetermined 1150 years after Christ; howsoever the Roman correctors of Gratian do tell us, that now the case is altered, and that "it is most certain, and must be held for most certain, that the sacramental confession of mortal sins is necessary, used in that manner, and at such time, as in the Council of Trent after other councils it is appointed." But the first council wherein we find any thing determined touching this necessity, is that of Lateran under Innocent the Third, wherein we heard that transubstantiation was established: for there it was ordained, that " *Omnis utriusque sexus fidelis*, every faithful one of either sex, being come to years of discretion, should by himself alone, once in the year at least, faithfully confess his sins unto his own priest; and endeavour according to his strength to fulfil the penance enjoined unto him, receiving reverently at least at Easter the sacrament of the Eucharist: otherwise, that both being alive he should be kept from entering into the Church, and being dead should want Christian burial." Since which determination Thomas Aquinas, in his exposition of the text of the fourth book of the Sentences, distinct. 17, holdeth the denial of the necessity of confession unto salvation to be heresy; which before that time, saith Bonaventure, in his Disputations upon the same fourth book, was not heretical; forasmuch as many Catholic doctors did hold contrary opinions therein, as appeareth by Gratian.

' But Medina will not admit by any means that it should be accounted " strictly heresy;" but would have it said that "it savours of heresy." And for this decree of confession to be made once in the year, he saith, that it "doth not declare nor interpret any divine right of the thing, but rather appointeth the time of confessing." Durand thinketh that it may be said that this statue containeth " an holy and wholesome exhortation of making confession, and then adjoineth a precept of the receiving of the Eucharist, backed with a penalty;" or if both of them be precepts, that "the penalty respecteth only the precept of communicating of the transgression whereof knowledge may be taken), and not the precept of confession;" of the transgression whereof the Church can take no certain notice, and therefore can appoint no certain penalty for it. But howsoever, this we are sure of, that the canonists afterwards held no absolute necessity of obedience to be required therein, as unto a sacramental institution ordained by Christ for obtaining remission of sins; but a canonical obedience only, as unto an useful constitution of the Church. And therefore, where Gratian in his first distinction *De Pœnitentia* had, in the 34th chapter and the three next following, propounded the allegations which made for them, who held that men might obtain pardon for their sins without any oral confession of them, and then proceeded to the authorities which might seem to make for the contrary opinion; Johannes Semeca,* at the beginning of that part, upon those words of Gratian, *Alii e contrario testantur*, putteth to this gloss: " From this place until the section, *His auctoritatibus*, he allegeth for the other part, that sin is not forgiven unto such as are of years without confession of the mouth; which yet is false," saith he. But this free dealing of his did so displease friar Manrique, who, by command of Pius Quintus, set out a censure upon the glosses of Canon Law, that he gave direction these words, " which yet is false," should be clean blotted out. Which direction of his, notwithstanding, the Roman correctors under Gregory XIII. did not follow; but letting the words still stand, give them a check only with this marginal annotation : " Nay, it is most true, that without confession, in desire at least, the sin is not forgiven."

' In like manner, where the same Semeca holdeth it to be the better opinion, that confession was " ordained by a certain tradition of the universal Church, rather than by the authority of the New or Old Testament," and inferreth there-

---

* Johannes Semeca flourished about the year 1200. He was an honest German, who opposed the exactions of Pope Clement IV.

upon, that it is "necessary among the Latins, but not among the Greeks, because that tradition did not spread to them;" friar Manrique commandeth all that passage to be blotted out; but the Roman correctors clap this note upon the margin for an antidote: "Nay, confession was ordained by our Lord, and by God's law is necessary to all that fall into mortal sin after baptism, as well Greeks as Latins." And for this they quote only the 14th session of the Council of Trent; where that opinion is accursed in us, which was held two or three hundred years ago by the men of their own religion, among whom Michael of Bononia,* who was prior-general of the order of the Carmelites in the days of Pope Urban the Sixth, doth conclude strongly out of their own received grounds, " that confession is not necessary for the obtaining of the pardon of our sin;" and Panormitan, the great canonist, professeth that the opinion of Semeca doth much please him, which referreth the original of confession to a general tradition of the Church; "because," saith he, "there is not any clear authority which sheweth that God or Christ did clearly ordain that confession should be made unto a priest." Yea, " all the canonists, following their first interpreter, say that confession was brought in only by the law of the Church," and not by any divine precept, if we will believe Maldonat; who addeth notwithstanding, that "this opinion is either already sufficiently declared by the Church to be heresy, or that the Church should do well if it did declare it to be heresy."

'And we find indeed that in the year of our Lord 1479, which was thirty-four years after the death of Panormitan, by a special commission directed from Pope Sixtus the Fourth unto Alfonsus Carillus, Archbishop of Toledo,† one Petrus Oxomensis, professor of divinity in the University of Salamanca, was driven to abjure this conclusion, which he had

* Michael of Bononia, in the age of Urban VI., must have flourished about the year 1380.

† Alfonsus Carillus, Archbishop of Toledo, presided there from A.D. 1446 to 1483. His character may be seen in Prescott's 'History of Ferdinand and Isabella.'

before delivered as agreeable to the common opinion of the doctors, "that confession of sins in particular was grounded upon some statute of the universal Church, and not upon divine right." And when learned men for all this would not take warning, but would needs be meddling again with that which the Popish clergy could not endure should be touched (as Johannes de Selva, among others, in the end of his treatise *De Jurejurando*, Erasmus, in divers of his works, and Beatus Rhenanus, in his argument upon Tertullian's book *De Pœnitentia*), the Fathers of Trent, within seventy-two years after that, conspired together to stop all men's mouths with an anathema, that should deny sacramental confession to be of divine institution, or to be necessary unto salvation. And so we are come to an end of that point.'—*Answer to a Jesuit*, p. 95.

Bishop Jeremy Taylor, whose 'Dissuasive from Popery' ought to be deeply studied, will speak next:—

' That confession to a priest is a doctrine taught as necessary in the Church of Rome, is without all question; and yet that it is but the commandment of men, I shall, I hope, clearly enough evince; and if I do, I suppose the charge laid against the Church of Rome, which is the same Christ laid against the Pharisees, will be fully made good, as to this instance; for this is one of the sorts of that crime, to say, " Dixit Dominus, Dominus autem non dixit;" to pretend a rite to be of divine institution when it is not so, but " humanum inventum," " a device of man's brain." The other (which is, still supposing an institution to be human and positive, yet to urge it with the same severe religion, as they do a divine commandment), I shall consider in other instances. For the present the inquiry is concerning auricular confession, and its pretended necessity. The first decree concerning it was in the Lateran Council; in which "every person of years of discretion is commanded to confess all his sins to his own priest, at least once in the year; or to another priest, with the leave of his own; otherwise while he is living, he must be driven from entrance into the Church; and when he is dead he must have no Christian burial." This is very severe; but yet here is no damnation to them that neglect it; and the duty is not pretended to be by divine commandment: and therefore, lest that severity might seem too much to be laid upon human law, they made it up in the new forge at Trent; and there it was decreed that, " To confess all and every mortal sin, which, after diligent inquiry, we remember, and every evil thought or desire, and the circumstances that change the nature of the sin, is necessary for the remission of sins, and of divine institution; and he that denies this, is to be anathema."

'Whether to confess to a priest be an advisable discipline, and a good instance, instrument, and ministry of repentance, and may serve many good ends in the Church, and to the souls of needing persons—is no part of the question. We find that in the Acts of the Apostles divers converted persons came to St. Paul, either publicly or privately, "and confessed their deeds;" and burnt their books of exorcism, that is, did what became severe and hearty penitents, who needed counsel and comfort, and that their repentance should be conducted by wise guides. And when St. James exhorts all Christians " to confess their sins to one another," certainly it is more agreeable to all spiritual ends, that this be done rather to the curate of souls, than to the ordinary brethren. The Church of England is in no way engaged against it, but advises it, and practises it. The Calvinist churches do not practise it much, because they know not well how to divest it from its evil appendages, which are put to it by the customs of the world, and to which it is too much exposed by the interests, weaknesses, and partialities of men. But they commending it, shew they would use it willingly if they could order it unto edification. " Interim quin sistant se pastori oves, quoties sacram cœnam participare volunt, adeò non reclamo, ut maximè velim hoc ubique observari." And for the Lutheran Churches, that it is their practice, we may see it in Chemnitius, who was one of greatest fame amongst them; and he is noted to this purpose by Bellarmine; only they all consent that it is not necessary nor of divine institution; and being but of man's invention, it ought not to pass into a doctrine; and, as the Apostles said in the matter of circumcision, "a burden ought not to be put upon the necks of the disciples:" and that "in lege gratiæ, longè difficillimum," too, as Major observes truly, by far greater than any burden in the law of grace, the time of the Gospel. Let it be commanded to all, to whom it is needful or profitable; but let it be free, as to the conscience precisely, and bound but by the cords of a man, and as other ecclesiastical laws are, which are capable of exceptions, restrictions, cautions, dispensations, rescindings, and abolitions, by the same authority, or upon greater reasons.

'The question then is, whether to confess all our greater sins to a priest, all that upon strict inquiry we can remember, be necessary to salvation? This the Church of Rome now affirms; and this the Church of England and all Protestant Churches deny; and complain sadly that the commandments of men are changed into the doctrines of God, by a Pharisaical empire, and superstition.'*

Archbishop Bramhall, than whom a higher Church of England man, a more enlightened opposer of Popery and a more constant supporter at the same time of the Protestant element in our Church, could not be found, writes as follows:—

'What are those corruptions then, which we have "pared away" from the Romish shrift? First, that they have tricked it up in the robes of a Sacrament, obtruding it upon the world as absolutely necessary to salvation, and that by Divine institution; contrary to their own schools. Gratian concludes it with, "*Lectoris judicio reservatur.*" "It is referred to the judgment of the reader;" and cites Theodore, Archbishop of Canterbury, for his opinion. The Glosser refers the original to an universal tradition; to whose opinion Scotus inclines. Bonaventure saith, that it was "insinuated by Christ, instituted by the Apostles, and promulged by St. James." Panormitane makes the original of it human; with whom side Petrus Oxomensis,† Erasmus, Rhenanus.

---

* 'Dissuasive from Popery.'
† He was also called 'Petrus Oosma.'

And Lyranus,—that in times past it was not so rigidly observed. Secondly, that they have restrained it to a particular and plenary enumeration of all sins. " Who can tell how oft he offendeth; cleanse Thou me, O Lord, from my secret faults." But without this, say they, the priest cannot give true judgment. No? Why? Christ said not, "*what* sins ye remit," but "*whose* sins;" giving this caution to the Presbyters, to attend more to the contrition and capacity of their confitents than to the number and nature of their sins. Thirdly, they make it to be meritorious at the hands of God, and satisfactory for sins, not by way of complacence only, but even in justice. Thus in the doctrinal part.

'In the practice there are corruptions also, which deserve to be "pared away;" though this author cannot see to distinguish between the body and the botches, between the institution and the corruptions. As, that they do first absolve a man from his sins, and then bid him to make satisfaction; contrary to the practice of the ancient Church. Then, that it hath been used as a picklock to open the secrets of states and princes. Most certain it is, that many have, and too many daily do, convert it to their own advantage.' *

I would refer also to the whole of Bishop Bull's Sermon on the Necessity of Works of Righteousness, wherein he not only exposes 'the trade of auricular confession,' but refutes the Romish doctrine of attrition, which is so closely connected with it, proving it to be, in his own words, 'a doctrine so dangerous, so damnable, that it seems itself sufficient to unchristian and unchurch any society of men that shall teach and maintain it.' 'Indeed,' says Bishop Bull, 'there is no society of Christians in the world, where antinomianism and libertinism more reign, than among the Papists, into whose very faith they are interwoven, and men are taught them by the definitions of their Church. It is no wonder so many vicious persons, especially when they come to die, turn Papists, and no visitants are so welcome to them as the Roman confessors. They find them very easy and comfortable doctors for men in their desperate case, and admire their

* Bramhall's Works, Anglo-Catholic Library, vol. v. p. 222.

rare invention, who have found out a shorter way to heaven, and a readier one to escape hell and damnation, than the Scriptures ever discovered, or their former ministers of the Church of England, following the guidance of the Scriptures, durst warrant to them. And what broken plank, yea, what flag or reed will not a drowning man lay hold on? O how pleasant a thing is that which they call the bosom of the Roman Church! how willingly do those forlorn wretches cast themselves into it! where they are promised, and in their deluded imaginations enjoy, that rest and security, which they could not anywhere else, no, not in the word and promises of God, find. But alas! when they thus say Peace, peace, unto themselves, behold, sudden destruction cometh upon them, and within a minute after they are launched out into eternity, a sad and dreadful experience convinceth them what a sorry refuge they fled to.

'It is evident, that the Church of Rome, in teaching this vile doctrine, aims only at her own interest and advantage, and hath no regard at all to the honour of God and the good of souls. It is absolutely necessary, she saith, for a sinner to make an auricular confession to, and be absolved by, a priest, though God hath nowhere said so: but it is not necessary for him to be contrite, or to repent of his sins out of the love of God, though God Himself in His own word hath an hundred times said it is. That is necessary for the honour and gain of the priest. The trade of auricular confession must by any means be kept up, because from thence they reap no small gain; and besides by it they govern, not only the silly common people, but great men, and kings and princes, by becoming masters of their secrets. But is it not the doctrine of true contrition as necessary for the honour of God? Yes: but the promoting of God's glory in the salvation of souls is the least of their design or business. Indeed, it were easy to shew how the whole frame of the religion and doctrine of the Church of Rome, as it is distinguished from that Christianity which we hold in common with them, is evidently designed and contrived to serve the interest and profit of them that rule that Church, by the disservices, yea, and ruin, of those souls that are under their government.' *

Let it be remembered that the authors here quoted are men whom the Presbyterianizers in our Church brand as semi-papists, and their words will perhaps come with greater weight to those who, by a just abhorrence of the Presbyterianizing extreme in the Church of England, are inclined to think with too great partiality of the Romanizers.

The necessity of *confessio oris* (that it is necessary to confess our sins, not only to God, but also to the priest), was asserted by Thomas Aquinas, in Supplementiæ, Part. Quest. 8, Art. 1. Peter Lombard expressed himself more indefinitely on this point; Sent. iv. Dist. 17, Litt. B. The Ecclesiastical Institution of auricular confession was established by the fourth Council of the Lateran, under Pope Innocent III. This is the plain history of the doctrine, which is thus seen to be medieval and Romish, not Scriptural and primitive.

I may add that there are, in the Public Library, at Geneva, several volumes of manuscript written in the Vaudois patois, and illustrating the doctrine of those persecuted people who met with such hard measures from the Papal party in the thirteenth and fourteenth century. The following extract is taken from the volume numbered in the Library 208, p. 78; and is remarkable as furnishing a testimony to the opposition which the decree of the Fourth Lateran Council encountered at the period of its promulgation. The MS. is apparently of the early part of the fourteenth century; and it was copied by a friend who took some pains to decipher it:—

'DE LA PENANZA.

'De la qual Penanza nos tenem por fe e confessem purament de cor, qu'ella es besognuol a lome cagi por sfaczar lo pecca.

'A la qual se dev continuament amonestar, e amonestem, qu li pecca

'OF PENANCE.

'Concerning which Penance we hold for faith, and confess with sincerity of heart, that it is necessary for every man thus to put away his sin.

'On which, men ought continually to be admonished, and we do

* Bull's Works, Oxford Edition, vol. i. p. 12.

se confessen segond la forma de la primtiva gleisa, e requerir consells en las besognas a preyres prudent e savi de si. La forma e obligacion introducta novellament d'Ynocent terz, la qual solon husar comunament li preyr simoniach, se dev squivar e fugir d'li fidel: mas li remedis profectivole a dever conselliar a li pentent, como son lo dejun, l'oracio, l'almona, e las autras obras de satisfacion, nos confessem ess util e profectivole.

admonish, that their sins should be confessed according to the form of the primitive Church, and that they should require counsels in cases of need from priests of prudent character and known to them. The form and ordinance lately introduced by Innocent III., which the simoniacal priests commonly use, ought to be shunned and avoided by the faithful: but the remedies which may be profitably recommended to penitents, such as fasting, prayer, alms-deeds, and other works of satisfaction, we confess to be useful and profitable.

'La Confessio auricular facta tout solament al preyre . . . e la forma e husanza d'l'absolucio, e la . . . d'la penanza en numbre en pes e en mesura, segond la volunta del confessor, costa lo modo husa d'li preyre simoniach, e l'obligacion d'Ynocent terz, no es . . . de substancia, ne de . . . a la vera penanza.'

'Auricular Confession made all alone to the priest . . . and the form and usage of absolution, and the [injunction] of penance in number, in weight, and in measure, according to the will of the confessor, as is the mode used by the simoniacal priests, and the ordinance of Innocent III., is not of . . . the substance, nor of [the nature] of true penance.'

Here it may be remarked that the writer speaks of the obligation of every Christian to Auricular Confession as an ordinance of Pope Innocent III., not a decree of the council assembled by him. Which agrees with the account of this council given by Matthew Paris, who says that the several canons were read before the council by the Pope's authority, that some of the Churchmen then present were satisfied with them, others thought them burdensome; but he mentions no voting of the council on the question.

Note XXIV., p. 221.

Quotations from St. Chrysostom may be seen in my Sermon on the Visitation of the Sick, in which this subject is alluded to. Other quotations may be seen in Bingham, who bserves: 'Chrysostom is not the only person that maintains this assertion. St. Basil says the same thing before him : " I do not make confession with my lips, to appear to the world; but inwardly in my heart, where no eye sees; I declare my groanings unto Thee alone, Who seest in secret, I roar within myself: for I need not many words to make confession : the groanings of my heart are sufficient for confession, and the lamentations which are sent up to Thee, my God, from the bottom of my soul." In like manner, St. Hilary makes confession necessary to be made to God, only ; for, commenting on the fifty-second Psalm, he tells us David teaches us that confession is necessary to be made to none but God, Who hath made the olive fruitful with the hope of mercy for ever and ever. And St. Ambrose as plainly says, that tears poured out before God are sufficient to obtain pardon of sin, without confession made to man. His words are, " Tears wash away sin, which men are ashamed to confess with their voice. Weeping provides at once both for pardon and bashfulness : tears speak out faults without horror; tears confess our crimes without any offence to modesty or shamefacedness." So again, speaking of St. Peter's tears, he says, " I find not what Peter said, but I find that he wept ; I read of his tears, but I read not of his satisfaction ;" meaning that verbal confession was not simply necessary to obtain pardon. And in this sense, St. Austin, expounding those words of the Psalmist, " I said I will pronounce or declare my own wickedness against myself unto the Lord, and so Thou forgavest the iniquity of my heart," says, he had not yet pronounced it, but only promised that he would pronounce it, and yet God forgave him. He had not yet pronounced it, but only in his heart; his confession was not yet come to his mouth, yet God heard the voice of his heart : his voice was yet in his mouth, but the ear of God was in his heart ; which implies, that God accepts and pardons the penitent and contrite heart, even before any formal declaration is made by vocal confession either to God or man. In another place, he speaks of confession as no ways necessary to be made to man. What have I to do with men, that they should hear my confessions, as though they could heal all my diseases? He also frequently tells us, with all the rest of the ancient writers, that a great many of those which the Romanists now call mortal sins, were daily pardoned upon no other confession but the fervent and devout use of the Lord's prayer, " Forgive us our trespasses, as we forgive them that trespass against us." Which evidently shews, that he did not believe auricular confession is necessary for expiating all manner of mortal sins. Maximus Taurinensis delivers his opinion almost in the same words as St. Ambrose does: " Tears wash away sin, which the voice is ashamed to confess. Therefore tears provide at once both for men's modesty and salvation ; they neither make men blush in their petitions, nor disappoint them of pardon in asking." He adds, " That tears are a sort of silent prayers ; they ask not pardon in words, and yet deserve it (that is, in his style, procure it), they declare not the cause, and yet obtain mercy. Nay, the prayers of tears are many times of more advantage than those of words ; because words often prove deceitful in prayer, but tears never deceive. For words sometimes declare but half the business ; but tears always express the whole affection." Prosper, who was St. Austin's scholar, follows his doctrine: for speaking of private sins committed by the clergy, he says, " They shall more easily appease God, who being not convicted by human judgment, do of their own accord acknowledge their offence ; who either do discover it by their own confessions, or else, others not knowing what they are in secret, do voluntarily inflict the censure of excommunication upon themselves ; and being separated (not in mind, but in office)·from the altar, to which they did minister, do lament their life as dead ; assuring themselves, that God being reconciled unto them by the fruits of effectual repentance, they shall not only receive what they have lost, but also being made citizens of that city which is above, they shall come to everlasting joys." Cassian also assures us, that this was the doctrine of the Egyptian fathers. For he says, Pinuphius, the Egyptian abbot, gave this advice to the monks that were under him : " Who is it that cannot humbly say,

I made my sin known unto Thee, and mine iniquity have I not hid? that by this confession he may confidently adjoin that which follows: And so Thou forgavest the impiety of my heart. But if shamefacedness so draw thee back, that thou blushest to reveal them before men; cease not by continual supplication to confess them unto Him from whom they cannot be hid, and to say, I know my iniquity, and my sin is against me alway: to Thee only have I sinned, and done evil before Thee, whose custom is both to cure without publishing our shame, and to pardon sins without accusing or upbraiding." These are plain testimonies, evidently shewing, that the ancients did not believe the necessity of auricular confession, or urge it as a thing absolutely necessary to absolution and salvation."*

After making some other observations, Bingham sums up the points of difference between the Primitive Church and the modern Church of Rome, on this question as they are arranged in a treatise of Daillé's, under no fewer than thirty heads. 1. He argues from the practice of all other Churches in the world beside the Roman. The doctrine of the necessity of Auricular Confession is taught by no other denomination of Christians, not the Ethiopians nor the Indians of St. Thomas, nor the Babylonians or Chaldeans, nor the Armenians, nor the Jacobites, nor the Greeks, in the manner of the Romans. 2. He shows, that whereas the priests in the Roman Church are nicely instructed in the business of Auricular Confession, and teach and minister it daily to the people, as the noblest act of their office; there is nothing of all this to be found in the genuine writings of the ancient Christians. 3. Whereas Auricular Confession is continually mentioned by the Roman writers among the religious acts of all sorts of men, clergy, monks, laity, princes, private men, noblemen, plebeians, men, women, &c., there is nothing of this among the ancient Christians. 4. In the ancient Church, Christians were bound by no law, as now they are in the Roman, to confess their sins to a priest, before they came to the Lord's table to receive the Eucharist;

* Bingham, book xviii. chap. iii. sec. 2.

which he demonstrates by eight reasons, and the testimony of Chrysostom, Pelagius, Austin, Dorotheus, the Council of Chalon and Hincmar. 5. In the Roman Church it is usual for everyone to make his Auricular Confession at the point of death; of which there are no footsteps among the ancients. 6. The Romish writers are very full of Auricular Confession in describing any of the sicknesses, or calamities, or wars, or shipwrecks, or journeys, or other hazardous undertakings of their people: but there was no such practice among the ancients. 7. The ancients in describing the persecutions of the Church, or the conflicts and trials and last agonies of their confessors and martyrs, never mention Auricular Confession, which yet abounds everywhere in the Romish writers, when they make any such relations of the lives or deaths of their martyrs. 8. The ancients had no solemn times appointed for Auricular Confession, as Easter, Christmas, Lent, the greater festivals and the Friday and Saturday fasts, which are now everywhere spoken of in the Romish writers, as solemn times of confession. 9. The ancients say nothing of miracles done in or by confession, which the Romanists continually boasted of. 10. The ancient Pagans never objected to the Auricular Confession of the primitive Christians, as the modern Pagans do to those of the Roman communion. 11. The ancient Church knew nothing of heretics opposing Auricular Confession, because, there was no such thing enjoined; but since it was appointed by the Council of Lateran, anno 1215, many have been condemned as heretics for opposing it. 12. The primitive bishops often declare that they were ignorant of the sins of their people; particularly this is said by Chrysostom, Austin, Innocent and Leo, Bishops of Rome: which is an argument, that they were not revealed to them by sacramental confession. 13. The first man that instituted any private confession was St. Anthony, who appointed his monks to write down their thoughts, and communicate them one to another: but this was nothing to sacerdotal confession; for these monks were only laymen. 14. The ancient writers have none of these intricate questions and disputations about Auricular Confession, which so much stuff the books of the modern casuists in the Church of Rome. 15. The Fathers never interpret those passages of Scripture, which the Romanists produce for Auricular Confession, in their sense, but most of them to a contrary meaning, 16. The Fathers, in those books which they wrote professedly of repentance, never urge Auricular Confession as a necessary part of repentance. 17. The Fathers acknowledge only three sorts of repentance : the ante-baptismal, for all manner of sins; the quotidian or daily repentance, for lesser sins of incursion ; and the public penance of lapsers, falling into more heinous sins; but Auricular Confession appertains to none of these. 18. Gregory Nyssen says expressly, there were some sins, such as covetousness, which the Fathers before him endeavoured to cure, not by any canonical punishments, but only by the public exhortations of the word and doctrine: which will not consist with the doctrine of Auricular Confession. 19. Nectarius wholly abrogated the office of the penitentiary priest; which argues that there was no necessity of Auricular Confession. . . . 20. His next argument is drawn from those passages of Chrysostom Hilary, Basil, Ambrose, Maximus, Taurinensis, and St. Austin, . . . asserting, that remission of sins may be obtained of God by contrition only, without any oral confession. 21. The Fathers allow salvation to be attainable even by those relapsers who fell again into sin after their first public penance, though they had no liberty either to make confession or receive absolution. His 22nd, 23rd, and 24th arguments are drawn from the testimonies of Cassian, and Julianus Pomerius or Prosper, and Laurentius Navariensis. 25. To these he adds two considerable testimonies of Bede. 26. And the concessions of Erasmus, Beatus Rhenanus, and Rigaltius, who freely own that the Romish Auricular Confession was not in use in the Primitive Church. He shows that there was a change made of the ancient discipline in the ninth age, when private penance enjoined by the priest began to be pretty frequent and common. 28. And yet this differed vastly in many particulars from the confession established afterwards in the Council of Lateran. For still it was believed that confession made to God was sufficient to salvation. 29. In the following ages also Goffridus Vindócinensis, Peter Lombard, and Gratian say there were many who still held, that confession to God alone was sufficient without confessing to the priest. And Gratian particularly, having cited the authorities on both sides of the question, leaves it to the judgment of the reader to take which he pleases: because each opinion had wise and religious men to authorize and defend it. Which argues, that in Gratian's time, the question about the necessity of Auricular Confession was not so determined as it was afterwards in the Council of Lateran, and the Council of Trent. This is also acknowledged by Aquinas, Bonaventure, and Antonine, who say, that in the time of Gratian and Lombard the question about the necessity of such confession was only problematical, and what might safely be disputed both ways, and that it was no heresy to deny it; but after the determination of the Church made under Innocent III. in the Lateran council, it was to be reputed heresy for any man to assert, that it was sufficient to confess a man's sins to God, without making confession to a priest also. 30. Thus the doctrine of Auricular Confession was established in the thirteenth century, and not before; and even after that there wanted not witnesses, such as Wickliff and Huss, and Semeca, and Michael of Bononia, and Petrus Oxoniensis, to bear testimony against its novelty, to the time of the Reformation. This is the short account of those thirty arguments, which the learned Mr. Daillé uses to show the novelty of the Romish doctrine concerning Auricular Confession, which the curious reader, who desires to see them more fully deduced and confirmed, may consult in our author's elaborate work, for his farther satisfaction. *

NOTE XXV., p. 221.

The word Protestant is antagonistic to the word Popish. It was a crafty device to make it stand opposed to the word Catholic. The following observations are from the *Quarterly*

* Bingham, book xviii. chap. iii. sec. 4.

Review, vol. lxix., and have been generally attributed to Mr. Sewell :—

'Though the Bible has been abused by the licentiousness of private interpretation, they never omitted the opportunity of magnifying it, in its true interpretation, as " the only infallible rule of faith ; " as " containing all the principles of faith and points of salvation," as needing no associate, no addition of any authority as equally infallible, nor more perspicuous than itself to supply what it wants." Though the service of the Church was threatened to be stripped of all decency and order, they speak soberly and cautiously of ceremonies. Though Episcopacy was made a badge of Antichrist, they do not reduce all religion to a matter of Church discipline. Though the doctrine of faith had been perverted to the wildest excesses, there is no mention in them of justification by works, or of works at all, without immediate and solemn reference to the faith which alone can sanctify them. These points, and many others of their doctrinal teaching, might be advantageously examined. For much of this caution and comprehensiveness of view they were undoubtedly indebted to the proximity of Popery, and to their thorough acquaintance with its nature, and dread of its poison. Yet apparently they had more to fear from Puritanism than from Popery; and if we in this day might be reluctant to retain the name of Protestant, from the fear of being confounded with sectarians, much more might they. And yet, Catholic as they were both in language and in spirit, they use it boldly and prominently. As the believing Jews, when other Jews refused to believe, were compelled to distinguish themselves as Christians; and as the Christian Church, when heretics also called themselves Christians, was compelled to add the name of Catholic, so Catholic Christians, when one great branch of the Church, retaining the same title, is spreading the grossest errors, must distinguish themselves as Protestants. They are Protestant, as the " Latin or West Church " (so Field has proved), " wherein the Pope tyrannised before Luther's time, was and continued a true Protestant Church, condemning those profane and superstitious abuses which we have removed; and groaning under that tyranny, the yoke whereof we have now cast off." They are Protestants, as the Church Catholic itself is Protestant against the sins and follies of heathenism; as every Christian in every age and every country is appointed by God himself to be a witness and protester against evil. If, indeed, the acts we rebuke are no sins, then to protest is a crime. If they are sins, yet sins of the past, now buried and forgotten, to rake them up unnecessarily may well be condemned. If we judge them by our own private judgment, we intrude on the rights of our superiors, and so we sin. And if they be distant and weak, and no danger exists of infection, we may well spare ourselves and others the pain of declaring against them. But whether the deeds of Popery be sins or not—whether they be dead and buried, or alive and in full vigour—whether our Church has spoken on them, and we are bound to speak with her voice—whether in the silence and debility of the Church Catholic she was not bound to speak, when no other voice could speak so strongly—and whether there is not danger from Popery now in the very heart of the country; danger, which calls on us all to rouse the weak and the strong together to vigilance against their greatest enemy—unhappily need not be asked. We are not, and dare not be, Protestants, in the sense which some few may wrongly affix to the word, as discarding all guides to truth but our own self-will: in this sense Protestantism is worse than folly: it may be worse than Popery: but as remonstrating and warning all around us against the eruptions of Popery, we cannot cease to be Protestants, without ceasing to do our duty as Christians. It is our glory and our happiness to be Christians—our safeguard and consolation to be Catholics—our sad and melancholy duty, a duty which we never can abandon till Rome has ceased to work among us, to be Protestants.

' " My Lords," said Laud, " I am innocent in this business of religion, as free from all practice, or so much as thought of practice, for any alteration to Popery, or any way blemishing the true Protestant religion established in the Church of England, as I was when my mother first bare me into the world."

'"If I had blemished the true Protestant religion"— "the number of those persons whom, by God's blessing upon my labours, I have settled in the true Protestant religion established in the Church of England"—"I pray God, His truth (the true Protestant religion here established) sink not" —"God of His mercy preserve the true Protestant religion amongst us."

'This was the common language of Laud, the martyr of the Puritans.

'So Bramhall, while rightly denying that "Protestancy is of the essence of the Church," any more than the weeding of a garden is the essence of a garden, does not scruple throughout the whole of the same treatise to use the word as the right denomination of men, whom he describes in the same place as "endeavouring to conform themselves in all things to the pattern of the Primitive Church," as "ready to shed their blood for the least particle of saving truth."

'So Hammond, speaking of those who preached resistance to the lawful magistrate :—

'" Such as these, if they must be called Protestants, are yet in this somewhat more than that title ever imported, I may say, perfect Jesuits in their principles." " This doctrine [of non-resistance] purely Protestant,"—the contrary of which, "by God's providence, hath formerly been timeously restrained, and not broken out to the defaming of our Protestant profession."

'So Nicholson:—

"The laws are now silent, and any man may be now anything, so he be not an old Protestant of the Church of England."

'So Sanderson is not afraid to say :—

"When we have wrangled ourselves as long as our wits and strength will serve us, the honest, downright, sober English Protestant will be found in the end the man in the safest way, and by the surest line."

'Nor is he ashamed to avow his "zeal for the safety and honour of my dear mother, the Church of England, which hath nourished me up to become a Christian and a Protestant (that is to say, a *pure pute* Christian, without any addition or epithet)."

' " Protestants," says Laud, " did not get that name by protesting against the Church of Rome, but by protesting (and that when nothing else would serve) against her errors and superstitions. Do you but remove them from the Church of Rome, and our protestation is ended, and the separation too. Nor is protestation itself such an unheard-of thing in the very heart of religion. For the sacraments, both of the Old and New Testament, are called by your own school ' visible signs protesting the faith.' Now, if the sacraments be *protestantia*, signs protesting, why may not men also, and without all offence, be called Protestants, since by receiving the true sacraments, and by refusing them which are corrupted, they do but protest the sincerity of their faith against that doctrinal corruption which hath invaded the great sacrament of the Eucharist and other parts of religion? especially since they are ' men which must protest their faith by visible signs and sacraments.' "

' " They are the Protestants," says Stillingfleet, " who stand for the ancient and undefiled doctrine of the Catholic Church against the novel and corrupt tenets of the Roman Church. And such kind of protestation no true Christian, who measures his being Catholic by better grounds than communion with the Church of Rome, will ever have cause to be ashamed of."

' So Hickes, though fully alive to the "wicked, absurd, and unchristian doctrines, which atheistical, heretical, and other seducing teachers taught in his day, under the name of Protestants," does not therefore repudiate the name, but declares that " the Protestant religion of the Church of England is but another name for primitive Christianity, and a Protestant for a primitive Christian, who protests against all the corruptions of the Gospel Popery."

' We may not indeed distinguish ourselves solely as Protestants, or without express declarations of Catholic principles, especially where the name is likely to confound us with sects, and doctrines, which a Catholic Christian repudiates. The word has been used too carelessly, and a false meaning popularly given to it, which must be condemned and corrected. But as yet, while no other badge exists to mark to the world, and especially to the poor and the weak, the duty of guarding against Popery, instead of dallying with its temptations, and palliating its corruptions, we cannot prescribe it. It is a sign—a little sign, but one most looked to—by which a large number of Christian minds within the Church, in a time of natural alarm and jealousy, test our attachment to the Church, and our repudiation of errors which they have been taught—and taught most rigidly—to regard with dread. For their sakes we are bound to be sparing of our own liberty and tender of their consciences. If a French army is closely besieging a town in which we live, we have no right to dress ourselves up as French soldiers and walk about the streets, or to refuse to give our English pass-word, though by this refusal we may alarm none but women and children. We have no right to alarm anyone. He who really desires the restoration of Christian unity will desire, most of all, to recall to the fold of the Church her own sheep. If he dreads to offend Papists by the word Popery, he will dread to offend Puritans by rejecting the word Protestant. If he fears that it will confound him with dissenters, he must fear alike lest the word Catholic should confound him with Popery—unless, indeed, he be wholly insensible to the evils of Popery, while keenly alive to the evils of Puritanism— unless the presence of Church government in the one is to cloak over all errors of doctrine, while the neglect of it in the other is to blot out all truth of doctrine—unless Popery in his sight be only holy, and Puritanism only sinful—unless he close his eyes to all the wickedness which the one has essentially produced, and to all the goodness with which the other has been accompanied—such as earnestness, energy, personal piety, study of the Scripture, prayer, self-denial, charity, zeal for what it believes to be truth, jealousy of all that seems to trench on the supremacy of God, or to substitute the creature for the Creator.'

NOTE XXVI., page 222.

'Be it therefore known unto him (the Jesuit) that no kind of Confession, either public or private, is disallowed by us, that is any way requisite for the due execution of that ancient power of the keys which Christ bestowed upon his Church. The thing which we reject is that new picklock of sacramental confession, obtruded upon men's consciences, as a matter necessary to salvation, by the canons of the late conventicle of Trent, where those good Fathers put their curse upon everyone that either shall "deny that sacramental confession was ordained by divine right, and is by the same right necessary to salvation;" or shall "affirm that in the sacrament of penance it is not by the ordinance of God necessary, for the obtaining of the remission of sins, to confess all and every one of those mortal sins, the memory whereof by due and diligent premeditation may be had, even such as are hidden, and be against the two last commandments of the decalogue, together with the circumstances which change the kind of the sin; but that this confession is only profitable to instruct and comfort the penitent, and was anciently observed only for the imposing of canonical satisfaction." This doctrine, I say, we cannot but reject, as being repugnant to that which we have learned both from the Scriptures and from the Fathers.

'For in the Scriptures we find, that the confession which the penitent sinner maketh to God alone, hath the promise of forgiveness annexed unto it, which no priest upon earth hath power to make void upon pretence that himself or some of his fellows were not first particularly acquainted with the business: "I acknowledged my sin unto Thee, and mine iniquity have I not hid; I said, I will confess my transgressions unto the Lord; and Thou forgavest the iniquity of my sin." And lest we should think that this was some peculiar privilege vouchsafed to the man who was raised up on high, the anointed of the God of Jacob, the same sweet psalmist of

Israel doth presently enlarge his note, and inferreth this general conclusion thereupon: "For this shall every one that is godly pray unto Thee in a time when Thou mayest be found." King Solomon, in his prayer for the people at the dedication of the temple, treadeth just in his father's step. "If they turn," saith he, "and pray unto Thee in the land of their captivity, saying, We have sinned, we have done amiss, and have dealt wickedly; if they return to Thee with all their heart, and with all their soul, &c., forgive Thy people which have sinned against Thee all their transgressions wherein they have transgressed against Thee." And the poor publican, putting up his supplication in the temple accordingly, "God be merciful to me a sinner," went back to his house justified, without making confession to any other ghostly father, but only the Father of spirits; of whom St. John giveth us this assurance, that "if we confess our sins, He is faithful and just to forgive us our sins, and to cleanse us from all unrighteousness." Which promise, that it appertained to such as did confess their sins unto God, the ancient Fathers were so well assured of, that they cast in a manner all upon this confession, and left little or nothing to that which was made unto man. Nay, they do not only leave it free for men to confess or not confess their sins unto others, which is the most that we could have; but some of them all seem, in words at least, to advise men not to do it at all, which is more than we seek for.

'St. Chrysostom, of all others, is most copious in this argument, some of whose passages to this purpose I will here lay down: "It is not necessary," saith he, "that thou shouldst confess in the presence of witnesses: let the enquiry of thy offences be made in thy thought; let this judgment be without a witness; let God only see thee confessing." "Therefore I intreat and beseech and pray you, that you would continually make your confession to God. For I do not bring thee into the theatre of thy fellow-servants, neither do I constrain thee to dicover thy sins unto men: unclasp thy conscience before God, and shew thy wounds unto Him, and of Him ask a medicine. Shew them to Him that will not reproach, but heal thee. For although thou hold thy peace, He knoweth all." " Let us not call ourselves sinners only, but let us recount our sins, and repeat every one of them in special. I do not say unto thee, Bring thyself upon the stage, nor, Accuse thyself unto others; but I counsel thee to obey the prophet, saying, Reveal thy way unto the Lord. Confess them before God, confess thy sins before the Judge, praying, if not with thy tongue, yet at least with thy memory; and so look to obtain mercy." " But thou art ashamed to say that thou hast sinned. Confess thy faults then daily in thy prayer. For do I say, Confess them to thy fellow-servant, who may reproach thee therewith? Confess them to God, who healeth them. For, although thou confess them not at all, God is not ignorant of them." " Wherefore then, tell me, art thou ashamed and blushest to confess thy sins? For dost thou discover them to a man, that he may reproach thee? Dost thou confess them to thy fellow-servant, that he may bring thee upon the stage? To Him who is thy Lord, who hath care of thee, who is kind, who is thy Physician, thou shewest thy wound." " I constrain thee not, saith God to go into the midst of the theatre, and to make many witnesses of the matter. Confess thy sins to Me alone in private, that I may heal thy sore, and free thee from grief." " And this is not only wonderful, that He forgiveth us our sins, but that He neither discovereth them, nor maketh them open and manifest, nor constraineth us to come forth in public and disclose our misdemeanours; but commandeth us to give an account thereof unto Him alone, and unto Him to make confession of them."

'Neither doth St. Chrysostom here walk alone. That saying of St. Augustine is to the same effect: "What have I to do with men, that they should hear my confessions, as though they should heal all my disease?" And that collection of St. Hilary upon the two last verses of the 52nd Psalm that David there teacheth us "to confess to no other," but unto the Lord, "who hath made the olive fruitful with the mercy of hope (or, the hope of mercy) for ever and ever." And that advice of Pinuphius, the Egyptian abbot, which I find also inserted among the canons, collected for the use of the Church of England in the time of the Saxons, under the title, " De Pœnitentia soli Deo confitenda ": " Who is it that cannot humbly say I made my sin known unto Thee, and mine iniquity have I not hid, that by this confession he may confidently adjoin that which followeth : And Thou forgavest the impiety of my heart? But if shamefacedness do so draw thee back that thou blushest to reveal them before men, cease not by continual supplication to confess them unto Him from whom they cannot be hid, and to say, I know mine iniquity and my sin is against me alway; to Thee only have I sinned, and done evil before Thee, whose custom is, both to cure without the publishing of any shame, and to forgive sins without upbraiding." St. Augustine, Cassiodore, and Gregory made a further observation upon that of the 32nd Psalm: " I said, I will confess my transgressions unto the Lord; and Thou forgavest the iniquity of my sin"; that God, upon the only promise and purpose of making this confession, did forgive the sin. " Mark," saith Gregory, " how great the swiftness is of this vital indulgence, how great the commendation is of God's mercy, that pardon should accompany the very desire of him that is about to confess, before that repentance do come to afflict him; and remission should come to the heart, before that confession did break forth by the voice." So St. Basil, upon those other words of the Psalmist, " I have roared by reason of the disquietness of my heart " (Psalm xxxviii. 8), maketh this paraphrase : " I do not confess with my lips, that I may manifest myself unto many ; but inwardly in my very heart, shutting mine eyes, to Thee alone, who seest the things that are in secret, do I shew my groans, roaring within myself. For the groans of my heart sufficed for a confession, and the lamentations sent to Thee my God from the depth of my soul."

'And as St. Basil maketh the groans of the heart to be a sufficient confession, so doth St. Ambrose the tears of the penitent. " Tears," saith he, " do wash the sin, which the voice is ashamed to confess. Weeping doth provide both for pardon and for shamefacedness: tears do speak our fault without horror; tears do confess our crime without offence of our shamefacedness." From whence he that glosseth upon

Gratian, who hath inserted these words of St. Ambrose into his collection of the Decrees, doth infer, that "if for shame a man will not confess, tears alone do blot out his sin." Maximus Taurinensis followeth St. Ambrose herein, almost verbatim. "The tear," saith he, "washeth the sin which the voice is ashamed to confess. Tears therefore do equally provide both for our shamefacedness and for our health: they neither blush in asking, and they obtain in requesting." Lastly, Prosper, speaking of sins committed by such as are in the ministry, writeth thus: "They shall more easily appease God, who being not convicted by human judgment, do of their own accord acknowledge their offence; who either do discover it by their own confessions, or, others not knowing what they are in secret, do themselves give sentence of voluntary excommunication upon themselves; and being separated (not in mind but in office) from the altar to which they did minister, do lament their life as dead, assuring themselves that God being reconciled unto them by the fruits of effectual repentance, they shall not only receive what they have lost, but also, being made citizens of that city which is above, they shall come to everlasting joys." By this it appeareth, that the ancient Fathers did not think that the remission of sins was so tied unto external confession that a man might not look for salvation from God, if he concealed his faults from man; but that inward contrition, and confession made to God alone, were sufficient in this case. Otherwise, neither they nor we do debar men from opening their grievances unto the physicians of their souls, either for their better information in the true state of their disease, or for the quieting of their troubled consciences, or for receiving further direction from them out of God's word, both for the recovery of their present sickness, and for the prevention of the like danger in time to come.

' "If I shall sin, although it be in any small offence, and my thought do consume me, and accuse me, saying, Why hast thou sinned? what shall I do?" said a brother once to abbot Arsenius. The old man answered, "Whatsoever hour a man shall fall into a fault, and shall say from his heart,

'Lord God, I have sinned, grant me pardon,' that consumption of thought or heaviness shall cease forthwith." And it was as good a remedy as could be prescribed for a green wound, to take it in hand presently, to present it to the view of our heavenly Physician, to prevent Satan by taking his office, as it were, out of his hand and accusing ourselves first, that we may be justified. But when it is not taken in time, but suffered to fester and rankle, the cure will not now prove to be so easy; it being found true by often experience, that the wounded conscience will still pinch grievously, notwithstanding the confession made unto God in secret. At such a time as this then where the sinner can find no ease at home, what should he do but use the best means he can to find it abroad? "Is there no balm in Gilead? is there no physician there?" No doubt but God hath provided both the one and the other for recovering of the health of the daughter of His people; and St. James hath herein given us this direction: "Confess your faults to one another, and pray one for another, that ye may be healed. According to which prescription, Gregory Nyssen, towards the end of his sermon of repentance, useth this exhortation to the sinner: "Be sensible of the disease wherewith thou art taken, afflict thyself as much as thou canst. Seek also the mourning of thy entirely affected brethren to help thee unto liberty. Shew me thy bitter and abundant tears, that I may also mingle mine therewith. Take likewise the priest for a partner of thine affliction, as thy Father. For who is it that so falsely obtaineth the name of a father, or hath so adamantine a soul, that he will not condole with his son's lamenting? Shew unto him without blushing the things that were kept close; discover the secrets of thy soul, as shewing thy hidden disease unto thy physician. He will have care both of thy credit and of thy cure."

'It was no part of his meaning to advise us that we should open ourselves in this manner unto every hedge-priest; as if there were a virtue generally annexed to the order, that upon confession made, and absolution received from any of that rank, all should be straight made up; but he would have us communicate our case both to such Christian brethren, and to such a ghostly father, as had skill in physic of this kind, and out of a fellow-feeling of our grief would apply themselves to our recovery. Therefore, saith Origen, " look about thee diligently unto whom thou oughtest to confess thy sin. Try first the physician, unto whom thou oughtest to declare the cause of thy malady, who knoweth to be weak with him that is weak, to weep with him that weepeth, who understandeth the discipline of condoling and compassionating; that so at length, if he shall say anything, who hath first shewed himself to be both a skilful physician and a merciful, or if he shall give any counsel, thou mayest do and follow it." For, as St. Basil well noteth, " the very same course is to be held in the confession of sins, which is in the opening of the diseases of the body. As men therefore do not discover the diseases of their body to all, nor to every sort of people, but to those that are skilful in the cure thereof; even so ought the confession of our sins to be made unto such as are able to cure them, according to that which is written, " Ye that are strong bear the infirmities of the weak," that is, take them away by your diligence. He requireth care and diligence in performance of the cure : being ignorant, good man, of that new compendious method of healing, invented by our Roman Paracelsians, whereby a man " in confession of attrite is made contrite by virtue of the keys ; " that the sinner need put his ghostly father to no further trouble than this, " Speak the word only, and I shall be healed." And this is that sacramental confession devised of late by the priests of Rome ; which they notwithstanding would fain father upon St. Peter, from whom the Church of Rome, as they would have us believe, received this instruction : " that if envy, or infidelity, or any other evil did secretly creep into any man's heart, he who had care of his own soul should not be ashamed to confess those things unto him who had the oversight over him; that by God's word and wholesome counsel he might be cured by him." And so indeed we read in the apocryphal Epistle of Clement, pretended to be written to St. James, the brother of our Lord; where in the several editions of Crab, Sichardus, Venradius,

Surius, Nicholinus, and Binius, we find this note also laid down in the margin: *Nota de confessione sacramentali,* " Mark this of sacramental confession." But their own Maldonat would have taught them that this note was not worth the marking: forasmuch as the proper end of sacramental confession is the obtaining of remission of sins by virtue of the keys of the Church; whereas the end of the confession here said to be commended by St. Peter, was the obtaining of counsel out of God's word for the remedy of sins. Which kind of medicinal confession we well approve of, and acknowledge to have been ordinarily prescribed by the ancient Fathers for the cure of secret sins.' *

Archbishop Usher is supposed by some to have been a Presbyterianizer, but this is hardly consistent with his being a friend of Archbishop Laud.

In vol. xv. of his works, published by Dr. Elrington, there is a letter (cxc.) to the Most Rev. William Laud, Archbishop of Canterbury, in which (1) he excuses himself for not having sooner congratulated him on his promotion to Canterbury; which he there does with all the warmth of a sincere friend and admirer. 'I may truly say thus much for myself,' writes Usher, 'that since the time I received the letter you wrote me the day before you began your journey into Scotland, no day hath passed hitherto wherein I have not made particular mention of you in my prayers unto Almighty God, who both graciously heard my request, and granted therein as much as my heart could desire.'

But further, the high opinion which he entertained of Archbishop Laud induced him to exert all the interest he possessed to secure his appointment to the Chancellorship of the University of Dublin. The following are the words of Usher to Laud, in the same letter: 'By the death of your predecessor, our University of Dublin was left to seek a new chancellor, whom I advised to pitch upon no other but yourself; which they did with all readiness and alacrity. If your Grace will deign to receive that poor society under the shadow of your wings, you shall put a further tie of

* Archbishop Usher's 'Answer to a Jesuit,' p. 75.

observance, not upon that only, but upon me also, who had my whole breeding there.' This letter not being so quickly responded to as Usher had expected, he wrote a second letter to Laud, urging upon him the necessity of taking this high office upon him.

During Usher's residence in Wales a book was published under his name, by Mr. Downham, entitled 'A Body of Divinity; or, the Sum and Substance of the Christian Religion.' Of this Body many editions have been published, and on the credit of its contents a character has been made for, and fixed upon Archbishop Usher, most singularly at variance with his true one. Although the book was disowned by him and declared 'to be in divers places deponant from his judgment,' and 'could not by any means be owned by him,' yet edition after edition of this work has been published by those who were aware of the primate's disavowal and disapproval of the work: and every advocate of Supralapsarian doctrines quotes in his support the opinions of Archbishop Usher, as put forth in this 'his Body of Divinity'! The letter to the editor disavowing the work is as follows:—

'Sir,—You may be pleased to take notice that the Catechism you write of is none of mine: but transcribed out of Mr. Cartwright's catechism, and Mr. Crooks and some other English divines, but drawn together in one method as a kind of common-place book, where other men's judgments and reasons are strongly laid down, though not approved in all places by the collector: besides that, the collection (such as it is) being lent abroad to divers, in scattered sheets, hath for a great part of it, miscarried; the one half of it (I suppose) well-nigh, being no way to be recovered, so that so imperfect a thing, copied verbatim out of others, and in divers places dissonant from my own judgment, may not by any means be owned by me. But if it shall seem good to any industrious person to cut off what is weak and superfluous therein, and supply the wants thereof, and cast it into a new mould of his own framing, I shall be very well content that he make what use he pleaseth of any of the materials therein, and set out the whole in his own name; and this is the resolution of

'Your most assured loving friend,
'JA. ARMACHANUS.
'May 13, 1645.'

As some persons have expressed their disappointment that Dr. Elrington has not published 'the Body of Divinity' among the works of the Archbishop, that learned divine remarks: 'Had the authorship been a matter of doubtful evidence, there might be a plausible ground for that complaint, but there can be none for not publishing among the works of Archbishop Usher what Archbishop Usher declared was not his.'

The Calvinistic and Supralapsarian character which has so long and so gratuitously been given to Archbishop Usher (built on the supposition that this work was his), vanishes as untrue, made for him, and assigned to him for party purposes.

This digressive vindication of an eminent divine will be pardoned by all who know the intrinsic value of Usher's writings. At the same time it will be observed that the importance of the citations from his Answer to the Jesuit consists in the many quotations he has produced from the Fathers, and in the reference to historical facts, which his unquestioned learning enabled him to make.

NOTE XXVII., page 222.

It is added, 'Then, if he humbly and heartily desire it,' but only then, 'the priest shall absolve him.'

'As for the ministerial sentence of private absolution,' says Hooker, 'it can be no more than a declaration what God hath done; it hath but the force of the prophet Nathan's absolution, "God hath taken away thy sin:" than which construction, especially of words judicial, there is not anything more vulgar. For example, the publicans are said in the

Gospel to have justified God; the Jews in Malachi to have blessed proud men, which sin and prosper; not that the one did make God righteous, or the other the wicked happy; but to bless, to justify, and to absolve, are as commonly used for words of judgment, or declaration, as of true and real efficacy; yea, even by the opinion of the Master of Sentences. It may be soundly affirmed and thought that God alone doth remit and retain sins, although He have given power to the Church to do both; but He one way, and the Church another. He only by Himself forgiveth sin, who cleanseth the soul from inward blemish, and looseth the debt of eternal death. So great a privilege He hath not given unto His priests, who notwithstanding are authorized to loose and bind, that is to say, declare who are bound, and who are loosed. For albeit a man be already cleared before God, yet he is not in the Church of God so taken, but by the virtue of the priest's sentence; who likewise may be said to bind by imposing satisfaction, and to loose by admitting to the holy communion.

'Saint Hierom also, whom the Master of the Sentences allegeth for more countenance of his own opinion, doth no less plainly and directly affirm: "That as the priests of the law could only discern, and neither cause nor remove leprosies; so the ministers of the Gospel, when they retain or remit sin, do but in the one judge how long we continue guilty, and in the other declare when we are clear or free." For there is nothing more apparent than that the discipline of repentance, both public and private, was ordained as an outward means to bring men to the virtue of inward conversion: so that when this by manifest tokens did seem effected, absolution ensuing (which could not make) served only to declare men innocent.'*

There is, indeed, a difference to be marked between the notion of absolution in the Church of Rome and that entertained by the Church of England. In the Church of Rome absolution is regarded as a judicial act; but by the Church of England it is held to be declaratory only. 'Absolution,' the Papists say, 'declareth indeed, but this is not all, for it likewise maketh innocent; which addition being an

* Hooker, book vi., 'On the Absolution of Penitents.'

untruth proved, our truth granted hath, I hope, sufficiency without it, and consequently our opinion therein neither to be challenged as untrue nor as unsufficient.'*

Absolution is, in truth, nothing more than a verbal and authoritative application to individual persons of the great doctrine of Justification by Faith.

We are sinners. Because of our sins we are justly afraid to participate in the sacred ordinances of the Church, to receive the sacrament of the Lord's Supper, or in any way to draw near to the throne of glory and of grace. But we, though sinners, believe in Jesus Christ; our faith is counted for righteousness; and, being thus justified sinners, we do, as being in Christ, what out of Christ we should not dare to do, we join with angels and archangels, and all the host of heaven, in offering our sacrifice of prayer and praise.

How beautifully is this carried out at the commencement of our morning and evening service; an addition to the Prayer Book made by the Reformers. We first confess our sins to God: and as much as say, we are unworthy to take part in this service: then the ambassador of the King of kings rises in his place, and in pronouncing the Absolution says in effect: 'Ye are, as ye have confessed, sinners, and, as such, unfit to approach God: nevertheless, if ye truly repent, and unfeignedly believe the Holy Gospel, I have authority to pronounce you to be in a state of justification, and as Christian men, men to whom faith is imputed for righteousness, you may unite with the holy ones of God in this sacred and pleasant exercise.'

The same meaning is to be attached to the confession and absolution in the office for the holy communion; the absolution being the form by which this fundamental truth is brought to bear upon our souls.

When the Church, at the Reformation, restored us to our Christian liberty, and no longer required us to make a special confession of sins to the priest, she directed the absolution to be pronounced every day upon those who desire to receive it. She permits it also to be pronounced upon the sick, because

* Hooker, book vi. p. 95.

they cannot attend the public administration of the ordinance. Will anyone say, if this be so, if it is our contrition which is accepted by God for the sake of our Lord Jesus Christ, the absolution is a work of supererogation? Let us see. Suppose you had been a traitor to your country, and that you were dwelling in a foreign land; suppose also, that you had repented of your sin and that proof of your repentance had been conveyed to your sovereign; suppose, moreover, that from the general expressions used by your injured sovereign, you felt sure that he would receive you again into favour: would you not nevertheless feel it satisfactory, before returning to your country, to have some formal writ made out and duly signed by the ambassador of your sovereign residing in the strange country in which you have taken up your abode? However certain you might feel of the favour of your sovereign, still you would think it expedient to have your pardon, signed and sealed with the customary forms: you would not feel grateful to the ambassador, your gratitude would flow entirely to the sovereign his master; the act of the ambassador would be merely ministerial, but of his ministerial services you would avail yourself. If the ambassador were to refuse to act, he would be punished, and his evil deed would not damage you, but you would feel, if he were prepared to act, that your reception by your sovereign would not be what you would desire it to be, were you to despise the regulations he has made; and you would seek from his ambassador a certificate, or such documents as might be legally necessary.

I shall conclude this note with another quotation from the judicious Hooker:—

'It standeth with us in the Church of England, as touching public confession, thus:

'First, seeing day by day we in our Church begin our public prayers to Almighty God with public acknowledgment of our sins, in which confession every man, prostrate as it were before His glorious Majesty, crieth against himself, and the minister with one sentence pronounceth universally all clear whose acknowledgment so made hath proceeded from a true penitent mind; what reason is there every man should not, under the general terms of confession, represent to himself his own particulars whatsoever, and adjoining thereunto that affection which a contrite spirit worketh, embrace to as full effect the words of divine grace, as if the same were severally and particularly uttered with addition of prayers, imposition of hands, or all the ceremonies and solemnities that might be used for the strengthening of man's affiance in God's peculiar mercy towards them? Such complements are helps to support our weakness, and not causes that serve to procure or produce His gifts, as David speaketh. The difference of general and particular forms in confession and absolution is not so material that any man's safety or ghostly good should depend upon it. And for private confession and absolution it standeth thus with us:

'The minister's power to absolve is publicly taught and professed, the Church not denied to have authority either of abridging or enlarging the use and exercise of that power; upon the people no such necessity imposed of opening their transgression unto men, as if remission of sins otherwise were impossible; neither any such opinion had of the thing itself, as though it were unlawful or unprofitable, save only for these inconveniences which the world hath by experience observed in it heretofore. And in regard thereof, the Church of England hath hitherto thought it the safer way to refer men's hidden crimes unto God and themselves only; howbeit, not without special caution for the admonition of such as come to the holy sacrament, and for the comfort of such as are ready to depart the world. First, because there are but few that consider how much that part of divine service, which consists in partaking the holy Eucharist, doth import their souls; what they lose by neglect thereof, and what by devout practice they might attain unto: therefore, lest carelessness of general confession should, as commonly it doth, extinguish all remorse of men's particular enormous crimes, our custom (whensoever men present themselves at the Lord's table) is, solemnly to give themselves fearful admonition, what woes are perpendicularly hanging over the heads of such as dare adventure to put forth their unworthy hands to those admirable mysteries of life, which have by rare examples been proved conduits of irremediable death to impenitent receivers; whom therefore, as we repel being known, so being not known we cannot but terrify. Yet, with us, the ministers of God's most holy word and sacraments, being all put in trust with the custody and dispensation of those mysteries wherein our communion is, and hath been ever, accounted the highest grace that men on earth are admitted unto, have therefore all equally the same power to withhold that sacred mystical food from notorious evil-livers, from such as have any way wronged their neighbours, and from parties between whom there doth open hatred and malice appear, till the first sort have reformed their wicked lives, the second recompensed them unto whom they were injurious, and the last condescended unto some course of Christian reconciliation, whereupon their mutual accord may ensue. In which cases, for the first branch of wicked life, and the last, which is open enmity, there can arise no great difficulty about the exercise of his power; in the second, concerning wrongs, they may, if men shall presume to define or measure injuries according to their own conceits, be depraved oftentimes as well by error as partiality, and that no less to the minister himself, than in another of the people under him.

'The knowledge therefore which he taketh of wrongs must rise, as it doth in the other two, not from his own opinion or conscience, but from the evidence of the fact which is committed; yea, from such evidence as neither doth admit denial nor defence. For if the offender, having either colour of law to uphold, or any other pretence to excuse his own uncharitable and wrongful dealings, shall wilfully stand in defence thereof, it serveth as bar to the power of this kind. Because (as it is observed by men of very good judgment in these affairs) although in this sort our separating of them be not to strike them with the mortal wound of excommunication, but to stay them rather from running desperately headlong into their own harm; yet it is not in us to sever from the holy communion but such as are either found culpable by their own confession, or have been convicted in some public, secular, or ecclesiastical court. For who is he that dares take upon him to be any man's both accuser and judge? Evil persons are not rashly, and, as we list, to be thrust from communion with the Church, insomuch that if we cannot proceed against them by any orderly course of judgment, they rather are to be suffered for the time than molested. Many there are reclaimed, as Peter; many, as Judas, known well enough, and yet tolerated; many which must remain undescried till the day of His appearance, by whom the secret corners of darkness shall be brought into open light.

'Leaving, therefore, unto His judgment them whom we cannot stay from casting their own souls into so great hazard, we have, in the other part of penitential jurisdiction in our power and authority to release sin, joy on all sides, without trouble or molestation unto any. And, if to give be a thing more blessed than to receive, are we not infinitely happier in being authorized to bestow the treasure of God, than when necessity doth constrain to withdraw the same?

'They which, during life and health, are never destitute of ways to delude repentance, do notwithstanding oftentimes, when their last hour draweth on, both feel that sting which before lay dead in them, and also thirst after such helps as have been always, till then, unsavoury. St. Ambrose's words touching late repentance are somewhat hard: "If a man be penitent and receive absolution (which cannot in that case be denied him) even at the very point of death, and so depart, I dare not affirm he goeth out of the world well; I will counsel no man to trust to this, because I am loath to deceive any man, seeing I know not what to think of it. Shall I judge such a one a cast-away? Neither will I avouch him safe. All I am able to say is, let his estate be left to the will and pleasure of Almighty God. Wilt thou be therefore delivered of all doubt? Repent while thou art healthy and strong. If thou defer it till time give no longer possibility of sinning, thou canst not be thought to have left sin, but rather sin to have forsaken thee." Such admonitions may in their time and place be necessary, but in no wise prejudicial to the generality of God's heavenly promise, " Whensoever a sinner doth repent from the bottom of his heart, I will put out all his iniquity." And of this, although it hath pleased God not to leave to the world any multitude of examples, lest the careless should too far presume, yet one He hath given, and that most memorable, to withhold from despair in the mercies of God, at what instant soever man's unfeigned conversion be wrought. Yea, because, to countervail the fault of delay, there are in the latest repentance oftentimes the surest tokens of sincere dealing; therefore upon especial confession made to the minister of God, he presently absolveth in this case the sick party from all sins by that authority which Jesus Christ hath committed unto him, knowing that God respecteth not so much what time is spent, as what truth is shewed in repentance.

' In sum, when the offence doth stand only between God and man's conscience, the counsel is good which St. Chrysostom giveth : " I wish thee not to bewray thyself publicly, nor to accuse thyself before others. I wish thee to obey the prophet, who saith, Disclose thy way unto the Lord, confess thy sins before Him; tell thy sins to Him, that He may blot them out. If thou be abashed to tell unto any other wherein thou hast offended, rehearse them every day between thee and thy soul. I wish thee not to confess them to thy fellow-servant, who may upbraid thee with them ; tell them to God, who will cure them; there is no need for thee in the presence of witnesses to acknowledge them ; let God alone see thee at thy confession. I pray and beseech you, that you would, more often than you do, confess to God eternal, and reckoning up your trespasses, desire His pardon. I carry you not into a theatre or open court of many of your fellow-servants, I seek not to detect your crimes before men; disclose your conscience before God, unfold yourselves to Him, lay forth your wounds before Him, the best Physician that is, and desire of Him salve for them." If hereupon it follow, as it did with David, "I thought, I will confess against myself my wickedness unto Thee, O Lord, and Thou forgavest me the plague of my sin;" we have our desire, and there remaineth only thankfulness accompanied with perpetuity of care to avoid that, which being not avoided, we know we cannot remedy without new perplexity and grief. Contrariwise, if peace with God follow not the pains we have taken in seeing after it, if we continue disquieted and not delivered from anguish, mistrusting whether that we do be sufficient, it argueth that our sore doth exceed the power of our own skill, and that the wisdom of the pastor must bind up those parts, which being bruised are not able to be recured of themselves.'*

NOTE XXVIII., page 223.

'Now concerning St. James's exhortation,' says Hooker, ' whether the former branch be considered, which saith, " Is any man sick among you ? let him call upon the ancients of the Church, and let them make their prayers for him ;" or the latter, which stirreth up all Christian men unto mutual acknowledgment of faults amongst themselves, " Lay open your minds, make your confession one to another ; " is it not plain, that the one hath relation to that gift of healing, which our Saviour promised His Church, saying, " They shall lay their hands on the sick, and the sick shall recover health ; " relation to that gift of healing, whereby the Apostle imposed his hands on the father of Publius, and made him miraculously a sound man ; relation finally to that gift of healing, which so long continued in practice after the Apostles' time? that whereas the Novatianists denied the power of the Church of God in curing sin after baptism, St. Ambrose asked them again, " Why it might not as well prevail with God for spiritual as for corporal and bodily health ; yea wherefore (saith he) do ye yourselves lay hands on the diseased, and believe it to be a work of benediction or prayer, if haply the sick person be restored to his former safety? And of the other member which toucheth mutual confession, do not some of themselves, as namely Cajetan, deny that any other confession is meant, than only that which seeketh either association of prayers, or reconciliation, or pardon of wrongs? Is it not

* Hooker, book vi.

confessed by the greatest part of their own retinue, that we cannot certainly affirm sacramental confession to have been meant or spoken of in this place? Howbeit, Bellarmine, delighted to run a course by himself where colourable shifts of wit will but make the way passable, standeth as formally for this place, and not less for that in St. John, than for this; St. John saith, "If we confess our sins, God is faithful and just to forgive us our sins, and to cleanse us from all unrighteousness;" doth St. John say, If we confess to the priest, God is righteous to forgive, and if not, that our sins are unpardonable? No, but the titles of God just and righteous do import that He pardoneth sin only for His promise sake; "And there is not (they say) any promise of forgiveness upon confession made to God without the priest;" not any promise, but with this condition, and yet this condition nowhere expressed.

'Is it not strange that the Scripture, speaking so much of repentance and of the several duties which appertain thereunto, should ever mean, and nowhere mention that one condition, without which all the rest is utterly of none effect; or will they say, because our Saviour hath said to His ministers, "Whose sins ye retain," &c., and because they can remit no more than what the offenders have confessed, that therefore, by the virtue of His promise, it standeth with the righteousness of God to take away no man's sins until by Auricular Confession they be opened unto the priest.

'They are men that would seem to honour antiquity, and none more to depend upon the reverend judgment thereof. I dare boldly affirm, that for many hundred years after Christ the Fathers held no such opinion; they did not gather by our Saviour's words any such necessity of seeking the priest's absolution from sin by secret and (as they now term it) sacramental confession. Public confession they thought necessary by way of discipline, not private confession as in the nature of a sacrament, necessary.'*

* Hooker, book vi.

NOTE XXIX., page 225.

Without attaching any undue importance to painful instances on record, the details of which cannot be alluded to without offence, and have been dwelt upon by some controversialists with too little regard to moral propriety, I will content myself with only a single quotation from a presbyter of the Church of Rome, on this subject. The author is Juan de Avila, one of the most eminent spiritual teachers of the Church of Spain, whose 'Spiritual Epistles' were translated and published in English, 'Permissu Superiorum,' in 8vo., 1632. He is giving the advice of his experience to a young preacher:—

'Let me also advise you not to give yourself too much to hearing the confessions of women, especially young women: for it is a perilous business, if a man has not some special gift of God, which may make him insensible to temptation. Turn your attention more to the profit of the men; for if you once begin to look after female penitents, you will have little leisure to devote to anything else; so apt are they to waste time in matters of little moment or benefit. And I would have your principal object be to preach; for you will do much, if you do this well; and as to confessing, neither altogether take up the practice, nor altogether leave it unregarded.'*

This sensible advice is from a man who was in his own country another Francis de Sales, or Borromeo. The words appear fully to justify the practice of the Church of England; and they are the more striking as coming from one who was himself obliged to suit his doctrine to the Council of Trent.

For the same reason I will give the following quotation from the late Rev. David O'Croly, who for upwards of twenty years performed the duties of a confessor in the Church of Rome, and whose statements, with reference to the confessional, are therefore entitled to great respect:—

'A priest in the chair of confession is the most arbitrary of judges. He acts without check or control. His admoni-

* Treatise i. Lett. 38.

tions, his commands, his decisions, his casuistry, are not the necessary result of fixed principles or acknowledged maxims, but of his own particular qualities or dispositions—of his caprice, of his ignorance, of his prejudices, of his perversity, of his profligacy. Yet confession, under all these forbidding circumstances, is announced, is trumpeted as a necessary means of salvation—a *secunda post naufragium tabula*, " a second plank after shipwreck ; " and the favour of heaven, the grace of God, the justification of the sinner, is restricted, as an adjunct, to human precariousness and profanation !

'But how is this machinery of confession made to work ? how is it brought into action ? In the country the poor people practise confession, for the most part through dread of public exposure. And how do they practise it ?—how do they prepare for it ? When they hear of the priest's arrival at the station-house, they quit their labour in the field or in the barn, hurry to the confessor, make a compendious recital of some sins they are in the constant habit of committing, and confessing, make some sort of a promise of amendment, as a matter of routine, receive absolution, hear the mass recited in Latin, take the blessed sacrament, pay the confession dues or battle with the priest, return to their labour with an obligation of repeating a number of rosaries within a given time, and think no more of the transaction. In the cities and large towns, confession is very generally neglected, except at the point of death.

'Does confession improve the morals ? It is said that a bad confession or a confession not clothed with the necessary conditions, not accompanied by a change of disposition and a firm purpose of amendment, superinduces the guilt of sacrilege, and adds immeasurably to the guilt of the pretended penitent. Must not this take place in most instances, from the mode in which confession is practised ; and if so, what improvement in public morals can result from it ? But this is only a theoretical argument. Let the question be decided by general facts. Are those who practise confession better conducted or less immoral than those who do not ? Are they better husbands, better fathers, better subjects, better citizens—less given to turbulence, to sedition, to lying, to injustice? Have the Roman Catholics the advantage of the Reformers in this respect? Compare nations together. Confession is universally practised in Spain and Portugal. It is not practised in England or Scotland. Is the state of morality, public and private, among the Spaniards and Portuguese higher in the scale of virtue than among Englishmen and Scotchmen? What was the state of morals throughout Christendom in the times of old when the benefits or evils of this practice were universally felt? History will not give a very creditable answer to the question. Will anyone venture to say that the Irish Roman Catholics, who go to confession at stations twice a year or once a year, as they would to a fair or pattern, are superior in virtue and good manners to their Protestant fellow-countrymen, who learn their Christian duties from the sacred Scriptures? Or that the Spaniards and Portuguese and Italians are superior, as men and as Christians, to the people of England, or Scotland, or Holland, or the Protestant States of Germany? Or that the Roman Catholics, taken collectively and individually, do not lose considerably by the comparison? And if so, is it right that malevolent, profligate priests—and many there are of this revolting description—should be enabled with impunity to lay snares for innocence, and to break into the sanctuary of private life, and make it a matter of conscience with weak-minded servants and labourers to ruin the interests of a good master and employer?'

I shall conclude this note with the following sensible remarks from a clergyman of the Church of England, who, although no Romanizer, has always ranked as a High Churchman:—

'The extent to which the confessors have thought it right to carry their examinations on subjects concerning which the Apostle recommends that they be not once named among Christians, and which may be seen either in Den's Theology, or Burchard's Decrees, c. 19, Paris, 1549, affords a melancholy, painful, and sickening subject for contemplation; especially, when it is considered that they were Christian clergy who did this, and that it was done in aid, as they supposed, of the Christian religion. The fearful effects of these examinations upon the priests themselves I will do no more than allude to; he who may think it necessary to satisfy himself upon the point may consult the cases contemplated and provided for (among others) by Cardinal Cajetan, in his 'Opuscula,' Lugd., 1562, p. 114. In the Bull of Pius IV., *Contra solicitantes in confessione*, dated Ap. 16, 1561 ('Bullarium Magn.,' Luxemb., 1727, ii. p. 48), and in a similar one of Gregory XV., dated Aug. 30, 1622 (Gregor. XV. Constit. Rom., 1622), p. 114, there is laid open another fearful scene of danger to female confitents from wicked priests, 'mulieres penitentes ad actus inhonestos dum earum audiunt confessiones alliciendo et provocando.' Against which flagrant dangers, and the preparatory steps of sapping and undermining the mental modesty of a young person by examinations of particular kinds, it is vain to think that the feeble bulls of the bishops of Rome can afford any security. These observations apply to the system of the Roman Church, peculiar to itself, of compelling the disclosure of the most minute details of the most secret thoughts and actions. As to encouraging persons whose minds are burthened with the remembrance of fearful sins, to ease themselves of the burthen by revealing it to one at whose hands they may seek guidance and consolation and prayer, it is a totally distinct question, and nothing but wilful art will attempt to confound them. On this point I see no reason to withdraw a regret which I have before expressed as to its disuse in the Church of England; for I cannot but believe that, were it more frequently had recourse to, many a mind would depart the world at peace with itself and with God, which now sinks to the grave under a bond of doubt and fear, through want of confidence to make use of ghostly remedies.'*

NOTE XXX., page 226.

'Concerning confession as it is a special act of repentance, the first thing that is to be said of it is, that it is due only

* Perceval's '*Romish Schism*,' p. 378.

to God; for He is the person injured; sin is the prevarication of His laws; He is our Judge, and He only can pardon, as He only can punish eternally. "Non tibi dico, ut tua peccata, tanquam in pompam, in publicum, proferas, neque ut te accuses, sed ut pareas Prophetæ dicenti, Revela Domino viam tuam. Apud Deum ea confitere, apud Judicem confitere peccata tua, orans si non linguâ, saltem memoriâ et ita roga ut tui misereatur." " I do not enjoin thee to betray thyself to the public ear, bringing thy sins as into a theatre, but obey the Prophet, saying, Reveal thy way unto the Lord. Confess to God, confess to thy Judge; praying if not with thy tongue, yet at least with thy mind, and pray so that thou mayest be heard:" so St. Chrysostom: and upon those words of St. Paul, "Let a man examine himself," he saith, " Non revelavit ulcus, non in commune theatrum accusationem produxit," &c. " He did not reveal his ulcer, he did not bring his accusation into the common theatre; he made none witness of his sins, but in his conscience, none standing by, God only excepted, who sees all things." And again, upon that of the psalm: "My sin is always against me;" " If thou art ashamed to speak it to anyone, say them daily in thy mind; I do not say, that thou confess them to thy fellow-servant, who may upbraid thee; say them to God. Ἀμάρτυρον ἔστω τὸ δικαστήριον, Θεὸς ὁράτω μόνος ἐξομολογούμενον. " Let this judicatory be without assessors or witnesses, let God alone see thy confession," " Quod si, verecundiâ retrahente, revelare ea coram hominibus erubescis, illi, quem latere non possunt, confiteri ea jugi supplicatione non desinas, ac dicere, Iniquitatem meam agnosco, &c., qui et absque ullius verecundiæ publicatione curare, et sine improperio peccata donare consuevit." So Cassian in the imitation of St. Ambrose: "If bashfulness call thee back, and thou art ashamed to reveal them before men, cease not, by a continual supplication, to confess them to Him from whom they cannot be concealed; who, without any pressing upon our modesty, is wont to cure, and without upbraiding, to forgive us our sins." And the Fathers of the Council of Caballon advanced this duty by divers sentences of Scripture:—" Ita duntaxat ut et

Deo, qui remissor est peccatorum, confiteamur peccata nostra, et cum David dicamus, Delictum meum cognitum tibi feci, et injustitiam meam non abscondi : Dixi, confitebor injustitias meas Domino, et Tu remisisti impietatem peccati mei," &c. "God is the pardoner of sins, and therefore let us confess to Him, and say with David : I have made my sin known unto Thee, and mine unrighteousness have I not hid ; I said, I will confess mine iniquity unto the Lord, and Thou forgavest the wickedness of my sin." But this thing is pressed more earnestly by Laurentius Novarriensis, who, because he was a Father of the fifth age, his words are of more use, by being a testimony that the ecclesiastical repentance, which we find to be now pressed by some as simply necessary, was not the doctrine of those times. "From that day in which thou goest out of the font thou becomest to thyself a continual font, and a daily remission. There is no absolute necessity of the priest's right hand ; from thenceforward God hath appointed thee to be thy own judge, thy own arbiter, and hath given thee knowledge whereby of thyself thou mayest discern good and evil; and because while thou remainest in the body thou canst not be free from sin, God hath, after baptism, placed thy remedy within thyself; He hath placed pardon within thy own choice, so that thou art not, in the day of thy necessity, indispensably tied to seek a priest; but thou thyself, as if thou wert a most skilful doctor and master, mayest amend thy error within thee, and wash away thy sin by repentance. The fountain is never dry, the water is within thee ; absolution is in thy choice, sanctification is in thy diligence, pardon is within the dew of thine own tears. Do not thou therefore look either for John or Jordan; be thou thy own baptist, viz., in the baptism of repentance. Thou art defiled after thou art washed, thy bowels are defiled, thy soul is polluted ; plunge thyself in the waters of repentance, cleanse thyself by abundance of tears, let compunction be plentifully in thy bowels—and the Lord Himself shall baptize thee with the Holy Ghost and with fire, and shall heap the fruits of repentance, and lay them up like wheat ; but the chaff of thy sins He shall burn with unquenchable fire." Many testimonies out of antiquity to the same purpose are to be seen ready collected by Gratian, under the title "De Pœnitentiâ."'*

The following quotation should be pondered seriously by the young clergy who are urging the necessity of Auricular Confession. They are the words of one of our soundest Churchmen :—

'Since there is no necessity declared in Scripture of confessing all our sins to a priest, no mention of sacramental penance, or confession, it must needs seem strange that a doctrine, of which there is no commandment in Scripture, no direction for the manner of doing so difficult a work, no office or officer described to any such purpose ; that a doctrine, I say, of which in the fountain of salvation there is no spring, should yet become, in process of time, to be the condition of salvation: and yet for preaching, praying, baptizing, communicating, we have precept upon precept, and line upon line: we have in Scripture three epistles written to two bishops, in which the episcopal office is abundantly described; and excellent canons established ; and the parts of their duty enumerated: and yet no care taken about the office of "father confessor." Indeed, we find a pious exhortation to all spiritual persons, that "if any man be overtaken in a fault, they should restore such a one in the spirit of meekness;" "restore him," that is, to the public peace and communion of the Church, from which by his delinquency he fell; and restore him also, by the word of His proper ministry, to the favour of God; by exhortations to him, by reproving of him, by praying for him : and besides this, we have some little limits more, which the Church of Rome, if they please, may make good use of in this question ; such as are, "that they who sin should be rebuked before all men, that others also may fear ; " which indeed is a good warranty for public dicipline, but very little for private confession. And St. Paul charges Timothy, that he should "lay hands suddenly on no man," that he be not partaker of other men's sins"; which is a good caution against the Roman way of absolving them that confess, as soon as they have confessed,

* Bishop Jeremy Taylor *on Ecclesiastical Penance*, edit. Heber, ix. 243.

before they have made their satisfactions. The same Apostle speaks also of " some that creep into houses, and lead captive silly women ; " I should have thought, he had intended it against such as then abused Auricular Confession ; it being so like what they do now ; but that St. Paul knew nothing of these lately-introduced practices ; and lastly, he commands everyone that is to receive the holy communion, " to examine himself, and so let him eat ; " he forgot, it seems, to enjoin them to go to confession to be examined : which certainly he could never have done more opportunely than here ; and, if it had been necessary, he could never have omitted it more indecently. But it seems, the first Christians were admitted upon other terms by the Apostles than they are at this day by the Roman clergy. And indeed it were infinitely strange, that since in the Old Testament remission of sins was given to everyone that confessed to God, and turned from his evil way, that, in the New Testament, to which liberty is a special privilege, and the imposed yoke of Christ infinitely more easy than the burden of the law ; and repentance is the very formality of the Gospel-covenant ; and yet, that pardon of our sins shall not be given to us Christians on so easy terms as it was to the Jews ; but an intolerable new burden shall be made a new condition of obtaining pardon. And this will appear yet the more strange ; when we consider, that all the sermons of the prophets concerning repentance were not derivations from Moses's law, but homilies evangelical, and went before to prepare the way of the Lord ; and John Baptist was last of them ; and that, in this matter, the sermons of the prophets were but the Gospel antedated ; and, in this affair, there was no change but to the better and to a clearer manifestation of the divine mercy, and the sweet yoke of Christ ; the disciples of Christ preached the same doctrine of repentance that the Baptist did, and the Baptist the same that the prophets did, and there was no difference ; Christ was the same in all, and He that commanded his disciples to fast to God alone in private intended that all the parts of repentance transacted between God and our consciences, should be as sufficient as that one of fasting, and that other of prayer: and it is said so in all; "for, if we confess our sins, He is faithful and just to forgive us our sins, and to cleanse us from all unrighteousness." It is God alone that can cleanse our hearts, and He that cleanses us, He alone does forgive us; and this is upon our confession to Him: His justice and faithfulness are at stake for it; and therefore it supposes a promise: which we often find upon our confessions made to God, but it was never promised upon confession made to the priest.

'If we consider whether this thing be reasonable, to impose such a yoke upon the necks of the disciples, which upon their fathers was not put in the Old Testament, nor ever commanded in the New; we shall find, that, although many good things might be consequent to the religious and free and prudent use of confession; yet, by changing into a doctrine of God, that which, at most, is a commandment of man, it will not, by all the contingent good, make recompense for all the intolerable evils it introduces. And here, first, I consider that many times things seem profitable to us, and may minister to good ends; but God judges them useless and dangerous: for He judges not as we judge. The worshipping of angels, and the abstaining from meats, which some false prophets introduced, looked well, and pretended to humility, and mortification of the body; but the Apostle approved them not: and of the same mind were the succeeding ages of the Church; who condemned the dry diet and the ascetic fasts of Montanus, though they were pretended only for discipline; but when they came to be imposed they grew intolerable. Certainly men lived better lives when, by the discipline of the Church, sinners were brought to public stations and penance, than now they do by all the advantages, real or pretended, from Auricular Confession; and yet the Church thought fit to lay it aside, and nothing is left but the shadow of it.

'This whole topic can only be a prudential consideration, and can no way infer a divine institution; for though it was as convenient before Christ as since, and might have as now had the same effect upon the public or private good then as now, yet God was not pleased to appoint it in almost forty ages; and we say, He hath not done it yet. However, let it be considered, that there being some things which, St. Paul says, are not to be "so much as named" amongst Christians, it must needs look indecently, that all men and all women should come and make the priest's ears a common sewer to empty all their filthiness; and that which a modest man would blush to hear he must be used to, and it is the greatest part of his employment to attend to. True it is that the physician must see and handle the impurest ulcers; but it is because the cure does not depend upon the patient, but upon the physician, who, by general advertisement, cannot cure the patient, unless he had a universal medicine, which the priest hath: the medicine of repentance, which can indifferently cure all sins, whether the priest know them or no. And therefore all this filthy communication is therefore intolerable, because it is not necessary: and it not only pollutes the priest's ears, but his tongue too; for, lest any circumstance, or any sin, be concealed, he thinks himself obliged to interrogate, and proceed to particular questions in the basest things. Such as that which is to be seen in Burchard, and such which are too largely prescribed in Sanchez; which thing does not only deturpate all honest and modest conversation, but it teaches men to understand more sins than ever they (it may be) knew of.'*

NOTE XXXI., page 229.

These statements have been fully proved before, but *ex abundanti*, two other quotations shall be given, the first from the judicious Hooker, the second from Archbishop Usher :—

'They bind all men upon pain of everlasting condemnation and death to make confessions to their ghostly fathers of every great offence they know, and can remember, that they have committed against God. Hath Christ in His Gospel so delivered the doctrine of repentance unto the world? Did

* Jeremy Taylor's '*Dissuasive from Popery*,' vol. xi. p. 30.

His apostles so preach it to nations? Have the Fathers so believed, or so taught? Surely Novatian was not so merciless of depriving the Church of power to absolve some certain offenders, as they in imposing upon all a necessity thus to confess. Novatian would not deny that God might remit that which the Church could not, whereas in the Papacy it is maintained, that what we conceal from men, God Himself should never pardon. By which oversight, as they have here surcharged the world with multitude, but much abated the weight of confessions, so the careless manner of their absolution hath made discipline, for the most part, amongst them a bare formality; yea, rather a means of emboldening unto vicious and wicked life, than either any help to prevent future, or medicine to remedy present evils in the soul of man. The Fathers were slow and always fearful to absolve any before very manifest tokens given of a true penitent and contrite spirit. It was not their custom to remit sin first, and then to impose works of satisfaction, as the fashion of Rome is now; insomuch that this their preposterous course and misordered practices hath bred also in them an error concerning the end and purpose of these works. For against the guiltiness of sin and the danger of everlasting condemnation thereby incurred, confession and absolution succeeding the same, are, as they take it, a remedy sufficient; and therefore what their penitentiaries do think good to enjoin further, whether it be a number of Ave-Maries daily to be scored up, a journey of pilgrimage to be undertaken, some few dishes of ordinary diet to be exchanged, offerings to be made at the shrines of saints, or a little to be scraped off from men's superfluities for relief of poor people, all is in lieu or exchange with God, whose justice, notwithstanding our pardon, yet oweth us still some temporal punishment, either in this life or in the life to come, except we quit ourselves here with works of the former kind, and continued till the balance of God's most strict severity shall find the pains we have taken equivalent with the plagues which we should endure, or else the mercy of the Pope relieves us. And at this postern-gate cometh in the whole mart of Papal indulgences so infinitely strewed that the pardon of sin, which heretofore was obtained hardly and by much suit, is with them become now almost impossible to be escaped.'*

'We find,' says Archbishop Usher, 'that Lawrence, Bishop of Novaria, in his "Homily de Pœnitentia," doth resolutely determine, that for obtaining remission of sins a man needeth not to resort unto any priest, but this his own internal repentance is sufficient for that matter. "God," saith he, "after baptism hath appointed thy remedy within thyself, He hath put remission in thine own power, that thou needest not seek a priest when thy necessity requireth; but though thyself now, as a skilful and plain master, mayest amend thine error within thyself, and wash away thy sin by repentance." "He hath given unto thee," saith another, somewhat to the same purpose, "the power of binding and loosing. Thou hast bound thyself with the chain of the love of wealth: loose thyself with the injunction of the love of poverty. Thou hast bound thyself with the furious desire of pleasures; loose thyself with temperance. Thou hast bound thyself with the misbelief of Eunomius; loose thyself with the religious embracing of the right faith."

'And that we may see how variable men's judgments were touching the matter of confession in the ages following, Bede would have us "confess our daily and light sins one unto another, but open the uncleanness of the greater leprosy to the priest." Alcuinus, not long after him, would have us "confess all the sins that we could remember." Others were of another mind. For some (as it appeareth by the writings of the same Alcuinus, and of Haymo) would not confess their sins to the priest; but "said it was sufficient for them that they did confess their sins to God alone;" provided always that they ceased from those sins for the time to come. Others confessed their sins unto the priest, but "not fully;" as may be seen in the Council of Cavaillon, held in the days of Charles the Great; where, though the Fathers think that this had "need to be mended," yet they freely acknowledge that it remained still a question, whether men should only confess

* Hooker *on the Absolution of Penitents,* book vi.

to God, or to the priests also: and they themselves put this difference betwixt both those confessions, that the one did properly serve for the cure, the other for direction in what sort of repentance, and so the cure should be performed. Their words are these: 'Some say that they ought to confess their sins only unto God, and some think that they are to be confessed unto the priests: both of which, not without great fruit, is practised within the holy Church. Namely, thus, that we both confess our sins unto God, Who is the forgiver of sins (saying with David, "I acknowledge my sin unto Thee, and mine iniquity, have I not hid. I said I will confess against myself my transgressions unto the Lord: and Thou forgavest the iniquity of my sin"); and, according to the institution of the Apostle, confess our sins one to another, and pray one for another, that we may be healed. The confession therefore which is made unto God purgeth sins; but that which is made unto the priest teacheth in what sort those sins should be purged. For God, the Author and bestower of salvation and health, giveth the same sometime by the invisible administration of His power—sometimes by the operation of physicians.'*

The reader, in these Notes, has been presented with the testimonies of the Fathers, and the opinion of those learned divines of the Church of England who had written upon the subject of Auricular Confession. No modern theologian approaches the latter either in Patrology or in Biblical Exegesis. We have, then, I repeat it, the authority of the Primitive Church and of the Reformed Church of England, for saying that confession to man, though it may be a means of comfort to some, is necessary to no one, and that it is not to be numbered among the means of grace.

* *Answer to a Jesuit*, p. 91, printed at the Pitt Press, Cambridge, 1835.

LONDON : PRINTED BY
SPOTTISWOODE AND CO., NEW-STREET SQUARE
AND PARLIAMENT STREET

S. & H.

November 1876.

RICHARD BENTLEY & SON'S NEW WORKS.

I

UNDERGROUND JERUSALEM:
An Account of some of the Principal Difficulties encountered in its Exploration, and the Results obtained. With a Narrative of an Expedition through the Jordan Valley, and a Visit to the Samaritans. By CHARLES WARREN, Captain in the Corps of Royal Engineers, F.G.S., F.R.G.S., Assoc. Inst. C.E., late in Charge of the Explorations in the Holy Land. In demy 8vo. with Illustrations, 21s.

II

THE HISTORY OF ANTIQUITY.
From the German of Professor DUNCKER, by EVELYN ABBOTT, M.A., of Balliol College, Oxford. In demy 8vo.

III

THE CORRESPONDENCE OF HONORÉ DE BALZAC.
With a Memoir by his Sister, Madame de SURVILLE. 2 vols.

IV

OLD NEW ZEALAND:
A Tale of the Good Old Times, and a History of the War in the North against the Chief, Heke. Told by an OLD PAKEHA MAORI. With a Preface by the Earl of PEMBROKE. In demy 8vo. 12s.

V

LETTERS OF ELIZABETH BARRETT BROWNING TO R. H. HORNE, AUTHOR OF 'ORION.'
Edited by S. R. TOWNSEND MAYER. In 2 vols. crown 8vo. 21s.

VI

MEMORIALS OF THE SOUTH SAXON SEE AND CATHEDRAL OF CHICHESTER.
From Original Sources. By the Rev. W. R. W. STEPHENS, Prebendary of Chichester, Author of 'The Life and Times of St. John Chrysostom,' &c. In demy 8vo. with eight Illustrations and Plan of the Cathedral, 21s.

VII

PICTURESQUE HOLLAND:
A Journey in the Provinces of Friesland, Groningen, Drenthe, Overyssel, Guelderland, Limburgh, &c. By HENRY HAVARD, Author of 'The Dead Cities of the Zuyder Zee.' In demy 8vo. with ten Illustrations, 16s.

VIII

MOTHERS, WIVES, AND SISTERS IN THE OLDEN TIME.
By Lady HERBERT, Author of 'Three Phases of Christian Faith,' 'Impressions of Spain,' &c. In 2 vols. large crown 8vo. 21s. *[Continued on next page.*

RICHARD BENTLEY & SON, NEW BURLINGTON STREET,
Publishers in Ordinary to Her Majesty the Queen.

IX
STUDIES IN ENGLISH ART.
Gainsborough, Morland, Wheatley, Sir Joshua Reynolds, Stothard, Flaxman, Girtin, Crome, Cotman, Turner (in 'Liber Studiorum'), Peter de Wint, George Mason, Frederick Walker. By FREDERICK WEDMORE. In crown 8vo. 7s. 6d.

X
THE WITCHES' FROLIC AND THE BAGMAN'S DOG.
By THOMAS INGOLDSBY. Illustrated by an entirely New Art by JANE COOK, Author of 'The Sculptor Caught Napping.' In large 4to. 21s.

XI
AN UNREQUITED LOVE.
An Episode in the Life of BEETHOVEN. From the German of Dr. NOHL. In demy 8vo. 10s. 6d.

XII
THE LIVES OF THE ARCHBISHOPS OF CANTERBURY.
The Twelfth Volume, being the Index to the proceding Eleven Volumes. In demy 8vo. 15s.

*** *Only a limited number of this Volume printed.*

XIII
WITHIN THE ARCTIC CIRCLE.
Experiences of Travel in Norway and Lapland. By S. H. KENT. In 2 vols. crown 8vo. 21s.

ALSO,

NEW NOVELS
BY

MISS BROUGHTON.
MRS. EDWARDES.
ROBERT BUCHANAN.
MISS MATHERS (Authoress of 'Comin' thro' the Rye').
JULIAN HAWTHORNE.
THE AUTHORESS OF 'The Queen of Connaught.'
MRS. TROLLOPE (Authoress of 'Aunt Margaret's Trouble ').
MRS. ALEXANDER (Authoress of 'The Wooing O't ').
ALBANY DE FONBLANQUE.
PERCY FITZGERALD.

And other Authors.

RICHARD BENTLEY & SON, NEW BURLINGTON STREET,
Publishers in Ordinary to Her Majesty the Queen.

www.ingramcontent.com/pod-product-compliance
Lightning Source LLC
Chambersburg PA
CBHW020303240426

43673CB00039B/691